the Path throug

Also available from Grey House in the Woods

the Voice within the Wind
of Becoming and the Druid Way
Greywind

Arianrhod's Dance – a Druid Ritual Workbook
Julie White & Graeme K Talboys

the Path through the Forest

a
Druid Guidebook

Second Edition

Julie White
&
Graeme K Talboys

Grey House in the Woods

First published on the summer solstice in 2002 by
Grey House in the Woods
PO Box 8211
Girvan
Ayrshire
KA26 0WA
Scotland
www.greyhouseinthewoods.org

This edition published on the summer solstice in 2005

ISBN 0-9540531-4-1

Cover design by Redwind

Set in 9 point Comic Sans MS

CONTENTS

Before enlightenment you chop wood and carry water;
after enlightenment you chop wood and carry water.

ACKNOWLEDGEMENTS

Julie has been a pagan and a Druid for most of her life. She has a deep love for the land, sea, and sky, and also for helping others on the Druid Way. She trained as a Druid in an Order, where she was a tutor for many years, before leaving to form a Grove in Sussex. She lives in the South Downs with her partner and dog.

She would like to give special thanks to the following:

The Goddess.

Graeme, for without him this book would not have been possible. He gave me the courage and the chance to write it. He is my dear friend.

Barbara, Graeme's wife, for putting up with our long phone calls to each other when discussing chapters.

Spiral Light Grove, always a source of inspiration (and chocolate cake).

All my Druid friends (you know who you are).

Sussex Pagan Circle.

Dear Grove sisters, Kate and Fay.

My partner for listening to me, when he had no idea what I was going on about.

My dog, who reminds me when it's time to stop writing and eat.

*

Graeme has been Druid for many years. His first steps on the Way were taken in Sussex on the spiral path of a Harvest Hill. Although he trained formally in an Order, he was first and is once more a Hedge Druid, exploring now the deeper reaches of the Forest. He lives in Carrick with his wife and two cats.

He would like to give special thanks to the following:

Barbara - as ever a source of inspiration, a steadfast companion, the love of my life.

Julie, for without her this book would not have been possible. She knows parts of the Forest I have never explored and she has trusted me with her words – a friend unlike any other.

Pip and Martin for their faith and all their hard work.

Eileen, Gael, and Charis for all that they have taught me.

Greywind.

The Goddess for the gifts she has graciously entailed.

*

Julie and Graeme would both like to thank Fay Young for permission to use her beautiful Grove Prayer.

Summer Solstice 2002

It is not often that authors are accorded the opportunity to produce a new edition of their work. That we have been so blessed is due solely to all those people who bought the first edition and responded so positively to what we had to say. We would like, therefore, to thank them all. We would also like to reiterate our thanks to Grey House in the Woods and to Pip and Martin Faulks without whom...

The changes in this second edition are minor and do not alter the underlying ethos of our vision any more than they alter the content of what we have to say. There is a new chapter on deity to make good an alarming omission from the first edition, some of the material on ritual has been re-written to make it more compatible with *Arianrhod's Dance*, and we have corrected errors that crept in at the printing stage last time round.

Clas Myrddin ~ Summer Solstice 2005

PREFACE

This book, a companion to *Arianrhod's Dance*, is an introduction to the Druid Way. The content is comprehensive, but far from complete. Even taken as a subject of academic study, there is far too much to fit into one book. And being Druid goes well beyond academic study - it is both a material and spiritual way of life.

That said, we hope that this book (and its companion) will offer you sufficient information and inspiration to take your first steps on the path into and through the Forest. You can be confident that what you read is well considered and based, where possible, on what we know of ancestral thought and practice. It also derives from the combined experience of two Druids who have each been in the Forest for well over thirty years.

Please note that parts of 'Casting a Circle and Circle Working' are also to be found in *Arianrhod's Dance*. We make no apology for this. Although the books were written as companion volumes, we wanted each to stand alone and these sections rightly belong in both books.

Julie White
Graeme K Talboys

INTRODUCTION

A Druid is what we call someone who opens their mind, their heart, and their soul to the way in which our Celtic ancestors lived. Not in the detail, not as a fancy dress re-enactment, but with the totality of a vision of the world that is now lost to most people.

Through this vision, they see the world more fully. It realigns them and thus allows them to be reintegrated with that from which they have been divorced by modern society. And with the power this realignment endows, they are able to fulfil an important role - working to heal the hurts of the world and building a healthy future in which *all* the children of the Goddess may thrive in peace.

That is no easy task. This book was written to help. It was set down primarily for those who are considering whether to start out on the Druid Way and for those who are taking their first, tentative steps. There is a great deal of confusing and inaccurate advice and material available for such people. Some is obscure because of its antiquity; much of it is demanding because many experienced Druids who produce it find it difficult to remember what newcomers want and need in the way of guidance.

Far worse, however, is the fact that some of the material available has been made up by people pretending to have access to sources of knowledge denied to everyone else. These people are charlatans.

The source of a Druid's knowledge and wisdom is not found in books or ancient manuscripts, any more than their work in the world can be confined to a library. Indeed, the knowledge and wisdom of the Druid is freely available to us all. It is knowing how to recognize it when we see it that is difficult. There is no denying that we can all learn from books, but they are mere primers in an age when it is difficult to find an experienced Druid who will take you under their wing.

Besides, if these people have access to previously unseen, ancient texts and they are true seekers after knowledge; they should make their material available to others. Dressing it up in systems and lessons does nothing but make the author look foolish and casts a deep shadow over their integrity.

That is why this book contains nothing that is hidden; that is why it contains no obscure rites. There are rituals associated with the Druid Way – and for the serious seeker these are to be found in *Arianrhod's Dance*, a companion volume to this by the same authors.

However, rituals are an outward expression of what is already within. And to nurture what is within requires a dedication to a threefold path.

The first strand is the one in which you seek to know and channel the self. It is the most obvious place to begin. Having come to know one's self, it is then possible to move to the second strand in which one seeks the Light. For many, that is the goal, but the Druid Way recognizes a third strand in which one learns to channel the Light for the benefit of the world.

The Forest that is the Druid Way is there for all to see and there for all to explore. Everything you need to know is to be found within it, as long as you know how and where to look. From the outside, it can be daunting with seemingly deep shadows at its heart. Once within, however, you will find that the sun shines throughout and is at its brightest in the central grove that we all seek.

What a newcomer needs, and what we hope this book will offer, is an introduction to the main pathways into the Forest. Once these have been understood, the true seeker after knowledge will be able to go deeper into the literal and metaphorical forest for themselves, confident that they will not get lost, confident that they are equipped to learn from their experiences.

The Single Way

It has become popular in recent years for people to think they can build their own spiritual path by plundering the paths of others for the bits they like the best. This is cultural and spiritual imperialism of the worst kind, posing as an enlightened attitude. It is indicative of the consumer society in which we live and the way in which we are brought up to believe that anything in the world is there for our benefit and to be used as we will. Such an attitude runs counter to the very metaphysic that underlies the Druid Way – and all other genuine spiritual paths.

The question of the single Way has to be faced, despite the fact that some people have labelled it 'fundamentalism' or a 'doctrine of purity' (with overtones of fascism). The single Way is neither of these things. The Druid Way, for example, is a spiritual path derived from the Celtic metaphysic. It is very specific in its form. If bits are left out and other bits added, it ceases to be the Druid Way and it becomes ineffective as a spiritual force.

Anyone who sets out to travel the Druid Way is heading for the same goal as everyone else who undertakes a spiritual journey, whatever their chosen Way may be. So, if we are all heading for the same destination, why not take the same route? What harm in mixing and matching your approach?

There would be none if we were all the same and all at the same stage of spiritual development. But we are not. We all have different backgrounds, we come from different places, and we have different understandings of the world. The destination may be one we hold in common; the starting point is not.

Nor is the Way we choose simply like walking a path. That is why we prefer to use the term 'Way'. This has within its meaning the idea of a path and a journey, but it also has a broader meaning - of how we conduct ourselves as we travel along the Way.

There are two other reasons for keeping to a single Way. The first is to do with harmonics. By doing so, we integrate our energies and channel them in a common direction. This gives us greater strength and protection as well as minimizing the disturbance in our spiritual lives.

Think of a river in which different streams and currents contend with one another. The surface is rough and the undercurrents are dangerous. They can spin you round until you are dizzy and no longer have any sense of direction; they can pull you down and keep you under. Think of a river that splits into many channels and tries to go in different directions. It becomes sluggish and loses its way.

Many people do not take their spiritual health seriously, which is a mistake. Not only is this bad in itself, but it can also have serious effects on mental and physical well-being. Those who dabble in things they do not understand or use what they discover for their own hedonistic ends will hurt themselves. This, ultimately, is their own choice. However, they will also hurt others whilst disturbing things on many levels, and this they have no right to do.

The other reason for keeping to a single Way is that progress is only achieved if one takes it a step at a time, each step in the proper order. This is accepted as a sound principle in other forms of learning. You cannot, for example, learn calculus before you understand number. You cannot substitute algebra with a bit of French grammar along the way. You cannot taste the fruit before you plant the seed.

This is not to claim that the Druid Way is well or fully defined in the present day. It is not that kind of thing. It derives from the natural world, which changes and evolves. Part of being Druid is the constant striving to understand what we are and what we are becoming. To do that effectively we have to look beyond our own Way to other traditions and ways to help us fill the gaps in our understanding.

So it is that we all of us have interests in Native American Spirit Ways, in Shamanisn, in ancient Chinese philosophy, in Buddhism, in Christian Gnosticism, and so on. However, an 'interest in', no matter how deep, should not be confused with a 'commitment to' or a 'commitment to becoming'.

This has only touched on the subject. Commitment to a Way is a form of meditation on a grand scale. It is the gradual calming of the mind over many years. To begin with, the enquiring mind darts hither and yon in search of knowledge. The more it learns the more it begins to see patterns. As it settles into a particular pattern, the knowledge it has gathered is assimilated and begins to fall away. The more you know, the less you need to know.

As that knowledge falls away it reveals a growing wisdom upon which the mind centres and finds rest. In that wisdom we may, ultimately, find enlightenment. In that enlightenment, we find the means by which we can serve the world.

It is not our intention in this to scare you, simply to point out that there are very real dangers to your spirit if you do not take care of it. Fear takes no one forward. The only lesson you learn is to despise your teacher. Openness and understanding are much better. The more you learn, the better you can protect yourself simply through the fact that your spirit is strong and true.

For now, it is enough to study the Forest and study the tree. It is all there.

Questions

If you have come this far and you are still determined to learn more, you have already begun to take your first steps along the Druid Way. If that is the case, there are a number of points of which you should be aware.

The Druid Way is a spiritual discipline that has, in its essence, much in common with other spiritual disciplines. What makes the Druid Way unique is that it is rooted in a particular place and a particular culture. The understanding we aim for is brought to light through the history, language, peoples, events, and understanding of what, for want of a more precise term, we call the Celtic World. This is a complex issue that is explored later on.

The point is that your psyche is moulded by all the aspects of the place in which you live. That means (and there are *always* exceptions) that it is easier to approach the mysteries of the Way through what is familiar in terms of myth and folk tale. That is why the Druid Way works through the Matter of Britain and the myth and folklore that gave birth to those tales. That is why its sacred groves are of oak.

Through working with the commonplace, the everyday, the familiar (and the sometimes despised), we are more readily able to pull aside the veil and come to understand the Truths that lie behind these things - Truths that are common to all peoples.

Nothing is carved in stone, because the living world that is our teacher changes and evolves. There is no Druid 'Bible'. There were and are no Druid charismatic leaders. And no one Druid knows everything there is to know. What we offer herein is the result of many years of our own learning along with a consensus that has been reached by many others. However, the Forest is vast and there are many places of purest wilderness.

What we offer are ways by which you may better come to know and understand the world; ways by which to develop your relationship with the world. That relationship is unique to you. And as you learn, you will find that the wisdom you gain will eventually take you onwards, beyond the Forest. Not out the other side, but beyond.

To be Druid is a means to an end. It is of no worth as a Way if it is not travelled to its destination. You may never get there, but you will have progressed. What the destination might be is revealed to you by the Goddess for that is at the heart of your personal mystery, at the heart of your relationship with the world.

If, at any time, you decide you want to take a break away from what you are doing or if you want to stop altogether, that is your absolute and unquestionable right. After all, it is entirely possible that you come to feel this is not the path for you. No one will be offended by any rejection or any argument that is honest – Druids hold Truth to be the most essential of virtues.

If you decide you want a break it can be as long as you like. Even if it is twenty years and you want to come back after that, that is fine. You are in charge!

With all that said, we would like you first to reflect on and respond to a number of questions. These are not intended to try to get you to change your mind. We simply want you to begin to clarify certain things. You may change your ideas as time goes on, but the important thing now is that you get into the habit of thinking carefully about everything, of questioning everything, and trying to answer every question. That is, we know from experience, a tall order, but it does become easier as you progress.

To make the task easier, keep a journal. In this, you can write down your thoughts, reactions, dreams, poems, the titles of books, quotations... As time goes by you will be able to relate back to things and see how you have moved on from where you were.

Simplicity is of the essence. If you have complicated thoughts and ramble for two pages trying to express them, they may not mean much to you when you read them in a year's time. Try poetry instead of prose as this often pushes you to encapsulate an idea in just a few words. At the same time, do not regard it as a chore. There are times when thoughts, ideas, feelings, and understanding cannot be put into words - these are the truest of our mysteries.

Honesty is also of the essence. This will be a private journal. You can put what you like into it and use it as a reference. You can also express yourself as fully and as ripely as you wish.

In some respects, it is a bit like making a map of your journey through the Forest. We will offer you the ways in and some basic thoroughfares to follow; symbols to use and signs to watch for; hints on good ways to travel and the etiquette to be followed; but you will no doubt want to look at everything that catches your eye.

So, to begin.

❖ Do you stand before the Forest of your own free will? That is, are you here because of your own search rather than because of pressure from someone or something else? It does not matter whether this is a step toward the Druid Way or a step away from everything else. Both steps take you in a particular direction. But they must be your steps.

- ❖ Do you wish to learn? It may sound a strange question, but many approach the Forest because they want to impose their vision on it. It cannot be done.
- ❖ Do you realize that if you enter the Forest, it is a serious venture that will change your life and affect those around you?
- ❖ Do you still wish to learn?
- ❖ Do you understand that once you reach the boundary of the Forest, you alone must decide whether you wish to enter? No one can force you. No one can shape you. No one can decide for you. We can show you the way, but you must walk the path for yourself.
- ❖ Do you realize that this book (or any other book) cannot make you Druid? It can only teach you the markers on the route to the Forest and give you a grounding in Forest craft.
- ❖ Do you understand that even if you learn well, the mysteries will only be revealed to you if you are truly ready and the Goddess so grants it? She may have her reasons for keeping the mysteries from you and you must accept this.
- ❖ Do you understand that to be Druid is a complete thing? It is not just for high days and holy days. It is for all days and all thoughts and actions, no matter how trivial they may seem. It is for all relationships with the world.
- ❖ Do you understand that, above all else, to be Druid is to Serve and that to Serve is to immerse one's self in the light of Truth that one may radiate it to the entire world?

A last word. The more involved you become with the Druid Way, the more you become Druid, the more you attune yourself with the underlying rhythms of the universe, the more out of tune you are likely to feel with the World (that is, with the workings of mankind – see the Glossary). It is not, therefore, a journey to be taken lightly.

It may be that you already feel at odds with the World and you are seeking a structure to your own feelings. For you this is not such a problem. However, before you set foot on the Forest path remember those about you - your family and friends - and how this will affect your relationships with them, even if you keep your journey a secret. Indeed, a secret journey may bring changes to you that others do not understand.

Consider, then, whether you should tell your nearest and dearest about what you are going to do. In some respects, it will make life easier, especially when you need quiet time to yourself. Consider, also, what you are going to tell them. A sensible first step may simply be to express an interest. You are committed to nothing, but you are not likely to spring unwelcome surprises on anyone either. And if you have a particularly close partner, it may just be that they want to make the journey with you.

*

May you be blessed with the cauldron's gift
may the breath of inspiration touch you
may your voice always sing
may the Light reach within you
may you learn from the Land
may the seed you plant be fruit for your children
may calmness be your mantle
may wisdom blaze out from the depths of your soul
may Truth be at the heart of you

PART ONE

HOW THE WORLD CAME TO BE

THE MEANING OF THE WORD 'DRUID'

It was classical Greek writers who first recorded the word *Druidae*. The earliest known references survive from the second century BC, but come to us third hand as quotations via Diogenes Laertius, a Greek living in the third century AD, who wrote *Lives and Opinions of Eminent Philosophers*.

What the Greek authors actually had to say about Druids may be found elsewhere. Our present concern is with the meaning of the word. For some, the search for meaning is a dry and fruitless topic. And whilst it is true that words derive their meaning in large part from their context and use, a search for the origin of the name of something does help to illuminate the origins of the thing itself.

The etymology of 'Druid' is uncertain, but there is one thing on which everyone agrees. For all that its earliest known appearance in writing is in Greek, the word is undoubtedly Celtic. Beyond that, there is consensus, but no certainty. A number of plausible interpretations have been made over the centuries, but debate continues.

Some leading Celtic etymologists, including Rudolf Thurneysen, Holger Pedersen, Henri d'Arbois de Jubainville, and Whitley Stokes saw the word as being composed of two parts. The *dru* element they regarded as an intensive whilst the *wid* element means 'to know' or 'to see'. The composite meaning of Druid, therefore, was seen as being something like 'very knowing', or 'all seeing'. As the name for an intellectual caste, this is entirely apposite if somewhat dull and un-Celtic in its flavour.

This is further complicated by the equally viable interpretation of *vid* as the root for Celtic words that refer both to knowledge and to trees. That the two share a common root is indicative of the importance of trees to the Celts.

Closer to the Celtic spirit would be an interpretation that gives us *dreo,* meaning 'truth', as the first element. The composite then means 'one who sees the truth'. Seeing, of course, encompasses both knowing and understanding. Given that Truth is a central tenet of the Druid Way, and was of great importance in the everyday lives of Celtic peoples, this meaning may reflect more accurately the function of the Druid in society.

Other commentators have looked to more contrived readings of the word to elicit a meaning. Davies derived 'Druid' from the British *dar*, which he gives as 'superior' and *gwydd*, which he gives as 'a priest'. This was presumably in an attempt to provide a meaning for and connection with *gowydd* or *ovydd*, 'a subordinate priest'. Toland thought the word *drud*, in old British, signified 'a discreet or learned person'. The basis for these particular interpretations is obscure.

Less contrived is the derivation offered by Pezron. He offers the idea that 'Druid' is from the Celtic *deru*, 'oak', and *hud*, 'enchantment' – citing Pliny on the Druids' attachment to performing rituals in the presence of the oak.

These, however, are minority views. Most modern authorities agree with the classical authors who stated that the title of 'Druid' is derived from the Celtic words for 'oak', combined with the Indo-European root word *wid*. This combination gives us a word that means something like 'one with knowledge of the oak', or 'one who sees the oak'.

Support for this can be found in the widespread survival of the word for 'oak' in a whole host of related languages.

Dair	Irish (*Drui* – druid)	*Doire*	Gaelic
Dervo	Gaulish	*Derw*	Breton
Derwen	Welsh (*Derwydd* – druid)	*Druh*	Sanskrit
Drus	Greek	*Dre/Dry*	Saxon

These all derive from what is thought to be a single Indo-European root word of great antiquity. This does not necessarily mean that the caste that became known as Druids also pre-dates the Celts, although the more we learn of the past, the smoother seems to have been the transition from one culture to the next.

The oak did not stand alone as a special tree for ancestral Celts or the Druids. Indeed, surviving texts from Ireland (where Druids kept their place in society for much longer than in other Celtic countries) refer to other trees more often than the oak, which has led some to question the 'oak' etymology.

There are also those who argue that there is an etymological difference between the root *dur* as given above and the root *dru* from which Druid derives. They are correct to point to the more generalized interpretation of *vid* as 'tree' (and of *dur* as both 'knowledge' and 'door'). However, this ignores the fact that the word we use now is a Latinized form of the original Celtic.

We know the oak was important to the Druids and we also know that it was likely to have been regarded as the father of all trees (in the sense of eldest and protector rather than the more literal sense of progenitor). The oak symbolized both the forest, which had been the home and constant neighbour of European peoples from the earliest times, and the Forest.

Other words in the Celtic languages strengthen the general connection with trees in that many words for knowledge, wisdom, magic, and the like are also derived from the root that gave us the words for trees and forest. Knowledge, wisdom, and trees were inextricably linked, therefore, in the minds of early peoples and their rites and rituals were performed in the presence of the most venerable of the trees, the oak.

The oak is a climax tree. That is, it appears in mature forests and is the pillar around which all else comes and goes. It provides the structure and continuity that holds the rest of the mature forest together. It is also host to an unprecedented number of animal and insect species.

The wisdom of the Druids had its origins in a time when oak forests covered Europe and were an integral part of all aspects of life. This was at the beginning of the Neolithic period when Goddess worship was thought to be universal.

The oak, in particular, and trees in general, provided materials for all aspects of life – wood, shelter, fuel, food. Indeed, the acorn was still regarded as an important foodstuff in twelfth century Ireland. Those who knew the oak (that is, those who knew the trees, those who knew the forest) stood a better chance not just of survival, but of comfortable living. The greater the wisdom, the greater the level of comfort.

French Celticist J. de Cambray pointed out the fact that the Celts, in common with many other peoples, believed that humans were descended from trees – specifically the oak tree, which they held to be the father of their race. Their priests and wise men were, therefore, interpreters and oracles of the ancestors.

The degree to which ancestral Celts believed they were descended from the oak is uncertain. It is unquestionably part of their mythology, but ancestral Celts were a sophisticated people who understood the role of mythology far better than many people today. They may have embraced it as a Truth, symbolically or literally, but not as the whole Truth.

Proto-Celtic Indo-Europeans and the earlier peoples of Europe very likely had analogous beliefs, which they approached in similar fashion. They were certainly a people of the forest even more than the Celts. They were steeped in its magic and it was far from being a place of fear or darkness, as some fatuous academics would have us believe. A place to respect, without a doubt, but our early ancestors were far too much a part of the forest ever to fear it.

It was from these peoples and their priests that the Druids 'inherited' their wisdom. It is also possible that the name and the function of the caste to which it belongs were also inherited from these earlier peoples. Indeed, the Celts were not a 'new' people, merely the same people who had developed a culture sufficiently distinct from the old for us to give it a name.

Knowledge of the oak, knowledge of the forest, can easily be seen as purely pragmatic. Yet those who knew the lore of the forest and the paths that ran through the forest would have been well aware of the less tangible dimensions of their existence, highly conscious of their place in the great web of life. Moreover, in such a rich environment that provided them with all their needs and more, these people would have had plenty of time to contemplate and explore the mysteries that surrounded them.

There is a further depth to the meaning, especially for a people who knew they were an integral part of the natural world. Knowledge of the oak would also have meant having the same knowledge that the oak has – perceiving and understanding the world as the oak and the forest perceives and understands it. That would mean being part of the forest, taking the long view of life, the slow view – adopting wood sense.

Druids, indeed, were the oaks of human society. They appeared when the 'forest' was sufficiently mature and stable to support them. In turn, they provided the structure for society, provided the continuity, nurtured all living beings and allowed the other trees (for some people are birches, others are yews, some are willows, others still hazel, and so on) to flourish and co-exist.

Even in this short discussion, it is easy to see that there is much upon which to meditate. This is not a case where accepting one meaning in any way invalidates any of the others. They have all been arrived at through a sensible study of the problem. That one is more likely than the others simply provides a core about which the other relevant meanings may orbit, the relative weight of each one offering due influence to the whole.

It is indicative of the whole field of study that definitive answers are not to be found. However, a sense of the essence may be detected in the air like an elusive scent, blended from many flowers. Whilst it is instructive and fun to try to decide what individual flowers are contributing, it is much more important to remember, savour, and learn from the synthesis – elusive as it may be.

THE CELTS

Context

Druids were Celts. The Druid caste was an integral part of Celtic society, providing essential functions within society and acting as a cohesive force that bound the different tribes together. We cannot understand the modern Druid Way without understanding ancestral Druids. We cannot do that without first considering the context within which they existed and operated.

The history of the Celts is, perhaps, the most extraordinary of all the peoples who have inhabited the European landmass and its islands. Their language, culture, and traditions have survived for several millennia despite the major impact of the Romans, Goths, Huns, Vandals, Saxons, and Normans along with many other cultural and religious influences. Indeed, despite all this, they have left a distinct and indelible mark on the world.

The likeliest explanation for such survival is in the fact that the Celts are neither a race nor a nation. They were unified by non-material aspects of being - intangibles such as language and thought, belief and skills – all born out of a metaphysical stance that imbued both society and person.

National borders came and went; invaders came and went with them. In the end, the Celtic peoples have outlived them all, for it is important to remember that Celts still exist in their millions – despite the many modern and insidious attempts to destroy their living culture.

An explanation for the power of their vision and the indelible mark it has made on the world is harder to find. One suspects it lies in the fact that the Celtic peoples were intuitively and emotionally in tune with their world. Wherever they went, they took their essential vision with them and found it reflected in what was already there.

However, it goes further, for the way in which they saw the world and the ways in which they expressed that vision touch us directly without the need to intellectualize. They had the ability to see and live in the everyday world as poets of the divine.

Although ancestral Celts recognized the distinction between poetry and farming, the exquisite metal work they produced and house building, art, religion, politics, and all the rest, they knew that these were only distinctions and nothing more - symptoms of the inadequacy of human communication. They also knew that farming is a spiritual and political endeavour, that devotion to the gods is entirely practical. Yet, in knowing it, they did not intellectualize it as we do. For them it was simply how you did things, how you looked at the world – and that was enough.

It is an important point to grasp. We view the world in a very different way to our ancestors. We are brought up in a social system that accepts certain concepts as axiomatic – some of which were formulated only in the last century and which seemed strange to our grandparents when they were first voiced. Other notions have come into being over a much longer period and are now rarely questioned within the mainstream. It is one of the tasks of the modern Druid to rediscover our ancestor's way of thinking and of viewing the world.

Proto-Celts
The Celts came into being as a recognizable culture along with the development of iron smelting and other technologies for the working of the metal. But this culture did not appear overnight. Metal working skills had been around for centuries and it seems likely that the culture began to develop its distinctiveness during the late Bronze Age. Indeed, a number of factors – not least being the degree of equality afforded women along with the degree of Goddess worship – suggest that Celtic culture had its origins in and was a direct descendant of Neolithic Great Goddess culture.

The Bronze Age people who were the immediate ancestors of the Celts are known only by the name given them by archaeologists – Urnfielders. The designation is derived from their habit of burying their dead in urns laid out in flat cemeteries that resemble fields of the dead. Their home was eastern Europe where they had lived for centuries in a relatively static culture.

These people probably spoke an early form of Celtic, identical with or closely related to the common Indo-European language of the Neolithic and early Bronze Age. They built hilltop enclosures, developed a warrior society in response to the pressures that scattered them westward, and were successful farmers practising crop rotation. Indeed, the only major difference between them and the Celts was iron and burial practice.

Around 1200BC, the settled life of the Bronze Age peoples of Europe was set on his head. Nomads from the eastern steppes of what is now Russia began to move westward. They moved down into the Mediterranean, upsetting the politics of the area on a massive scale. It was this that caused the Urnfielders to develop as warriors, refining their bronze making techniques to produce the armour and the heavy bronze swords that were prized and feared by warriors everywhere.

When in the eighth century BC the Cimmerians, an obscure people from north of the Caucasus, began to move into the region occupied by the Urnfielders, they brought the two final elements that mark the beginning of Celtic culture. Iron. The horse.

Hallstatt

The earliest stage of the development of the Celts is known as the *Hallstatt*, named for a small village in the Salzkammergut of Austria. It was here that a cemetery associated with the salt mines was discovered, with evidence of a distinct cultural type.

Salt was, with iron, the major currency of the Hallstatt Celts. Salt had been mined for centuries before the emergence of Celtic culture, but it became instrumental in the rise of the people. They not only traded the salt, but they used it to produce salted fish and meats. This allowed them to travel long distances without the need to waste time hunting along the way.

Although salt and iron produced a surplus of wealth, it was farming that formed the basis of Celtic economy. The quality of farming in the region, already advanced in many of its techniques, was greatly enhanced by the introduction of iron. Fields were more easily ploughed, opening up areas with heavier soils. Woodland could be felled more efficiently. The strength of the metal meant that tools lasted longer and could be smaller and more delicate.

Farming became immensely productive. More land was made available. Yields increased. Livestock products could be sold further afield as the meats could be preserved. The area became prosperous and the Celts flourished. Inevitably, increased leisure time and greater life expectancy meant a growth of the population.

With the growth of population came an inevitable expansion. The arrival of the Cimmerians had already started to push the Celts westward. By the time that Hallstatt Celts were well established in Austria, Celtic culture had spread into most of western Europe and the south-eastern corner of Britain.

By the sixth century BC, trade with Mediterranean Greek colonies had pulled the centre of Hallstatt power from its original homelands around the upper Danube and surrounding area, to the upper Rhine, encompassing south-west Germany, Switzerland, and Burgundy.

These trading links not only greatly increased the wealth of the Hallstatt Celts, but also introduced the first notions of what we now consider one of the hallmarks of Celtic culture - artistic expression. There is no doubt that such a wealthy people as the Hallstatt Celts were able to indulge their aesthetic appreciation, but it had been mostly through imported materials. The cross-fertilization of ideas and techniques that strong trading links brought was to lead, eventually, to a new stage in the development of Celtic culture.

In 540BC, the Greeks and the Carthaginians went to war. As a result of Carthaginian victories, Greek trade routes along the Mediterranean were cut off and the power base of the Hallstatt Celts was deprived of a major source of its trading wealth. Within a period of two generations, when those trade routes began to re-open, much had changed in the Celtic world.

La Tène

What prompted the changes beyond the collapse of trade with the Greeks is uncertain. No doubt, domestic political changes occurred, as those who had previously provided wealth and stability were no longer able to do so. There was certainly a shift in the structure of Celtic society.

La Tène culture is differentiated from Hallstatt culture by a difference in burial practice, which in turn reflects the changes in social structure. Hallstatt Celts buried their elite in rustic wagons with their weapons and other grave goods – an indication that the farmers were also the warriors and chieftains. La Tène Celts buried their elite with two wheeled chariots. This marks a shift from a society of fighting farmers to a society of warriors supported by farmers.

Also apparent is a development of all those skills needed to produce the goods that had formerly been obtained by trade from Greek sources. This flowering of artisan skills is amply reflected in the burial chariots – magnificently constructed vehicles that are in all respects superior to any other form of chariot in existence at that time.

La Tène culture takes its name from an archaeological site on Lake Neuchâtel in the west of Switzerland. La Tène means 'the shallows' and it was a site held sacred by the Celts for they made votive offerings to whatever deity resided in the waters at this point. A mass of iron swords and other weapons had been sacrificed along with everyday ironwork, woodwork (including an entire wheel), as well as skeletons. All of these items would have been precious and expensive. We do not know in what state the bodies were when they entered the water, but there is no evidence of human sacrifice.

La Tène culture was a development of Hallstatt culture, but it was also more vigorous. This is very likely the result of the need to be self-sufficient. Whereas before Celts relied on trade to provide themselves with a good proportion of their needs, the breaking of trade links meant they had to provide everything for themselves.

The innate skills and sophistication of the Celtic peoples came into their own. They quickly adapted to the new circumstances and within a few generations, we see not just a flowering of skills, but a great social revolution.

There were other consequences. In order for a people to be self-sufficient, they must control all aspects of their life. As a result, the Celtic world increased in size. Whereas Hallstatt Celtic remains are found in central Europe as far south as the Alps and in to south east Britain, by the fifth century BC La Tène culture had expanded well beyond these boundaries.

Eventually La Tène Celts were to be found in Ireland, Britain, northern and western Spain, virtually the whole of France (and eventually all of it), northern Italy, Switzerland, Belgium, the Netherlands, western Germany, the Czech and Slovak Republics, Romania, Bulgaria, and the republics of the former Jugoslavia as far south as the northern borders of Macedonia. They even colonized a part of central Turkey, which became known as Galatia after its people. Moreover, they traded well beyond these borders.

By this stage, Celts begin to figure in the earliest written accounts of the classical world. These brief accounts are both respectful and not a little fearful. Respectful in that the authors recognize Celts as every bit their equals in all aspects of life; fearful in that they recognized they had no means by which to prevent Celtic expansion into their territories.

In the fifth century BC, Celts from Switzerland and eastern Gaul moved into Italy, settling in the north and venturing as far south as Sicily. In 387BC, Celts under the leadership of an individual named Brennus marched into Rome and sacked the city. Thus began the Romans' single-minded hatred of the Celts.

The Celts were not interested in creating an empire, as the Romans were later to forge. Having defeated their enemies, they did not try to impose their political or religious beliefs on those they had beaten. They were not conquerors in that sense. What they wanted was land on which to settle and get on with their lives.

In 295BC, the Romans began their long expansion out of Italy. By 225BC, they had northern Italy within their influence. For all that, it was another hundred years before the Romans had established sufficient control of their home territory for them to feel confident enough to take on the Celtic peoples and absorb them into their ever-growing empire.

During this period, the Celtic world was expanding in other directions. They marched through Greece, the Balkans, and even entered Macedonia in 279BC – destroying the hub of what had been Alexander's vast empire.

Their success as warriors soon meant that Celts were in great demand as mercenaries. It was this that led to the foundation of Galatia. Mercenaries were also to be found in the Syria of the Selucid kings, Judea of Herod the Great, Carthage until its impending defeat by Rome, and even Egypt of the Ptolemy pharaohs.

The Celtic troops of Ptolemy II actually attempted a *coup d'état*, but it was put down. It did not stop Ptolemy and his successors from using other Celts. Indeed, Cleopatra VII (the last of the Ptolemies) had an elite bodyguard composed of 400 Celtic warriors. It was this unit that was given as a gift by Octavian to Herod the Great.

The expansion of Celtic influence came to an end in the second century BC. The countries of the eastern Mediterranean began to reassert their independence. The Cimbri of Jutland joined forces with the Teutones and harried the Celts of north-western Europe. And finally, the Romans began their long conquest of the Celtic realms.

Under subversive influences from Rome, Gaul was thrown into political turmoil in the middle of the first century BC. It is a technique still in use today by the great imperial powers of western society. They enforce monopolistic trading treaties. They covertly encourage turmoil, providing weapons and training for malcontents who would otherwise have little impact on their own society. Thus weakened, any society is wide open to military or economic domination by outside forces.

Julius Caesar used this to his personal advantage as well as the advantage of Rome. With Gaul in turmoil and unable to present a united front, he was able to tear the country apart, piece by piece. However, for all his boasting and the picture he paints of himself in his writings, Gaul was not a walkover. It was a seven-year campaign of unremitting and bloody warfare during which he signally failed to make any inroads on Britain and which left Gaul a rebellious and unsettled province. When Caesar was assassinated, Gaul was still not wholly under Roman control despite his defeat of Vercingetorix.

In central Europe, Celtic culture became increasingly diluted through occupation by and trade with Rome. The last remaining stronghold of La Tène Celtic culture, and the place that saw its greatest flowering was Britain and Ireland. Ironically, it was the final upheaval to pre-Christian Celtic society in Britain that both prompted a new and vigorous phase of artisanship and opened many of the trading links with Rome that led to the eventual weakening of Celtic unity. This upheaval was the migration of the Belgae.

Many historians refer to this migration as an invasion. This is nonsense. The evidence of tribal names shows that many Celtic tribes had a presence on both sides of the Channel – an arrangement that may have developed from the Celtic practice of fostering. There may well have been a Belgic presence in Britain, which opened its arms to its continental cousins who came as refugees from Roman occupied Gaul.

Britain was to prove an even more difficult prospect than Gaul for the Romans. Whilst some tribes were happy to accept the Roman presence, and whilst the legions were established throughout most of the territory now known as England by the end of the first century AD, they were never able to establish a convincing presence in west Wales, Cornwall, Highland Scotland and never, as far as we know, even considered the conquest of Ireland. And even where they were established, they did not have things their own way.

The best known of the rebellions against Roman rule was the uprising of the Iceni and other tribes under the rule of their queen who is now known as Boudicca, a corruption of the Celtic word for 'victory'. And victory it nearly was; yet the unremitting and tireless machine of the Roman army broke Boudicca's loose confederation.

Rome's retribution was relentless with the destruction of towns and villages and the salting of fields, allowing whole tribes to starve – those, that is, that they did not butcher or send to Rome as slaves.

Yet the spirit of Celtic Britons was not broken, any more than the Druids were wiped out – as so many historians have carelessly assumed. Throughout the Roman occupation of Britain, there were rebellions and there was trouble. Although the cohesive power of the Druids was dispelled in the south-east, they had been far from destroyed.

Celtic peoples continued to live and work under the occupation, and it was they who were left to defend the country against increasing Saxon incursions when Rome removed its protection at the beginning of the fifth century AD. By this stage, the withdrawal of Rome was far from clear cut. Many of the soldiers who were ordered to protect the Roman heartland had strong ties with Britain through family and marriage. Many deserted.

During the fifth century AD, much of the wealth that Britain generated was used to pay for training warriors, replenishing hillforts, and building other defensive works. The Saxon invasions were fought and kept in check. For several generations, the Saxon presence was confined to the south-eastern corner of Britain, their power broken at the battle of Badon.

However, the Saxons, like the Romans, were unremittingly warlike and the Celtic lands were slowly occupied once again by a people who were far less tolerant of Celtic ways than the Romans had ever been. However, for all their savagery, the Saxons were unable to occupy more territory than the Romans. The western extremities of Britain remained largely untouched, despite attempts to enter and occupy.

The wheel turns. By the time the Saxons had settled and adopted many of the farming, social, and cultural practices of their Celtic vassals and become a more peaceable and enlightened society, they found themselves subjected to the invasions and cruelties they had practised in the past. First came the Danes, raiding and nearly taking the country by force. Then the Norman storm troopers ravaged the land.

On the fringes of all this - the fringe becoming ever smaller and more remote - were the Celtic peoples of the West. And, as many times before, such adversity produced a new flowering of Celtic culture – this time with Christianity as the leavening force.

During the slow and violent growth of Saxon Britain, Ireland was becoming renowned throughout Europe and beyond as a centre of learning. The universities, many of them once druidic colleges, flourished – producing beautiful books and writing down much that had until that time only been held in the memory of Druids.

This revival was not confined to Ireland. Native Irish, Scots, and Welsh missionaries travelled throughout the north of Europe, establishing Christian monasteries and setting up schools. At one stage, what we now call Celtic Christianity (a blend of the Celtic metaphysic, Druid teachings, and Christian Gnostic teaching) was set to rival Rome in its dominance of Europe. Even now, Roman Christianity owes most of its basic teaching to a movement it once considered heretical.

It was the Normans, backed by Rome, who completed the seeming subjugation of the Celtic world with their castles and economically engineered famines, their outlawing of the use of Celtic languages and practices. Yet neither they, nor successive dynasties of English kings and protectors, succeeded completely. For Celtic peoples and Celtic culture still exists.

Culture

Culture is a big word. Moreover, when we use it in connection with ancestral Celts we are faced with an enormous problem. In our present and hugely disarticulated society, the term 'culture' is used to refer to specific aspects of that society – generally speaking, the aesthetic. That is, culture generally refers to the arts – painting, music, poetry, literature, drama, opera, dance, sculpture, pottery, and so on.

These things are referred to as if they were separate entities that existed within society, but without having concern for other aspects of society such as science, technical and artisan skills, manufacturing, farming, politics, religion, philosophy, and so on.

The notion that aesthetic pursuits can be separated from the rest of life is derived from the metaphysic upon which modern society is founded. This evolved in tandem with the idea of science; each reinforcing the other until we have came to an underlying metaphysic that is materialistic and analytic, ignoring the realities of the world.

Ancestral Celts would have found the modern attitude to the arts incomprehensible. Indeed, they would have found our whole way of life to be based on ideas entirely alien to their own. It is this, more than any other thing, that differentiates us from our ancestors; it is this more than any other thing that we must grasp if we are to be truly Druid.

It is true that ancestral Celts had art, music, architecture, and all the rest – distinctive forms of expression that we can identify and study. It is also true that these derived from the metaphysic underlying all that Celts were, just as modern aesthetic sensibilities are derived from materialistic and analytic thought. And in that which is the same also lies that which makes one world so different from the other.

Where modern thought disarticulates the differing facets of our life, the metaphysical basis of Celtic thought unified them. Nor is it just modern thought that differs so much from the Celtic view. The seeds of the way in which people of western society see the world today were first sown in classical antiquity by Greek philosophers and the Romans who absorbed them into their somewhat barren and militaristic culture.

It goes a long way to explaining the antipathy between the two peoples. It goes a long way to explaining why most people today consider the people of classical antiquity to have been civilized whilst the Celts are still thought of as uncouth barbarians.

One of the major hurdles we must overcome is that in talking of Celtic culture, we cannot talk about art or dance or architecture as if they were abstract pastimes indulged in by an artistic elite parasitical to society. Indeed, aesthetics as a whole is an idea that is alien to the Celtic metaphysic.

All aspects of Celtic life were connected, each reflected in the other. The whole was to be seen in each facet; each facet defined by the whole. Bards, for example, were not poets as we understand them. They used poetic forms to fulfil specific functions within society.

Druids were not an isolated elite who went their own way in pursuit of esoteric knowledge. They were people who held the picture of society in their heads, who held the many nations and tribes together in their loose confederation. They were doctors, teachers, lawyers, diplomats, and priests.

Farmers were not just people who grew food. They worked and nurtured the land that was held by each tribe in sacred trust; they held the knowledge and passed it on and worked to improve their understanding.

Warriors were not members of a permanent standing army. Apart from the bodyguard of the chief or monarch whose peacetime duties were akin to that of a police force, the others carried out their everyday and mostly agricultural tasks – men and women alike.

Even as an intellectual concept, it is difficult for most modern people of western society to grasp. All things are related. Yet for Celts, it was not an intellectual exercise. It was the way of things, a way that had survived down the millennia and which had produced a vibrant society that, at its height, was as sophisticated as any on the planet – then or now.

Perhaps the easiest way to gain an insight into Celtic culture and to see how it differed from classical culture is by concentrating on the way in which Celts decorated their artefacts.

Celtic decoration as it is commonly recognized is La Tène. Jewellery, weapons, pots, caskets, horse and vehicle harnesses, were rarely plain and were never produced for their own sake. Even jewellery served a purpose in that it was used for pinning clothing, as symbols of status, gifts in ritual bonding, or sacrifices to the gods and goddesses. Yet the decoration was invariably elaborate and highly skilled. Even simple patterns were executed with great skill and an eye for sophisticated design.

The most easily recognized of all these motifs was the sinuous knotwork designs that adorned everything from early period carved bowls through to the richly decorated books of the Christian monasteries. Such designs have become popular of late, but all too often, they are divorced from the very practical objects that they once adorned.

We would perhaps say that every object produced was an act of worship but that, again, is to see it through modern eyes. All life was an act of worship, because the belief and action of each Celt was intimately associated with their belief in the gods and goddesses, with their belief in the sacredness of life. Even a simple cooking pot would reflect this idea of the sacred in all things, the cauldron being a central symbol in the notion of the Otherworld. Decoration was a manifestation of this unity of being.

This can be seen in the flowing lines and sinuous forms, which speak of an understanding of the cyclical nature of existence and of the way in which the natural world flows and curves. Nor was this decoration a crude imitation of the world about them. It was a sophisticated interpretation of the visible world and a symbolic representation of the forces that underpinned that world.

What is more, the decoration was of relatively small, personal, and portable objects. Not only did Celts know they could take it with them to the next world, but they also had no desire to leave behind them vast monuments to their own egos.

Contrast all this with Greek and Roman artistic expression, which is idealistic rather than symbolic, linear, large scale, and invested in things they hoped would live on after they had died, to remind those still alive of their existence - vast and gaudy tombstones.

Religion

When discussing culture and the Celtic metaphysic, it is impossible to disentangle them from Celtic religious beliefs. Again, we must tread warily in making such statements. This is not because the life of the Celt was religious in the sense that we might now understand it. They were not zealots or evangelists (to borrow words from other traditions). Such ideas would have seemed absurd, worth a full-blown Bardic satire. It is simply that the metaphysic that underlay all of Celtic being was a view of the world that was essentially spiritual.

Nor must we fall into the trap of so many scholars in assuming that ancestral Celts were, in some way, primitive. Even the Hallstatt people – the first distinct culture we know as Celtic – were highly sophisticated. Moreover, Celtic culture developed in sophistication from that point forward. They did not, for example, worship the Sun or the trees. To claim so would be as absurd as saying that Christians worship crosses.

Ancestral Celts had no need of organized religion. That, too, was foreign to their nature. There was no holy book. There were no religious leaders. What existed was an all-pervading understanding of the panentheistic nature of the world.

Talk, too, of Druids having a separate cult is absurd. Druids were an integral part of Celtic society. Of all people, they adhered to its social mores, as they were keepers of the law and upholders of Truth, witnesses to its existence.

The pre-Christian Celts were, then, a religious people. Life was a spiritual journey. Every breath, every action, and every thought had a spiritual and religious dimension. Everything was done in reference to the gods and goddesses and to the world of spirit. One only has to consider the many prayers that have come down to us from Celtic regions. Although they are now thinly clothed with a Christian veil, their pagan origin is clear and they constantly refer to the everyday events of life.

Nor was Celtic religion universal in the sense that they all worshipped the same deities. Their underlying beliefs were held in common, but each tribe expressed this in their own way in keeping with the locale in which they lived and which had shaped them. Each tribe had its own deities, its own totems, and its own ways of worship, which were usually kept private (rather than secret). If giving an oath, a Celt would often say 'I swear by the gods my tribe swears by' in order to protect their own sources of spiritual strength and well-being.

As well as this, there seem to have been some deities and folklore themes held in common by all Celts. In some cases, it is possible to relate this to the family structure of the gods and goddesses. Those that the tribes held in respect tended to be the children of those who were universally regarded.

For all this, we have no idea whether the Celts had a name for their religion. Given that it was such an integral part of everyday life, it is unlikely that they ever bothered to distinguish it by naming it. Of one thing we can be certain – it was not called Druidry or Druidism. Druids acted as priests and they certainly shared the beliefs of all other Celts, they may even have presided over a unifying cult, but the teachings of the Druid did not constitute a religion.

Like most religions of the ancient world, and many today, Celtic religion was polytheistic. There are just over 370 names of Celtic deities extant with indications of others whose names have not survived. Most of these occur once or are confined to relatively small localities. These local deities were probably connected with specific tribes, and are often referred to as *teutates*. Some twenty names occur with greater frequency and are to be found (sometimes in cognate form) across the entire region once inhabited by the Celts.

Most deities were conceived of as having human form. One only has to consider the many depictions of deity that began to appear after the Celtic world had contact with classical Greece. Depictions of animals also figure largely in carvings and statues that are associated with religious practice and it is therefore reasonable to assume that animals were recognized as having spirit and spiritual ancestors. They certainly figure widely in the tales and mythologies that have come down to us, often as sources of wisdom. Indeed, many of the poems and tales that have an initiatory element contain sections in which humans and animals shapeshift.

Animal and god names also figure as elements in personal, place, and tribal names – Cunobelinus (hound of Belinus, the shining one); Camulodunum (the town of Camulos, a god of the Gauls); the many rivers named for Danu or Don; the Brigantes (the people of Brigantia or Brigid).

Cernunnos, indeed, seems to have been a major deity and there are convincing arguments that Cernunnos is a personal or variant name for The Dagda (the Good God – father of all deities). If this is so, then a picture of the triune nature of Cernunnos begins to emerge. As Lord of the Animals and bearer of the club that can destroy with one end and restore life with the other, the role of Creator, Preserver, and Destroyer is evident and the form and name of the chalk giant at Cerne Abbas becomes clear.

For all that this mighty and potent figure dominates, it is clear that the Celts believed their origins lay with the Mother Goddess, Danu. Her name means 'divine water from heaven' and she fell from the sky (as rain?), watered the sacred oak Bíle, and gathered to form the great Danuvius (Danube). From this union sprang the pantheon of gods and goddesses known, in Irish, as the Tuatha Dé Danaan and in Welsh as the Children of Dôn. More can be found on deity later in the book.

However, religion and belief are not simply about gods and goddesses. Belief encompassed all aspects of life and is reflected by many of the practices that fascinated those who encountered the Celtic world. For example, the notion of threes was not confined to aspects of deity. The triads of Wales and Ireland, used by the Druids as aids to teaching, are immensely powerful poetic forms, even now when they have come down to us in corrupt form and without the material to which they act as pointers. The Celts also saw people as body, soul, and spirit; divided nature into animal, vegetable, and mineral; knew the primary colours as red, yellow, and blue; ascribed the colours of red, black, and white to the mysteries; divided the worlds into three; endowed the Druids with three aspects.

Three was not the only number important to Celts. Each one was accorded its place, and they recognized the power of number as well as the connections and correspondences they accorded. However, where other numbers tended to be derived from the material world, three was the number most closely associated with religious and spiritual thought and thereby underlay the Celtic metaphysic. Indeed, the Celtic belief in the power of the three has been a major influence on another religion. Hilary, Bishop of Poitiers, whose work *De Trinitate* defined the concept of the Holy Trinity in Christianity for the first time, was a Gaulish Celt. The Celtic metaphysic underpins the whole of Christianity.

Another important aspect of the religious sensibility of Celts was their fascination with the head. The Celts believed not only that the soul was to be found in the head, but also that it was the seat and source of all that defined humans as humans. The head was venerated and it was considered a mark of respect to keep the head of a person that had been admired in life, be that friend or enemy. Heads were embalmed in cedar oil and kept as prized possessions, so highly revered that they were often given as offerings in sacred rituals.

Some have interpreted this as evidence that Celts were headhunters. This is plain nonsense. They did not kill others to get their heads. Heads were only taken after the person had died – in battle or naturally – and then only if they had been held in respect during their life.

Heads feature in many of the tales and myths of the Celts, talking after they have been severed from their bodies. Bran the Blessed (Bendigeid Fran) is one such example. Mortally poisoned, he orders his men to cut off his head before the poison reaches it. This they do, and on the journey back to Britain, the head of Bran talks, gives them advice, even tells jokes.

Perhaps the best known of tales involving decapitation is *Sir Gawain and the Green Knight*, a Welsh form of tales that are also to be found in Ireland connected to Cúchulainn. This poem is vibrant with mysticism and the tales associated with the cycle of the year.

Heads of all form feature widely in sculpture as well and the notion of the head as the seat of the soul survived well into the twelfth century. Walk into any ancient church or cathedral and you will be surrounded by severed heads – some lifelike, some grotesque, some foliate, all owing their existence to pre-Christian Celtic beliefs.

Celts believed the soul was indestructible, that there was an afterlife in the Otherworld, and that the soul returns to this world. Much has been made of the similarity of the beliefs of Pythagoreans and the Celts and much discussion has been wasted on who taught whom – classical scholars adamant that the Celts borrowed from Pythagoras and Celticists the opposite. In all likelihood, given the major differences between the beliefs, they were parallel developments.

Pythagoras's ideas (as far as we know them from second hand sources) were a form of karmic metempsychosis, the new body and its life being a reward or punishment for the life as it was lived before – a kind of snakes and ladders of the soul.

Celts did not believe in reward or punishment in the afterlife due in part, one suspects, to their highly developed sense of moral and legal justice in this world. Their idea of immortality was that of a changing of places. Those who died in this world were reborn in the Otherworld, a fabulous reflection of this reality. There they lived their lives and, when they died, they were reborn in this world.

When a child was born, Celts mourned for the death of that soul in the Otherworld. Death in this world was an occasion of joy for the rebirth of the soul in the Otherworld. This fits well with the notion of life and the world as cyclical, unlike present day obsession with material linearity. The Celts knew that death occasioned new life; that each year those things that had died would be reborn.

Valerius Maximus, writing in the first century AD, told that Celts 'lent sums of money to each other that are repayable in the next world, so firmly convinced are they that the souls of men are immortal'. When the dead were buried, grave goods according to their station and their wealth went with them. Personal belongings, imbued with the spirit of the person through constant use, were rarely left behind as heirlooms for the living.

So real was the Otherworld that it had physical location in the minds of our ancestors and was, indeed, a place that the living could visit and from whence, if they were careful, they could return. Arthur raided the Otherworld in search of a magic cauldron (the original Grail quest story); Bran travelled to islands in the West by boat; Cúchulainn journeyed to Hy-Falga; Oisín dwelt there for 300 years.

The Otherworld has many names. These were euphemistic and poetic references to a place that had its own seasons and cycles to which different names were attached. Annwn is the traditional Cymric name although it is also referred to as Caer Feddwid (the Court of Intoxication) and Caer Siddi (Court of the Gods). In Ireland it is referred to as Hy-Breasail (Breasail's Island – for which Brazil was later named); Dún Scaith (Fortress of Shadows); Magh Da Cheo (Plain of Two Mists); Tír na nOg (Land of Youth); Tír Tairnigiri (Land of Promise); Magh Mell (Plain of Happiness); and Tír na tSamhraidh (the Land of Summer). There are many other such names. Most paint a picture of an earthly paradise; others are more brooding; all are reflections of this world and the human experience.

Travelling to the Otherworld, by the living or the dead, involved a journey into the West. Whilst the living had to undergo adventures and dangers to make the journey, the dead had an easier time of it. Their souls gathered at special places and were ferried into the sunset. In Irish myth (which has remained the most uncorrupted by later redactors), the gatekeepers of the Otherworld are, appropriately, those from whom our first ancestors sprang – Danu and Bíle.

There was one day of the year when the doors between the worlds became visible and were opened. The festival of Samhain (conventionally celebrated after the sun sets on 31 October) marked this. Much debased now as Hallowe'en and a target for 'Christian' fundamentalists, it was a time to remember those who had died in the previous twelve months and may even have been a time when temporary interments were made permanent. It was also a time when the dead who had been wronged by the living were allowed to return and re-balance the scales.

As well as their beliefs, the moral code by which ancestral Celts lived their lives has come down to us in part. That which has survived is sufficient to see that it was at the heart of all their conduct, providing the moral axioms derived from their metaphysic and by which they lived all aspects of their lives.

According to Diogenes Laertius, the central principle of Celtic life (expressed appropriately in triadic form) was that they 'should worship the gods, do no evil, and exercise courage'. This sounds somewhat vague, but when we realize that this is underpinned by the central importance of Truth, it becomes an extremely powerful and highly moral stance by which to live.

Truth was the highest principle of all, the very power of creation, the foundation on which all the teachings of Druids were based. It is Truth that sustains the world.

So deeply embedded is Truth in the whole metaphysic of the Celts, that the word for 'truth' in Celtic languages is the linguistic root for words such as 'holiness', 'faithfulness', 'reality', and words connected with the idea of free will and responsibility. Another euphemism for the Otherworld was The Place of Truth.

To this, we can add, from the various early texts that have survived, that Druids taught there were certain other ideals to which people should aspire. They should live in harmony with the natural world, recognizing that spirit was in all things and that all actions had a sacred dimension. They should live in peace amongst themselves, not quarrelling or fighting, bringing their disputes to the law (which was highly developed). They should accept that death was a natural part of the cycle of existence. They should understand that the only evil was moral weakness.

Central to the Celtic idea of evil was a highly developed sense of what was right and what was wrong. These were encoded in complex laws and teachings, impressed on the people by the use of taboos. The responsibility for good moral living lay with the individual. Tribal living reinforced this and was a moral pressure of its own, but it was the individual who had to answer for their actions.

The whole concept of free will and personal responsibility for one's actions and one's moral welfare was deeply embedded in the Celtic psyche. In the fourth century AD the Celtic Christian theologian Pelagius was accused of reviving the 'Natural Philosophy of the Druids' when he applied this to Christian theology as a rebuttal to Augustine of Hippo's teaching of preordination. Pelagius was eventually declared a heretic although his teachings are now widely accepted by Christians. Augustine is still regarded as a saint.

There were a number of other Celtic philosophers and theologians working at the same time as Pelagius. The church in Rome considered them a real threat to its spiritual and secular power and they were all condemned as Pelagian heretics. Their teachings, derived from the Celtic metaphysic, are far closer to that of the Christ than were the teachings of the Church - one of the reasons that Christian Gnosticism found an early foothold in Britain.

It would not be possible to write on the religious beliefs of the pre-Christian Celts without mentioning sacrifice. The word 'sacrifice' has two distinct, interconnected meanings. The first is 'to give up something of value' and the second is 'to make sacred'. To do one invariably meant doing the other.

We know ancestral Celts sacrificed inanimate objects: swords, torcs, jewellery, chariots, statues, and even severed heads. We also know that animals were sacrificed, using methods commonly in practice for the slaughter of all animals at the time. Celts certainly did not delight in death and found cruelty to be abhorrent.

There is no evidence, other than the single and often quoted source of Poseidonius, that Celts sacrificed humans. Later Roman writers repeated this claim *ad nauseam,* mostly to justify their own barbarities against the Celtic peoples. Yet there is no hint of a tradition of human sacrifice from within Celtic culture or within extant Celtic literature. Given that this literature was collected and written down by Christian monks, who delighted in denigrating the pagan ways of their forebears, it is curious that even they have found no hint of it.

Recent archaeological finds that are said to constitute human sacrifice offer no such proof. Indeed, what we know of Celtic belief dictates against it. The methods posited, including the famous wicker man, are as ridiculous as the idea that you could cut mistletoe with a blade made of gold.

*

There is not the room here to give a more detailed exposition of Celtic history, the evolution of culture or religious ideas (for they have never been static), or the many archaeological wonders that have been discovered. Others have done this far better and in much greater detail. Some books are recommended, but many more have been written.

In reading them, which you must, it is important to keep open a critical eye. There are very few written from a Celtic viewpoint or with sympathy. Most are written by academics brought up in a tradition that values classical antiquity above all else and which regards the Celts and their forebears as little more than savages. Yet all that we know about Celts, their beliefs, and their conduct, militates against notions of savagery. They were a sophisticated, intelligent, and religious people with an extremely well developed social conscience.

THE DRUIDS

Origin of Druids

It was stated above that Druids were Celts and integral to Celtic society. This is undoubtedly true, but the picture is much more complex. Although Celtic culture as we now recognize it is defined by the Hallstatt and La Tène phases – this does not describe small groups of people who expanded their territory and imposed their vision on others. Rather, the Celts developed as a distinct people over a very long period of time and latterly adopted those practices by which we now recognize them.

Linguistic and genetic studies, along with advances in archaeological understanding, have traced the common stock that we now call Celtic back as far as 4000BC. These proto-Celtic peoples were spread throughout Europe and were themselves inheritors of the culture of Mesolithic peoples. Dramatic evidence of this continuity was found recently when genetic studies showed a direct descent from 9000-year-old remains found in the west of England to people living in the area in the present day. The gene pool has barely been muddied in all that time.

If proto-Celtic culture was indeed in place across Europe as early as 6000 years ago, then it coincides with Neolithic. This period marked a huge change in the relationship that people had with the land as its major feature is settled agriculture. The peoples of Europe flourished and spent a great amount of time and energy in constructing the huge earthworks, chambered tombs, and other mysterious features we find in our landscape.

As stone tools gave way to bronze, the great earth structures that were placed so carefully in the landscape were augmented with the stone circles that are popularly linked with Druids today. These were not built by Celts, but given the evidence presented above, it is now very likely that the Celtic culture was simply an evolution of the culture of the megalith builders. Druids were the rightful heirs to these wondrous structures.

What we know of ancestral Druids, however, marks a spiritual development for whilst they may have been rightful heirs to the stone structures – monuments of the mineral kingdom – they much preferred to work in their groves and with animal spirits. We have inherited this step forward and whilst we still work with the mineral, vegetable, and animal, we also now look to work with the most difficult of all kingdoms – the human.

To understand this work, it is important that we understand as best we can the fertile soil from which Druids grew, the nature of what they became, and the inheritance that they have left us.

We know precious little of the beliefs of the megalith builders. What we do know, however, has much in common with the greater understanding we have of Celtic and druidic belief and practice. They certainly did not lack imagination or organizational skills. Earthworks such as Silbury and the huge complexes such as New Grange, Avebury, and Stonehenge are every bit the equal of the pyramids and predate those piles of stone by many centuries.

This speaks not just of imagination and planning, but also of complex social structures in which the whole population of Britain must have been involved. And along with the major sites are many smaller local sites that, despite our ignorance of their purpose, have an integrity of design that speaks strongly of a shared metaphysic as well as a common and sophisticated mathematics.

It is this shared metaphysic that seems to have been transmitted through the generations from Neolithic peoples to the Iron Age Celts and beyond. The detail we can only speculate upon, but there are strong elements that cannot be denied. The Sun, for example, certainly seems to have played a central role, especially with the number of chambered tombs and sites open to the sky that align to midwinter sunrise – suggesting a whole cycle of belief and ritual connected with the rebirth of the Sun each year.

The huge earthworks that use and sculpt the land to suggest and enhance the female form, point to a view of the land as Mother Goddess and, therefore, as sacred. These works are often juxtaposed with water, which is connected with childbirth as well as being an important threshold between this world and the other.

To oversee the construction of such huge projects, it would have been necessary for there to be a universally dispersed group within society that shared the vision, the knowledge, and the understanding of their form and purpose – a caste of priest builders.

This caste would have been a cohesive force within society, mediating between the people and the divine. Their knowledge and understanding of the world would have been apprehended from nature and focused on the specific tasks they had undertaken. And although the monuments that have come down to us are the ones they created from stone and earth, the forerunners of these were constructed from wood. In this focus on timber and its central role in providing a bridge between the worlds is to be found the genesis of the Druids of the Celtic world.

Structure of the Druid Caste

Native Celtic sources tell us that there were three distinct groups – *Drui, Bard,* and *Fili* – that were considered especially important. Classical sources reflect this. Strabo in his *Geographia* writes:

> ...there are three classes of men held in special honour: the Bards, the Vates and the Druids. The Bards are singers and poets; the Vates are the interpreters of sacrifice and natural philosophers; while the Druids, in addition to the science of nature, study also moral philosophy. They are believed to be the most just of men, and are therefore entrusted with the decision of cases affecting either individuals or the public...

Strabo, it should be noted, used the work of Poseidonios as source material and Poseidonios is well known as an apologist for Rome. Any praise for the Celts or the Druids is therefore to be considered well earned. It should also be noted that both men and women were Bards, Vates, and Druids.

Most classical sources tend to see the division into three as a strict hierarchy of a single organization with Bards at the bottom, Vates in the middle, and Druids at the top. This is compounded by Julius Caesar's description of Gaulish society as having three divisions – the intellectuals called Druids (*Druides*), the military caste (*Equites*), and the people (*Plebs*). All of this is typical of the linear thinking of classical writers. Unfortunately, the notion of a single hierarchical order has been perpetuated by many of the modern Druid Orders.

Although there were distinct divisions within the intellectual caste, Bards and Vates were not only of equal standing one with another, they were both Druids. Druid was the name given to the intellectual caste, which also included philosophers, doctors, priests, astronomers, historians, and many more. Bards, Vates, and Druids did not constitute grades of a single order, although they did all work from a single view of the world. The confusion undoubtedly stems from the training that each of these had.

To become a Druid, one had first to become proficient in the basics of bardic knowledge. The Bard was the master of words and of song and it was through this medium that all else was accomplished. Although there were written texts, none of them

43

contained the teachings necessary to qualify so everything had to be memorized. To aid this prodigious feat, language was used carefully and in its most powerful metrical forms. The rhythms inherent in well-written verse make the words themselves easier to memorize, to recall, and to transmit accurately. Composing such verse and still keeping the sense and truth of the content ensures that it is carefully thought through and closely argued.

Learning the basics of the Bard's craft was probably much the same as taking a Bachelor's degree – although the term of study was far longer and much more rigorous. However, it did provide the student with the wherewithal to further their study in more specialist ways. It was a foundation course.

Those who wished to be Bards would continue with their bardic studies and would go on to earn their place within society by progressing through their equivalents of Masters and Doctoral degrees. That is, they would study more deeply and show that they had mastered their subject sufficiently to be able to teach it to others. From there they would work to make a significant and new contribution to the bardic legacy. In most cases this would undoubtedly be a major piece of original poetry (remembering that poetry was not composed for its own sake) or in exceptional circumstances a new metrical form. At this level, a Bard would be the intellectual equal of any other fully qualified Druid and there was no reason why those of exceptional talent should not then continue their studies in the other fields of study.

With the foundation of bardic studies achieved, one could elect to study to become a Vate (or Ovate as it is more commonly known these days) or a surgeon, or a judge, and so on. They would all then probably study at the next level a syllabus that had much in common, but which began to specialize more and more.

Talk of a syllabus should be approached with caution. Training was organic as befits the Celtic view of the world, yet there were many schools or colleges and it seems likely that the sheer volume of those who were studying would mean that a commonly followed syllabus was a necessity. This was, however, a long way from being a national curriculum!

Quite aside from those who intended to become Bards, Ovates, or any other type of Druid, there were many who were sent to the schools and colleges to receive an education that would allow them to hold their place in society. The Celts were an educated people and even those who did not attend the schools were 'literate' in the terms of an oral culture.

If children were to have schooling, they generally started at the age of seven. As children had no legal responsibility until they were fourteen, it is unlikely they went away before that age unless they were fostered (a fairly common occurrence). Even then they would generally stay with their foster parents and learn the basics within the community.

The nature and structure of Druid schools or colleges is unknown to us other than through folklore, which must be taken with more than a pinch of salt. Talk of huge complexes where thousands gathered to study is fanciful. Most Druids worked in the everyday world of Celtic society and much of the ordinary teaching would have taken place in the villages and towns.

Specialist instruction undoubtedly took place in out of the way places where students were able to concentrate on the prodigious amounts of material they had to memorize - free from the distractions of everyday life. Even so, these students would not have been isolated from everyday concerns for it is likely they would have cultivated their own food and seen to all the other everyday needs of their lives. This has led to the idea that the schools were the model for later Christian monastic settlements. This may be true, but too much should not be read into it.

As for the length of a Druid's training, a number of accounts have come down to us. Common to them all is the fact that it took in the region of twenty years to receive the education necessary to qualify as a Druid. Even if this includes those first seven years when a young Celt was at home with parents or foster parents, it meant that the youngest Druids were close to thirty years of age by the time they had returned to society and found their place.

The period of twenty years sounds suspiciously like a rounded figure. It may well have taken longer for some, and others may have qualified sooner, but buried in that figure is a significant number that may have set the symbolic length of training - nineteen years.

Ancestral Celts used a lunar calendar for mundane life and a solar calendar for the spiritual life that underpinned everything else. The nearest these two calendars get to coinciding is once every nineteen years (235 lunar months = 19 years, two hours, five minutes and ten and a half seconds). Nineteen is a significant number to the Celts and it is also cited by classical authors as important. The mention of Apollo's visit to the land of the Hyperboreans every nineteen years is an indication of this meshing of the lunar and solar calendars. Closer to home, in Geoffrey of Monmouth's *Vita Merlini*, Myrddin speaks of his nineteen apple trees, which may indicate the number of branches accorded this learned man.

The matter of content is much more complex. The only accounts of what was learned in the schools come from the early Christian period in Ireland. The Druid schools had disappeared by then to be replaced by schools for Bards, which existed in parallel to the great monastic schools. Despite the change of name and the removal of religious and legal function, Bards were probably teaching much the same as the Druids had always taught before they changed their name.

Those who attended bardic schools went through seven grades in twelve years. Amongst other things, they learned grammar, the use of ogham, philosophy, verse forms, and composition. They also committed many hundreds of poems and stories to memory.

The training of Druids would have followed along these lines but with much expanded subject matter and the opportunity to specialize in much needed skills. Healing was one such. A study of trees and plants would have enabled a rich understanding of the medicinal properties of flora, as well as the spiritual aspects of healing. There were hospitals in the Celtic world and they used music as part of their healing regime. Moreover, there were skilled surgeons who used tools that any surgeon today would recognize and use. Archaeological evidence suggests that major surgery was carried out successfully on a regular basis.

Druids were also engineers, architects, judges, teachers, philosophers of great renown, historians, theologians, poets and musicians, seers, astronomers and astrologers, magicians, walkers between the worlds, those that held the balance. They were also part of the ordinary world for, apart from the select few whose fame and renown brought them great wealth, the majority of Druids would have been part of village life, known by all, and intimately involved in the everyday existence of the people they served.

The Evolution and Survival of Druids and their Teachings

So, what happened to the Druids and how can we possibly claim a link between the activities of our ancestors of two millennia past and the work that we do today?

Most people assume that the Romans destroyed the Druids. They certainly tried, because Druids represented a cohesive force that tied Celtic society into a formidable alliance of tribes and peoples. It took Caesar seven long and bloody years to 'conquer' Gaul and even then, it was never fully accomplished. It was another 90 years before Rome felt sufficiently confident that Gaul was under their control for it to be safe to launch the invasion of Britain.

The long conquest was continued in Britain - sieges, bloody battles, rebellions, and seething discontent that lasted for centuries. And the Romans never controlled more than a half of the landmass. Rome itself often wondered whether it was worth the effort. It tied up many legions and Britain was a constant centre for rebellious attempts on Rome itself.

In Gaul and in Britain, the Romans were well aware that it was Druids who were the focus of unrest and revolt. It is often cited that a decisive attempt was made to crush the Druids in Britain when, in AD60, C. Suetonius Paulinus concluded a two year campaign in northern Wales by invading Anglesey. There is no evidence (other than Tacitus mentioning the presence of Druids in the resisting army) that this was an assault on druidic centres. It is far more likely that C. Suetonius Paulinus was after glory to match that of his military rival Corbulo.

That this attack on Anglesey comes at the same time as the Boudiccan revolt offers other intriguing possibilities. The Queen of the Iceni would certainly have been aware that a large proportion of Rome's military presence was involved in a bloody and prolonged campaign in Snowdonia. It is rarely appreciated how close she came to driving Rome from these shores for good.

We know that the power of the Druids was not broken in Britain (and never touched in Cornwall, Wales, Caledonia, and Ireland). When Rome formally withdrew its military protection of Britain in AD410, there were still Druids in the land. Which means the colleges and schools still existed. It also meant that Celtic society, as we well know from so much other evidence, was largely intact. Romanization was skin deep, often just wineskin deep.

The main source of information with respect to the survival of Druids and the religious practices of the Celts comes from the many pagan Romano-British temples. The Romans may have grafted on a few names to muddy our understanding, but they did little more. No more than the new religion that came out of Judea.

Quite when Christianity reached these shores is unknown. The tales of Joseph of Arimathea arriving some 30 or 40 years after the Crucifixion are part of Christian mythology, but mythology often has a basis in fact. Britain may well have been a haven for Christian Gnostics and others who found themselves persecuted both by the anti-Christian Roman Empire and by the non-mystical wing of Christianity that was fast evolving into a political Church.

These early Christians were tolerated and sometimes openly welcomed. They did not evangelize and their beliefs held much in common with the philosophies of the Druids. A distinct form of Christianity began to evolve within Britain and Ireland alongside the still flourishing native beliefs and the Druids who upheld them.

Rome considered this distinct form of Christianity to have been so tainted by druidic thought that the British heresy was hunted down and denounced with great savagery. Pelagius, in particular, came in for dreadful criticism and persecution for doctrines that are now readily accepted within Christianity.

All this was to no effect. For centuries, the Celtic form of Christianity and the native Celtic beliefs co-existed. Druidic colleges continued to produce Druids and they continued to teach the old ways.

Successive waves of Saxon invasion did little to alter this. The maps changed, with Celtic kingdoms pushed further and further toward the Atlantic fringe. The official religion became Christianity – itself subject to division and dictate from Rome that did little to destroy the Celtic vision. Yet there were still Druids.

Even when the priestly function was forbidden any but Christian priests and the Druid colleges were outlawed, Druids continued to exist. Many had actually embraced the Celtic form of Christianity and kept a great deal of Druid philosophy alive in this fashion. It is possible that the Culdees were just such a group. Others simply called themselves Bards and taught their skills in bardic colleges.

In the tenth century AD and possibly later, the Kings of Cashel in Ireland were still receiving Druids as gifts. Welsh Bards in the twelfth century AD wrote quite openly of the Druids that still lived and taught in their country.

Nor were these Druids idle or insensible to change. Toward the end of the first millennium, there was a massive flowering of native Celtic literature emerging from Ireland and from Wales. Christian clerics and monks produced most of what has survived, but their sources were purely pagan and many of these redactors were openly proud of their Celtic identity and their Celtic heritage.

From the seventh to the tenth centuries, the poems attributed to Aneirin, Myrddin, and Taliesin were written down, as were the tales we now know as *The Mabinogion*. Most of the great Irish epics were also written down during this period, a huge number of which are still only to be found in their original language.

All these texts are densely packed with mystical and magical information and speak to us (if we take the time to read them deeply enough) of all that the Druids knew and thought to share with future generations. Despite the fact that they were still strong and still an influence, they knew the world was changing.

The bardic colleges survived as formal institutions in Ireland and Scotland until the late seventeenth and early eighteenth centuries AD. The changing political scene saw their patronage destroyed by the sword or lured to London. Yet even then, there were clans in the Highlands and Islands that were sending their sons to be trained as Bards into the late eighteenth century.

It is at this point that two strands of druidic survival begin to present themselves: one to which most modern Orders subscribe and through which they proudly trace their genealogies; the other which has remained largely hidden, but which is there for the diligent to discover.

This can be presented in a slightly different way. One strand of survival has been carried through by an elite that has formed secret societies in order to preserve the knowledge passed on to them. The other strand is represented by a total absorption of druidic teaching into folk culture, its survival ensured by the very breadth of its dispersal.

Both are in fact the case, and each also has its discontinuities and its problems, not least of which is the antipathy between proponents of the two strands.

The so-called Druid revival that began in the late seventeenth and early eighteenth centuries AD is so well documented that it is not worth laying out here. Save to say that it is so riven with problems that these do need mentioning.

These gentlemen did much to rescue many texts from obscurity and did much to explore and revive interest in our native culture. At the same time, they did much to corrupt these texts – Edward Williams (his bardic name being Iolo Morgannwg – Iolo of Glamorgan) being the worst offender. There is also the suspicion, that will forever hang over these gentlemen, that they were frustrated by their lack of success within Masonic circles and thus created their own secret societies using selected native materials as their source.

The degree to which they corrupted ancient texts by filling in the gaps and trying to pass the whole thing off as ancient knowledge is unlikely ever to be known. That Edward Williams was a fine poet is beyond doubt, that he has cast a long and blighting shadow over the Druid Way is also beyond doubt.

Texts, however, only tell a small part of the story and a large part of the corruption occurred when they were interpreted in a way to make them fit an alien metaphysic. Thankfully, we are not entirely reliant on the patriarchal upsurge of material that has the dubious authority of a scholarship based on ideas intended to prove the moral superiority of Britannia in all its ages.

Being Druid (in any age) has little to do with book learning. It is a way of conducting one's self that comes from a particular way of viewing the world. The Celtic metaphysic has not been lost to us, but it is to be found in places that are difficult to understand simply because our whole approach to education and understanding the world has a different metaphysic and has become text based.

The metaphysic by which we must live (and by which we should interpret the ancient texts to unlock their meaning) is that second strand of survival, imbued so deeply in folk culture, in the ways of the village and country dwellers (the true pagans and heathens), that it surrounds us still and informs much of our daily life.

Tracing this strand from the late seventeenth century AD to the present day is difficult, but we do catch glimpses of its existence. Moreover, by its very widespread persistence, we can judge its vigour. However, it is important to understand that this was not a conscious dispersal of ideas and ways. Rather it was a reaction of ordinary folk to changes that a minority of society attempted to impose upon them.

In truth, it began earlier than the seventeenth century with the coming of the Tudor dynasty. The aristocracy of Wales moved to London and the patronage for the bardic schools went as well. Some of the Bards made the journey, but the schools began to fade. Bards and Druids dispersed and continued their teachings and upheld their ways in a much more amorphous form.

At the same time as the proliferation of Hedge Druids, there were attempts to 'civilize' the populace. It was the reaction against this that began the entrenchment of folkways. These should not be confused with the folk traditions revived and prettified by the Victorian middle and upper classes for their own amusement.

From the reign of Henry VIII onwards, we keep seeing laws and edicts given out to suppress the Old Religion and those who preach it. Some claim that these laws refer solely to Catholicism, but the evidence does not support this. Many state-sponsored lies were spread about Catholics (just as they were about Jews), but nobody believes that references to fertility rites and worship of animals had anything to do with suppression of Catholicism.

The Old Religion was that which had survived since before Christianity, and efforts to suppress it failed. It is, after all, hard to suppress something that is bred into almost every child. Even during the Civil War and its aftermath when Puritanism was at its height, the constant attempts to suppress the Old Religion (as it was still being called) were a complete failure.

It was not just political and religious edict that failed. An even greater threat to the integrity of the Celtic metaphysic came in the form of the Industrial Revolution. We now live in the wasteland created by that huge upsurge of greed and our Grail Quest is more important than ever, but we can work in the sure knowledge that the means to bring life back to the scorched earth is still with us.

All through this, the fire festivals were kept (in quite pure form until the twentieth century in some parts of Scotland) and churches went empty whilst whole villages held their celebrations elsewhere on the high hills and in the woods. Charms and old prayers were whispered over everyday activities. Herb-wives practised despite the threat to their lives. Customs that have been traced back to the Celts were still continued – the spirit of the old ways grew, evolved, and thrived.

Today, if you scratch the surface of our 'Christian' society, you will find the old ways are still kept to an astonishing degree. Next time you visit a shopping centre, for example, and see someone throw money into the fountain, they are unconsciously enacting what any ancestral Celt would have done at a holy spring or well.

Discovering that underlying Celtic metaphysic and re-aligning one's self to live by it as unconsciously as our ancestors is part of what being Druid is today. A brief look at that way of viewing the world will follow. The rest of this book will then introduce specific ways in which this can be enhanced and applied in order that, as a Druid, you fulfil the service that is at the core of a Druid's existence.

THE CELTIC VISION

Much is made in this book of the notion of a Celtic metaphysic; a view of the world specific to ancestral Celts upon which modern druidic thought and practice is based. This vision is not a modern construct based on wishful thinking, but an evolving attempt to understand how our ancestors viewed the world and how that view is of benefit to us today.

The idea that we see the world in a particular way is extremely important. This is not something we are taught to recognize; yet it is vital to an understanding of our material and spiritual existence. The major problem is that the underlying metaphysic of any people or culture is so deeply embedded in the psyche and in the institutions of cultural transmission (such as schools and museums), that we do not see it, let alone think to question it.

This is particularly relevant in today's world, as the current dominant metaphysic is extremely aggressive – perpetuating itself through violence rather than rightness. Based as it is on scientific materialism, the aggressiveness is inherent. Moreover, the aggression is increasingly aggravated by the as yet largely unconscious recognition of the fact that this metaphysic is an aberration leading us into the cramped and poisonous confines of a destructive cul-de-sac.

For the vast majority of human existence, people's view of the world has been of an entirely different kind. Indeed, many people still see the world in the way of our ancestors, a way that evolved as people evolved, and a way that reflected the facts of human existence within the natural world. It is only in the last few centuries that scientific materialism has come into being and has grown to dominate, spreading corruption in all its forms.

There is not the room in this book to go into this transformation in detail. It is dealt with ably elsewhere. Suffice it to say that scientific materialism turned more natural and more balanced forms of seeing the world inside out, whilst also introducing biases that favoured certain sections of human society over others and human society as a whole (the World) over everything else.

It was in this development that the world came first to include the World and then be dominated by it. This dominance, of course, can only be short lived. The World is already destroying the means by which it is supported.

This destruction is not just of the material means of support, which is becoming increasingly obvious for all to see. It is also the destruction of the social and of the spiritual. What is more, their destruction is an inevitable consequence of a metaphysic that sees everything simply as a material commodity for which there is a material price.

Social cohesion and spiritual existence have become marginalized to an alarming extent, deprived of the nourishing environment they once had. They now wither and their evolutionary progress has been stunted. And these are not abstract concepts, but aspects of human being. As they wither, so does humanity.

Spirituality is an articulated essence of humanity. It has life; it evolves - giving voice to the human condition at a given time and a given place. It may seem odd, in that case, that we seek a spiritual vision for today and tomorrow by looking far into the past. However, this is not a retrograde step, simply a matter of finding the place where we strayed from the path and looking for ways to get back on. And to do that we need to know what the path we strayed from was like.

That spirituality is an articulation of the human condition within space and time validates the diversity of spiritual expression. No form of expression is superior to any other; none is the sole or correct way. All are valid provided they are true forms of expression.

This book seeks to explore the basics of one of those forms of expression – a nature religion and pagan spiritual Way that has its roots in the lands of the Celts. To do that we must cast aside the assumptions we have been taught to make about the world. This is no easy task. Our whole way of life in the so-called western world is now built on the metaphysic of scientific materialism. Our education system continues to peddle the idea as if it were the one true way. Protest against the danger of the metaphysic is increasingly portrayed as terrorist in nature, yet many people are now beginning to see through the tawdry façade.

To be true to a return to a more benign metaphysic we must also see a return of the many different strands of spirituality that once existed. Moreover, if we take the time to sit and watch the world, we can find all the teaching we need to help reconnect us with things as they are, rather than as some people would have us believe them to be. If we concentrate on place as well as time, we will find a specific expression of our spirituality emerging.

We have other help in this task, for there was once a people that lived by these very ideas, who saw the world in a way that we now seek. It was their path we strayed from, their path to which we now wish to return. Through archaeology, historical sources, and through the artefacts and literature that ancestral Celts have bequeathed us, we can begin to reshape our minds and the way we see the world. It is this reshaping that creates within you the basic form of the Druid that you will become.

Our ancestors considered the whole world to be sacred. Certain places were held in especial awe, places where the boundaries between this world and the Otherworld were nebulous and open. They were no more sacred than anywhere else, simply places where certain ritual activity could best be carried out or focused.

What is more, they lived *in* the world. They recognized that they were part of it, integral to it, woven into the web of life as it danced its cyclical journey. They were able to identify at the deepest level with fellow creatures, with plants and trees, with the landscape, with the macrocosmic and the microcosmic. Many of the poems attributed to Taliesin demonstrate this in a remarkable way.

Accepting the cyclical nature of existence is a powerful and wholly different perspective to that with which we are inculcated. Scientific materialism is a metaphysic that is both linear and dualistic. These concepts are constructs of the World and have no place in wider existence. The consequences of their adoption have been widespread and destructive - of our material environment, of our bodies, of our minds, and of our spirit.

There is simply not the room here to develop these arguments more fully. Besides, a degree of trust is necessary in order to make the changes required - no matter how much we are convinced at an intellectual level. Being aware of an idea is just the first of many steps toward it forming the matrix by which we instinctively conduct all aspects of our life.

Living in the world and being able to identify with all aspects of it is a gift we have allowed to wither. By creating the World, we have led ourselves to believe that we can live independently from the rest of existence. A few moments thought will show that this is an absurd idea, that the 'independent' existence of scientific materialism is nothing more than suicidal parasitism.

This is not a call for a return to a non-existent idyllic past. We must continue to go round the circle sunwise; we must accept a collective responsibility for what has been done to the world. The world needs healing and the World desperately needs reforming. That is a matter of engagement, not of retreat. It is a retreat from the world that has brought us to this situation.

It is, ironically, by retreating from the World that we can reconnect ourselves with the world. By reconnecting with the world we soon realize that it is a living thing. And in common with all living things, it has a soul - a world soul that can re-ignite the soul within us and keep the flame burning bright and true.

Knowing the soul in the world is knowing that it is in the world that wisdom lies. You will not find it in books or the sayings of some messiah, but in gardens and the wilderness, in trees and oceans, in the flight of birds and the light of stars.

Knowing the world properly and accepting its wisdom opens the way to a realization of the wider Celtic metaphysic. All nature religions, of course, teach the wisdom of the world. Each has its own perspective for the desert has different lessons to offer from the mountains, the lakeside from the high plateau.

The north-western landscapes of Europe informed the vision of pre-Celtic and Celtic peoples. And as with all pagan belief, the vision was not just of the spirit, but also of the material. For nature religions accept that we are both spirit and matter and that each informs the shape of the other, that to survive within a given landscape demands of us that we behave in a particular way. Beneath all this, however, the principles are similar and present a threefold vision of and approach to all aspects of being.

In the first instance, the vision is one of cohesion. All things have spirit and are thus all connected, each a single note in the great song. The connection is one of synthesis, for all things move toward harmony and unity; the connection is one of creativity as the song is never static. Each new connection and combination of connections, if made in true spirit and in accord with nature, brings forward new variations and new themes.

All levels of life and living systems are recognized as being imbued with differing levels of existence. A tree, for example, is a living being, which may, in turn, belong to the larger living being that is the forest. The same is true with people. The family, the tribe, the Grove - all are living beings with a dynamic of their own.

Each of these also demonstrates the notion that the whole (at whatever level) is greater than the sum of its parts.

Mystical as this may seem, it is in fact a strong indication that ancestral Celts were far more attached to reality than are the adherents of scientific materialism. The notion of cohesion and the principles that are inherent within it are based on a sound understanding of the real world and of living within it, not on some abstract that is distorted to fit partial theories.

The second aspect of the Celtic vision is one of balance. Cohesion would not work if those things that moved toward unity were not in right balance. This can be seen in the wider context through various examples of manifestation. Material balance, for example, was a principle in which our place within the world was maintained only by feeding our need and not our greed. Celtic tales are full of the dire consequences visited on those whose greed gets the better of them. The Matter of Britain, with its central theme of the Wasteland and its redemption by attaining the Grail, is an exploration of this at many levels and has produced some of the most potent and beautiful literature the world has ever seen.

Balance is the ideal that should be worked for in all things, recognizing as it does that we must all make sacrifice and that we must be held responsible for our own actions. Balance at all levels, recognizing that we are, for example, creatures of spirit and matter and that we should nurture both for if one is neglected, the other will suffer. Balance, too, in more practical ways, for although ancestral Celts recognized the need for specialists within society, they were self-sufficient to a much greater degree than we are at present. This was self-sufficiency based not so much in the idea of doing everything for one's self, but of ensuring the transactions within society were as simple and as equitable as possible – sufficient for the self.

Observing the cycle of the seasons and working to the rhythms of nature was also a form of balance – for we are not talking here of a linear notion that is detached from the real world. Balance cannot be achieved by working to a formula; it requires an understanding of the world and a sensitivity to given situations that is lacking in modern western society.

The third aspect of the Celtic vision is that of truth. This is by far the most difficult for people to grasp as truth is all too often linked solely with the veracity of the spoken and written word. Yet it extends far beyond that into all aspects of being. Indeed, truth is the measure by which we assess the rightness or fitness of a thing, an action, or a thought. To judge truth we must know what the world is and what the world is meant to be. We must also know the World, for that too is subject to the measure of truth.

None of this easy. Truth never has been. Accepting truth also means accepting a number of other difficult and troubling approaches to life. For example, the primacy of truth means that wisdom is more important than information – yet modern society is pathologically obsessed with information, which often gets in the way of truth and certainly obscures understanding of the important things in life. It puts quantity before quality, commodifies knowledge, and distorts and corrupts education.

Truth also makes us face up to the moral aspect of human existence. A truthful existence is moral by very definition. Not moral in the sense that we normally hear about, for that is tied to the constructs of the World, but moral in the sense that we act in accord with the basic forms and 'laws' of nature. No place here for the sins and taboos of man-made religions that have become the dogmas over which increasingly vicious wars are fought. There is no truth in any of that. There is no point in any of that if, in the process, we have destroyed the very means by which we live.

Truth means we must acknowledge that we are involved in the world. We live in it, we are part of it, we must – if we are to be true – work towards its (and thus our own) welfare. That means a political awareness and involvement. Not party political (which is a codification of the greed of the World), but involved in the means by which the person and human society orders itself to live in the world. Every act of living truthfully is a political act in that sense, and one that makes a real difference in the world.

Understanding the world in the way outlined above brings with it appropriate behaviour for living in the world. For, most importantly, it must be appreciated that the Celtic metaphysic is not merely an intellectual stance. It must inform every breath of your life, every action, every thought, and every dream. It must be instinctive. And therein lies the magical transformation of being Druid; therein lies the goal we seek in order that we may become a force for good in the world and a channel for the Light, which remains true to the environment in which it was engendered.

PART TWO

THE SHAPE OF THE WORLD

BARD * OVATE * DRUID

The Celtic metaphysic is both complex and subtle. It is also extremely practical, reflecting the nature of the life of the people in whom it took shape. Whilst ancestral Celts may have happily supported an intellectual elite, they were in the main a farming people who were concerned with winning a living from the land. They knew that a successful living was only to be had by respecting the many levels of being that permeated their own.

This view of the world and this practical approach was the basis of all druidic thought. It is from this that present day Druids derive their sense of identity, their strength, and their purpose. They recognize that their fundamental beliefs and understandings are unchanged from those of their ancestors, but that a change of emphasis is occasioned by changes in society. So it is that the Druid of today works to learn how to restore the balances that their ancestors once worked to maintain.

In learning to become Druid in the present day we adopt an approach that explores the three branches of the Druid Way – that of the Bard, the Ovate, and the Druid. These are derived, as we have already pointed out, from the revivalist interpretation. That they are not ancestral does not necessarily invalidate their efficacy.

Because of the nature of our existence (with a material dimension in time) and because we do not live in ancestral Celtic society, we must become Druid in a certain way, learning basics and building slowly and carefully on these foundations. Unfortunately, this is all too often interpreted as following a hierarchical structure.

Nothing could be further from the truth. Bardic studies come first because they are the ones best suited to unlocking the mind's potential to understand the world in a new way. Through an emphasis on the arts (in the broadest sense of that term), we learn to see things as connected and as unified. We also learn to see things intuitively and to value that form of cognition as being as important as any other.

It is not until we have destroyed the artificial barriers that our society erects through its metaphysic that we are ready to handle studying those areas that are associated with the Ovate. It also means that once we begin to move beyond familiar bounds, we have an expanded means of expression available to us. Words alone cannot adequately describe the worlds that we must explore as an Ovate. And we must describe them in some way, as that is how we make sense of them for ourselves.

Having made the journey inwards and become familiar with the many other worlds and levels and layers of existence of which we are a part, having learned to attune ourselves with them (rather than forcing them to comply with us), we are then ready to guide others onto the Way as well as to do what Service we can in the name of the Goddess.

Moreover, as any Druid will tell you, once they begin teaching others, once they begin their Service in earnest, they also go back to basics and start all over again on a new cycle of learning. In this way, they bring an entirely new perspective to their connection with and understanding of the world. They are able to refine what they know and understand, coming that bit closer to wisdom.

To understand better the way in which the three branches are linked and flow one into another, it is worth meditating on the figure below.

Today a Druid will follow the threefold Way much as an eagle, watching keen-eyed and absorbing all into their stillness; much as a tree, fixing into their being all that they have absorbed; much as the sun, radiating the warmth and light of all that they have learned. In this triple form, they tread the triple path.

As a Bard, you are adopted by the birch tree, which makes the way fit for other trees to follow. Under its protection you should work to know and preserve the history of the Druid Way and its peoples; know and protect the places of the Way; express the Way in all its forms through arts, crafts, and all the actions of your life; keep alive the traditions of the Way; seek out and preserve the ancient wisdom; uphold the freedom to right expression; learn and understand and keep the sacred word; open doors with the power of the word; be a force for good in the world.

As an Ovate, you are adopted by the yew, greatest and most ancient tree of thresholds. Under its protection you should work to know, understand, and respect the trees and their ways; know, understand, and respect the creature peoples and their ways; know compassion and, in accordance with your skills, heal the hurts of the world; converse with your ancestors; explore and come to know the Summerlands; understand the mysteries of death and rebirth; cultivate intuition; open the doors of time and there travel freely; know ways of understanding what is to be.

As a Druid, you are adopted by the oak, father of trees from which we were all born. Under its protection you should work to achieve authority in ritual and ceremony so as to be able to guide others through the cycles of their life; understand, make, and keep right law; offer good counsel and advice; investigate and understand the universe; develop intellect; seek balance; get wisdom; teach; generate and regenerate.

These are by way of being vows that bind Druids to the work they undertake. They are also a guide to areas of study that a Druid should follow as they set out on the Way. They are a key to understanding both the Druid and the Way they follow. None of these things is easy and as they are merely starting points, it is obvious that being Druid is no simple task. It involves changing one's whole self in order that you have the knowledge, the strength, and the wisdom to effect real change in the world. Yet for all that it is a complex and consuming Way, it is also life affirming and emancipating - a Way of joy, passion and, ultimately, of great contentment.

CYCLES AND CELEBRATIONS

Introduction

Rituals, ceremonies, and celebrations are important manifestations of the Druid Way. Our ancestors' lives were filled with numerous ways of marking the many and varied occasions in life that needed observation and acclamation. These ranged from the simple prayers that accompanied domestic tasks through to the ceremonies and celebrations that lasted a complete lunar cycle and involved the whole community. Modern society has largely turned its back on such an approach to life and we are very much impoverished as a result.

Our ancestors' lives were held together and celebrated through interlocking cycles of ritual, ceremony, and celebration. Together, they constituted a framework that extended into both worlds and upon which everything else could be arranged and woven. After all, these were not the rigid and wholly solemn occasions we are used to in our own culture.

A prayer said over the loom to keep the lines from tangling was an integral part of the weaving process. You could not weave without it any more than you could weave without wool. The same is true of the huge communal festivals. They were special occasions, and they undoubtedly had their solemn aspects, but each was also a ceilidh – a time for villages and small tribes to gather and mix and talk and settle disputes and set up trading deals for the coming year; a time to sing and dance and meet and fall in love.

Even those ceremonies that were shorter, less communal, and of a more serious nature were times of social mixing. Funerals, for example, were accompanied by wakes; the solemnity of marriage was (and still is) balanced by the wedding feast. This does not mean that our ancestors did not take these things seriously, simply that the spiritual side of life was not separated out from other aspects of being.

Indeed, so important is this aspect of the Druid Way that there will not be room in this book to look at each of the major ceremonies, celebrations, rites of passage, and prayers in any detail. A companion volume, *Arianrhod's Dance*, explores these and the issues surrounding them more fully. We can, however, consider what it is that lies behind the impulse to celebrate and at what points and why this is made manifest.

The Circle

At the centre of our world shines the Sun. At the centre of our being shines the Soul. The two are one, radiating Light. This essential correspondence is one of the foundations of druidic thought and work. However, there can be no centre without a defining circumference just as there can be no circumference without a defining centre. Nothing exists in isolation. This relationship between those parts that help define each other is also a foundation of druidic thought and work. The centre and the circle.

However, this is no lesson in geometry. Circle and centre are no mere point surrounded by a continuous line. Both are dynamic symbols, made manifest in the world through the actions and thoughts of all living beings and of the systems in which they exist.

All formal Druid work takes place within a created circle (more correctly, a sphere, but it is easier to talk of a circle). A circle is made to delineate a space and participants stand within it to celebrate one of the eight annual festivals or sit for meetings or to mark important rites of passage. When a Druid works alone, they also create a circle within which to work. At the centre of each of these circles will be a light on which the thoughts of those present are concentrated.

This circle is a microcosm of the world into which we welcome the four quarters – symbolic representations of the spirit of the world at large. We work within and for the whole world. Our candle, our fire, our thoughts, our soul, our rituals - all these represent the Sun, the source of all life.

Yet there is more to the circle than this, for it is also a place in which we might work safely and without distraction. We retreat in order to connect more closely. We cut off the World in order that we might experience the world. Our work also makes us vulnerable, so we draw the circle as an act of protection. Moreover, we work only when we are strong enough. Nothing more than that can be asked of any of us. We use the strength and the skills we have and which we can develop.

In creating a safe and quiet place in which to work, we also provide ourselves with a place from which we can travel and to which we can return. It is a spiritual hearth, an anchor in this world that is also a doorway to so many other worlds.

Beyond our work, our rituals, and times of quiet and prayer, we are still Druid. All life takes place within the circle of our being. All our actions and all our thoughts resonate across every world we touch as we dance through our lives. Although we might set aside a place at certain times, it is vital to remember that the whole world is a temple and all things within it are sacred.

That is why we can cast a circle wherever we are, upon the ground or in our minds. That is why the Druids of old built no temples or places of worship. They had their places apart, the sacred groves and places of power, but they moved through the world and were part of everyday life, seen by the people as the roots of life, stabilizing the world. They were also seen as doorkeepers, allowing the people access to the many other worlds about them where their ancestors lived and where they, one day, would travel. And these people are us, for we each have many lives.

The days, the seasons, the planets and stars, the recurring rituals of life, each turning of the circle moves us on as much as it brings us back. We move, too, from the centre to the outer edges where we dance and back again, where we may be still. Progress of the linear kind is an illusion. If we do not go back, we do not go forward. If we do not go out, we cannot return.

Past, present, and future coexist. Some magics bridge these more surely and more quickly than others - a scent, a tune, a touch, a poem. These are simple things, but they are always the most potent. We learn and we develop in order that we may live simply. It is one of the great mysteries of our lives that only children and those who have travelled to the limits of sophistication have within them the seed that can blossom into the simplest and most beautiful of flowers - wisdom.

Cycles

Druids are at one with the World and with the universe. At least, that is the end to which they strive. We work to be in tune with all that is about us: the sky, the land, the sea, trees, plants, people, animals, dreams... The relationships we have with these things are not relationships between separate entities. The idea of an objective approach to the world is a falsehood. We cannot be separate from these or any other things. You are not here and those things over there. They are you and you are they.

We can be distinct and celebrate that distinction, but we are fundamentally related to all things and our being is easier if we understand that and come to know something of the relationship that exists. To do that we must strip away many of the notions bequeathed us by our education and by society at large. Moreover, as we strip those notions away, we must look with fresh eyes at the universe that is revealed.

The Druid Way is most deeply rooted in a part of the world that has distinct and ever changing seasons. The seasons and the change of the seasons have an effect on the world about us and on our physical and spiritual being. This goes beyond the simple effects of weather, length of daylight, and the emotional connections that we make. The cycle of change in the outer world is intimately related to the cycle of change in our inner life and from this, we can glimpse the many layers of the many cycles that involve the material and the spiritual, the tangible and the intangible.

We are often sensible of these changes and these connections without being truly aware of them. Like tidal forces, they move us as they move through us. We can be at their mercy without ever understanding what pulls us this way and that whilst also pulling us apart internally. This is not to say that these forces are necessarily dramatic or dangerous, any more than it is to say that such change is somehow a bad thing. Often, all we experience is a continual and vague disorientation - that feeling of never being quite in step with the rest of the World. Which is exactly true because we are, most of us, out of synchronization.

Is it us, or is it the rest of the World that is at fault here? It is neither. We are both at fault. We both have it within us to put things to rights. The problem is that we have been brought up in a society that has based its whole view of existence on a materialistic, analytic, and empirical system of thought that has common roots with what we now call science. In adopting such a system, society has divorced itself from the universe (by which we mean all things natural - and in this statement there is much to be considered) and concerns itself only with the World. In so doing it has striven to present the World as something that can exist in isolation from the universe and has acted accordingly, which is why the World today is in such a terrible state.

To escape from this and begin work as a Druid, it is important to unlearn a great deal and look at both the World and the universe afresh. That is no easy enterprise and one that may seem daunting. However, all journeys start with a single step, and that step is just one step away from the familiar. And that which is most familiar is ourselves.

Let us start with our life. The orthodox way of viewing our lives is as a straight line. We are born, we move inexorably through the years, we die. This is the legacy bequeathed us by several centuries of westernized thought. It is a bleak picture. True, the lines will run parallel, cross, tangle, but in the end the isolated line simply comes to an end. However, this way of looking at things does not concur with our experience of the universe, any more than it accords with the thinking of most other societies in most other times.

There is another way of viewing our lives. It is a way which lies deeply within us, usually unacknowledged, and which reflects the observable workings of the universe. Indeed, so much does this way lie at the heart of all things that it is recognized by all spiritual teachings as a primary form of existence. In our lives, at this level of incarnation, we recognize this way of looking at the universe as symbolized by the circle.

Although the circle is perhaps the simplest symbol of all in visual terms, it is infinitely complex both in its representation and in its interpretation. For all that, the most important thing to remember when contemplating any circle is that it is not a static symbol. The circle always moves - either turning about its own centre so that the circumference rotates or pulling you into and beyond the space that is contained within the circumference.

When applied to our lives, the circle immediately introduces the cyclical nature of being showing that death is not the end (for the circle has no end), but merely a stage in a cycle, which is followed by birth or rebirth.

By adopting the circle as a means of symbolizing our life, the connection with the rest of nature becomes apparent. The cycles of night and day, of the moon, of the seasons, all resonate one with another. More tellingly is the fact that the cycle of our life accords so closely with the seasonal cycle of the year. And from the two, our life and the seasons, we derive the ceremonial cycle of the year.

So it is that the winter solstice is the time when we celebrate that dark, still moment of potential, the moment when the Sun dies and is reborn after the longest night of the year. At that point and time of deepest darkness, we light a single flame that symbolizes the birth of the Sun-child, the Mabon. His strength will grow and nurture the land until, at the summer solstice, his strength reaches its peak. Then it begins to wane until the Mabon dies again to be reborn once more.

If we take that dark heart of winter, the solstice, as the time of birth (the greatest hope in the time of greatest shadow), we can see how the rest of the year unfolds accordingly as the circle turns. Springtime is the childhood and youth of the year in which all the potential that shimmered with promise at the time of rebirth shoots forth in glorious splendour. Summer is the early adulthood of the year, the brightest time of greatest strength, the time of work, the time in which things begin to mature. Autumn is the later adulthood of the year when all that has gone before comes to fruition and we gather our harvest. Winter is the old age of the year when death holds sway; it is a time for withdrawal, the time to sit by the hearth drawing warmth and comfort from what we have gathered. There, we pass on to others what we have learned before moving on to our next cycle, be it here or elsewhere.

Such analogies are still in common usage, even in these materialistic and 'linear' times, and show just how deeply ingrained within us is the recognition that life is cyclical. What we know of the Earth and the Sun, of the planets and the stars simply confirms all this.

The Earth rotates about its axis, the surface of the planet moving through its own shadow, into the light of the Sun, and then back into shadow. This movement gives us the dawn, the morning, noon, afternoon, dusk, evening, night - more distinctive at our latitudes than in the tropics where the sun appears to rise and set much more quickly. Whilst the Earth rotates about its axis it also orbits the Sun and, because the axis is not at right angles to the plane of the orbit, the light of the Sun is more concentrated in some latitudes than at others - an effect that varies as the Earth completes its orbital cycle.

The daily and yearly cycles reflect one another. Morning is the spring of the day, fresh and full of promise; flowers opening to the Sun. Noon is the summer, the Sun at its strongest. Evening is the autumn when we rest and gather what the day has offered, watching perhaps the sunset ablaze with autumn colours. Night is the winter, a time of cold and dark, a time to gather about the hearth and prepare for the next cycle.

There are lunar cycles as well. The dark moon, hidden to our eyes, resides in the winter of the month, presiding over the mysteries of death and birth. The first quarter is the waxing flower of the sky, spring of the month. The full moon, at its greatest strength, face full to the Sun is the summer of the month. Finally, the last quarter, the waning old age of the moon, is the autumn of the month.

These correspondences can be taken further, laying the cardinal points into their appropriate places, adding another dimension to our understanding of how these cycles relate one to another and to the universe as a whole, symbolized here by our immediate universe of the geographical landscape. If we face the rising Sun we face the east and this, then, is placed at the appropriate point on our circle where we have marked the morning. Following the circle round in a sunwise direction, we find that south is placed at noon, at summer, where the Sun is strongest. On to the west, the setting Sun, autumn, the place of the Otherworld. And to the north, the place of winter and midnight.

If we collate these correspondences, we have a circle thus:

winter
midnight
dark moon
death/rebirth
solstice

N

autumn   spring
evening   morning
last quarter   W   E   first quarter
old age   youth
equinox   equinox

S

solstice
maturity
full moon
noon
summer

Some may find these correspondences between our lives and the universe strange, but a little gentle meditation will show that they are to be expected. These cycles have so much in common because they stem from a single source - one we cannot fully hope to know - working through distinct but connected manifestations of its being. And the more we look at life and the universe, the more correspondences we will find. It is only in the World, the constructs of humanity, that we find these cycles disregarded and disrupted.

Of course, the situation is much more complex than the mere turning of a circle - no matter how many correspondences we may find. Nothing ever repeats itself exactly. That would defeat the purpose of returning to learn new lessons. In looking at the circle, as we have, we are looking at one manifestation, one cycle that turns within many others. Although each circle turns about a centre, that centre is never still. It too revolves about a centre that, in turn, moves about another centre.

All these cycles move at slightly different speeds and angles so that although we constantly return to the familiar, there is always something slightly new to contemplate. In this way, the circles become helices that turn ever on or spirals that move away from or toward a particular point. It is a dizzying prospect that is so vast and so complex we can never hope to understand even the tiniest part of it.

Because we cannot possibly come to comprehend the true nature and purpose of creation in this plane of existence, that does not mean we cannot work toward that end. The path of our lives and the material world as symbolized by the circle are outward events. They are effects, not causes. They are the rim of the wheel, which has no meaning in itself, but must be related to what lies at the hub and round which the rim ever turns.

In our small universe, the one that has most effect on our everyday lives, the one we can best hope to understand, all these planetary cycles relate to a single source or hub. It is the centre of gravity about which everything turns. It is the source of energy that provides the seeds of life to fertilize the womb of the Mother. It is the Sun.

If we look to our own life cycle, that small wheel turning within so many larger wheels, we see that it is the self or soul around which everything revolves. The soul incarnates and provides the gravity for our physical body to begin its turning dance. It seeds our spirit that we might cultivate a greater understanding of the unknowable.

So it is that the many cycles turn about the great mystery of our being, illuminated by the light of the Sun and the Light of the soul - one a physical and one a spiritual manifestation of the divine, both fiercely ablaze in the firmaments of our being.

The work of Druids revolves about this manifestation. It is one reason why so many people think of Druids as Sun worshippers. Yet that is one thing they are not, for that would be to debase the esoteric understanding that is to be found in the relationship between soul and Sun, the relationship between physical and spiritual, the relationship between the World and the universe.

Understanding that relationship is all-important. We can see it intellectually by studying the correspondences we have already discussed along with the many others we are sure you can find for yourself, yet there is much more to it than that. Intellectual understanding is fine but, as we have already said, it is insufficient if we are to move forward spiritually and strengthen ourselves for the tasks that we, as Druids, must perform.

We must go beyond the rational and try to understand with more than just our intellect. Indeed, in the end we have to move beyond the intellect for it is capable of comprehending only a small part of the universe. Yet we should never despise it, merely accept its limits and then use it to the full in order to reach the point where it can be allowed to rest.

Transrational understanding is as much a mystery as the things we come to understand by such a method and thus impossible to explain fully. It is an apprehension and understanding of things without the need to analyse or synthesize. It comes to us sometimes when reading poetry, or listening to music, or looking at a piece of artwork, or simply lazing on a sunny afternoon - that moment when we are released from normal modes of sensibility and find we are part of what we were formally observing from the 'outside'. If it has happened to you, you will know what we mean. If it is something you have yet to experience, be assured that you will and that it will be a joy.

To create the conditions for transrational understanding, Druids engage in two related groups of work. The first is connected with the cycle of eight festivals with which Druids mark the turning of the year. Ritual celebration is a gentle but powerful means of appreciating the laws and relationships of the universe as well as exercising the imagination. Through ritual and the celebration of the cycle of the year, you will be tapping into the power of the mythic cycles that turn in the same dance. Indeed, ritual is a means of enacting the myth and making manifest in our world the strands of the Otherworld to which we are most closely related.

The second group of work includes the activities, studies, meditations, and inner journeys that weave in between the festivals - work you have already started by reading this book. These prepare and exercise the mental, psychic, aesthetic, and spiritual dimensions of your being just as other methods can exercise the intellect.

The use of the imagination and its training are extremely important to any Druid. All early work is devoted to this through a practical exploration of what we now call 'the arts'. It is this that enables us to break free of the dominant world view into the wider Celtic metaphysic. Intellect is appreciated there, but understood for what it is - one of the many ways in which we come to understand the world.

Imagination is often denigrated by those who adhere to the materialistic metaphysic of the age. They do not see its intrinsic value. Yet the intellect cannot operate without it and even the most dedicated devotee of materialism makes extensive use of their imagination. Unfortunately, we are not taught to take our imaginative powers seriously or exercise them to their full extent. Without them, however, we cannot hope to understand things that fall beyond our direct experience of the world. Without them, there can be no compassion.

The Eightfold Year
The eightfold year of festivals and ceremonies is disputed by some Druids and many academics who claim it is a relatively modern invention. Whilst the name may be, there is plenty of evidence that ancestral Celts celebrated eight annual festivals. The lunar festivals (also referred to as the fire festivals) are not in any dispute. These take place at times roughly midway between the solstices and equinoxes. Known as Samhain, Imbolc, Beltane, and Lughnasad, they are well documented and have been celebrated for thousands of years.

The solar festivals take place on the solstices and the equinoxes. The evidence for the recognition of these days as sacred and worthy of celebration is based on several points that are often overlooked. The first is that the Celts had numerous and important light and solar deities in their pantheon. To suggest they would not have acknowledged the importance of these deities and the Sun to which they were linked is absurd. The second point is that the Sun itself was an object of esteem and recognized as essential to the agricultural life of the Celts. The third is that what little we know of Celtic calendars is that they were based on lunar cycles that were adjusted to stay in step with the solar cycle. Marking the equinoxes and solstices was by far the easiest way to calculate the times of the lunar or fire festivals. The fourth point is that a great deal of later Celtic myth embodies tales based on a solar cycle. The fifth is that when pagan festivals were appropriated by the Christian Church, they did not subsume the lunar festivals. Rather, they took over the solar festivals, which suggests they were far more important to the Celts as spiritual rituals.

Irrespective of the historical veracity of the eightfold year, Druids today celebrate the turning of the year with eight ceremonies. The Druid Way, after all, is not an academic reconstruction of the past, but a living spiritual tradition that has every right to evolve in keeping with the world in which it exists.

The eightfold year is not directly reflected astronomically on the horizon. If that is represented as a circle surrounding an observer, we get the following solar positions:

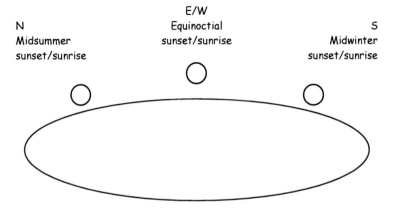

N	E/W	S
Midsummer	Equinoctial	Midwinter
sunset/sunrise	sunset/sunrise	sunset/sunrise

To understand this requires a knowledge of astronomy that enables the observer to comprehend that the Earth is a body in space like the Sun and the Moon. That Druids were astronomers with a sophisticated understanding of the intricacies of the measurement of time against astronomical bodies is well attested.

The Coligny Calendar

The Coligny Calendar was discovered in 1897 and named for Coligny near Bourg-en-Bresse in France, which is where it was found. It has been dated to the first century AD. Originally a single bronze tablet some 60 inches by 42 inches, it is now greatly fragmented. The tablet is engraved with a calendar of 62 lunar months and two additional, or intercalary, months.

The language used on the tablet is Gaulish, but the lettering is Roman. This has led to a great deal of discussion and controversy about the calendar. That it is Celtic is beyond dispute. That it is druidic is open to question, usually by those who tend to have an inflated estimate of the effect of Roman occupation on all aspects of Celtic life.

There are other problems connected with the calendar, not least of which is the length of lunar period used, but these do not necessarily cast doubt on its druidic origin. Too much emphasis on the minutiae of calculation based on a single and late example tends to obscure the basic principles upon which the calendar is based.

Ancestral Celts saw the day as running from sunset to sunset. This has left us (now that a day is artificially marked from midnight to midnight) with the legacy of such phrases as fortnight (fourteen nights) and se'night (seven nights or a week - less commonly heard these days), as well as the much used 'eve'. For example, Christmas Eve is - as we now reckon - the day before Christmas Day. Originally, it meant the dark period or evening of the same day.

Each month on the calendar begins on the day when the moon is full and is divided into two equal parts. The propitious part, in which the moon is waxing, is indicated by the word MAT, which means 'good'. The non-propitious part of the month is designated ANM, which stands for ANMAT - 'an-' being a commonly used prefix to designate an opposite of the word it prefixes.

This should not be taken to mean 'bad', as these words are also root words for those that mean 'active' or 'creative' and 'quiescent' or 'meditative'. Druidic lore, as we have already mentioned, places great importance on balance. Those things that materialistic thought tends to consider opposites (extremes on a linear formation) are in fact complementary and essential one to another (balancing segments and sectors of a circle or cycle).

This meant that each day, each month, and each year (beginning at Samhain) started with a period of growing darkness when one should meditate and rest. This was balanced by a time of work in the light.

The months on the calendar are named as follows:

Coligny Month	Gregorian Period	Probable meaning
Samonios	Oct./Nov.	Seed-fall
Dumannios	Nov./Dec.	Darkest-depths
Riuros	Dec./Jan.	Cold-time
Anagantios	Jan./Feb.	Stay-home time
Ogronios	Feb./Mar.	Time of ice
Cutios	Mar./Apr.	Time of winds
Giamonios	Apr./May	Shoots-show
Simivisonios	May/June	Time of brightness
Equos	June/July	Horse-time
Elembiuos	July/Aug.	Claim-time
Edrinios	Aug./Sept.	Arbitration-time
Cantlos	Sept./Oct.	Song-time

The intercalary month was known as Mid-samonios. This was used every four years or so to keep the lunar and solar cycles synchronized, producing a Celtic leap year. Even then, the cycle does not work itself out exactly.

The closest unit to a cycle that incorporates both lunar and solar calendars is known as the Golden Year, which is generally considered to be 19 solar years. It is in fact 19 years, two hours, five minutes, and ten and a half seconds, or 235 lunations. This mathematical diversion, whilst extremely interesting, is a little off the point. There is no doubt that Druids were extremely capable mathematicians and would have derived a great deal of joy and intellectual exercise from precise calculation. However, they were also part of the community in which they existed and would recognize that there were other factors involved in the need to keep a calendar.

Their main interest would have been ritual, ensuring that festivals and ceremonies took place at the correct time. However, such ritual was necessarily influenced by other factors. A festival that celebrated the harvest would be no good if precise calculation determined it should be held two weeks before the corn was cut.

Nineteen, as we have already mentioned, was a number of great importance to the Celts and their predecessors. Many Cornish stone circles have nineteen stones, as (it has been calculated) did many of the circles now lost to us. Nineteen was probably the number of years a person spent in training to be a Druid (one of the reasons why Myrddin in the *Vita Merlini* talks of his nineteen apple trees). There were 19 letters in the early Celtic alphabets. Later alphabets have since been modified. Modern Irish has only 18 whilst in the fifth and sixth centuries there is evidence (in the *Life of St Samson of Dol*) that the alphabet had expanded to 20, in keeping with the spread of ogham.

The point of all this is to show that Druids follow both a solar and a lunar cycle and reflect this in their ritual working. The lunar festivals were huge public festivals related to the agricultural cycle. And being agricultural, they were focused on the Goddess and her varying attributes relevant to the time of year. The cycle of four ceremonies (in conjunction with the solar celebrations) would have told a story that could be followed through the year.

Villages, tribes, and whole peoples gathered at these times to give thanks for the gifts of nature, to ensure a beneficent future, to conduct secular business, and generally to have a good time. They were open festivals in which the public participated in the outer mysteries – presided over by Druids who performed their priestly and legal functions, singing songs and ensuring that all went well, that nothing happened to upset the balance.

It is part of the ever-present paradox of spiritual life that these great, public, open ceremonies are connected with the moon and with firelight, which we associate with the night, with darkness, with things that are hidden. However, the evening was a time of rest and thus the most appropriate time for such celebration.

These days, the lunar festivals are usually celebrated on a single day, using conventional dates from the Gregorian calendar. Thus Samhain falls on 1 November, Imbolc on 1 February, Beltane on 1 May, and Lughnasad on 1 August. The Gregorian calendar is, however, a solar calendar and this tends to undermine the nature of the festivals. As they are lunar festivals they should, perhaps, follow a lunar cycle and be celebrated at specific phases of the moon.

Samhain as the time when the doorway between the worlds is open, as the time when greatest caution needs to be taken, as the time when no magic should be worked, is the time of the dark moon. Imbolc is celebrated on the first quarter of the moon, Beltane at the full moon, and Lughnasad at the third quarter. A fuller discussion of this can be found in *Arianrhod's Dance*.

In contrast with the lunar festivals, which were public and open celebrations of the outer mysteries, the solar festivals were quiet and contemplative affairs during which the inner mysteries were celebrated. It is likely that Druids retreated at these times and undertook private ceremonies in their groves as well as presiding over whatever public ceremonies were held.

The cycle of solar festivals was dedicated to the God, the Mabon who was the Son of the Mother Goddess. His story is told through the year as he grows from a newborn child at the winter solstice. His power waxes and then wanes until he dies at the far end of the year, born again to his consort and mother. The tale of the Sun Child and his incarnation as Arthur is discussed elsewhere.

The progress of the festivals (and all their names) is marked on the chart below, showing how they fall against the Gregorian calendar and the lunar cycles of the Coligny calendar.

Coligny Month	Gregorian Period	Festivals
Samonios	Oct./Nov.	Samhain (new moon closest to 1 Nov.)
Dumannios	Nov./Dec.	
Riuros	Dec./Jan.	winter solstice (21 Dec.)
Anagantios	Jan./Feb.	Imbolc (first quarter closest to 1 Feb.)
Ogronios	Feb./Mar.	
Cutios	Mar./Apr.	spring equinox (21 Mar.)
Giamonios	Apr./May	Beltane (full moon closest to 1 May)
Simivisonios	May/June	
Equos	June/July	summer solstice (21 June)
Elembiuos	July/Aug.	Lughnasad (last quarter closest to 1 Aug.)
Edrinios	Aug./Sept.	
Cantlos	Sept./Oct.	autumn equinox (21 Sept.)

The solar festivals are given their nominal dates. The astronomical solstices and equinoxes can fall as many as 36 hours either side. What is important to celebration is the day, rather than the moment, and this is how we currently calculate the days on which festivals and ceremonies fall. As you can see, it makes heavy use of the Gregorian Calendar. In times past, Druids would have made use of the great stone calculators and smaller wooden versions of their own to measure the lengths of daylight and the positions of sunrise and sunset as well as moonrise and moonset.

Rites of Passage
A Druid's Journey through Life, Death, and Life

Rites of passage are the rituals and ceremonies that mark a person's progress from one phase of their life to another. It can be a physical change, an alteration of roles, a shift in social status, a new connection, spiritual progression, whatever we feel has significance in our lives. These rites of passage are found in all societies and they reaffirm the specific values of the society in which they are performed.

Each of these changes is comprised of three stages. The first is the withering of and removal from the former status. This is often the most difficult to accept as well have a tendency to cling on to what we know, even if it is holding us back. The second is a state of transition that usually takes place within a circle or under the protection of a presiding Druid. The third is the newly acquired status.

We have little idea of what rituals ancestral Druids performed in the way of rites of passage, but we can make a calculated guess that, in common with most societies, they would have marked events such as birth, naming, puberty, marriage, and death. There may well also have been rites of initiation for those who became fully fledged Druids.

The main rites of passage performed by Druids today are marriage (handfasting), naming (of babies), death (funeral rites), and initiation (into Grades or the Way itself). We will take a brief look at these below. A full set of rituals will be found in *Arianrhod's Dance*.

As modern Druids, we can (and do) perform as many rites of passage as we like. They have evolved or been recreated from the old ones over the years. Many have the same purpose in our day-to-day society as they did in the past. Some modern Druids have added to these, especially in the US, where there is a greater emphasis on women's rites of passage, which can include 'croning'.

The croning rite is relatively new – a new-age invention - deriving from the original meaning of crone as 'Old Ewe', that is, a female beyond childbearing age. It has developed from the 'Wise Woman' concept of the old woman who knows all the stories of the tribe, is a healer, and generally highly respected. This status was originally given in the North American tradition to someone who was old. Strange, then, that some women are 'croning' in their early thirties.

Croning does not appear in Celtic tradition where it was accepted that age did not automatically bestow wisdom. Nor is it part of the Druid Way. Indeed, the crone in Celtic mythology (more properly the Cailleach) is most often associated with death and destruction - not an aspect that most women would willingly embrace.

It is, of course, up to the individual how they celebrate their life and its changes. However, it should always be born in mind that the Druid Way is based on the Celtic metaphysic and the Celtic appreciation of life. It is from this that our rites of passage should be derived.

Marriage

A Druid Wedding is often called a *Handfasting* - a term that simply means the joining of two people in a contract. The origin of the word is obscure, but it has a long history. The earliest extant use of the term is from AD1200 and Malory also uses it in *Le Morte D'Arthur*. It is more commonly used in the Craft, but is gaining popularity as a term with Druids.

A Druid marriage is not a legally binding ceremony; that, if needed, has to be done either before or after the event, at a Registry Office. However, the couple will, it is to be hoped, accept the rite as a serious commitment to each other in the sight of family, friends, ancestors, and the Goddess. This should be a union of soul with soul; a wonderful and joyous occasion where all those present honour and celebrate the couple's love for each other.

There are Druids who perform marriage rites with the option given to the couple to marry for a year and a day, this lifetime, or many lifetimes. Whether our ancestors pledged themselves over many lifetimes is unknown, although it does have a genuine ring to it. Trial marriages were an accepted part of ancestral practice and considered a sensible approach to such a serious undertaking. It means that the couple may dissolve the marriage after a year and a day. If they decide to stay together after that period, they are handfasted until parted by death.

Druid weddings are becoming very big functions these days. They used to be small gatherings of friends and family, in a woodland glade. Now they are taking on many of the traditions of Christian weddings, complete with bridesmaids, best man, and the hiring of locations. Although this is a matter of choice and taste, it is important to reflect on the importance of the rite and the tradition in which it is being proclaimed.

Despite the importance of the vows, there is much to celebrate. The formal handfasting is usually followed by a feast with music and dancing. One nice tradition connected with Druid weddings is toasting the happy couple with *Druid's Delight,* a quite lethal mixture of mead and champagne!

In the sad event that a couple decide to part (at the end of a trial marriage) or divorce (from a full commitment), a ritual can be performed by a Druid to define this. It is important that a couple gives thought to this and has the courage and sense to ensure the circle of marriage is properly closed down. Relationships do alter and we should accept this without the need to blame anyone or find ourselves caught in the vortex of energies that are not correctly channelled.

Naming

The Druid presiding over a Gorsedd (meeting of Groves) often carries out the naming of a child, though it can be done at a more private ritual. Many namings are done in the eye of the Sun, where the Druid lifts the babe high and the child is named and blessed. It is not like a christening where the child is then linked to the Church. The child will enjoy freedom until they are old enough to choose their own path. Again, this is a happy and joyous occasion for the whole family. However, it can look a bit daunting seeing the poor mite held up so high. Not for the faint-hearted!

Death and Funeral Rites

When someone dies, their family wants to do the best they possibly can for them. Many Druids and pagans do not get the burial rites they had wanted. Families often do not understand what it is to be Druid. In some cases, they do not know what the dead person's wishes were. It can even be a shock to a family to find out their loved one *was* a Druid, especially in a very Christian family.

With all this in mind, it is very important for a Druid (whatever your age) to write a will and to have it in writing what you want done in the event of your death. If there is a close friend or family member to tell, even better, but put it in writing as well and try to get it witnessed. Music you wish to be played can be compiled onto a tape or CD. These can be stored with your personal papers and, it is to be hoped, not used for a good long time.

There are two good reasons for all this. The first is that, when you die, you will get the funeral that you want. It makes your journey from this world to the next a little easier for you. It also gives you the opportunity to consider all aspects of your existence. The second reason is that you will save your loved ones a great deal of anguish and trouble. The loss of a loved is bad enough, especially if it is unexpected. Having to arrange the funeral that they would have wanted can be extremely harrowing. Organizing it all beforehand is your parting gift to them.

There are many things that funeral companies do that you are not obliged to have done, such as being embalmed, having an elaborate wooden coffin (such a waste), and having floral tributes (flowers flown half way round the world). You can have all Christian symbology removed from where the body bag or coffin is laid. You do not even have to be buried in a cemetery, but you or your family will need to obtain permission for you to be buried elsewhere. This can be longwinded and permission is not often given by the landowners.

Many funeral arrangers these days offer green or woodland burials. Theses are at sites (normally near a cemetery) that are suitable for the burial of bodies. They have to be well away from watercourses, because the bodies are normally in cardboard coffins that rot quickly, leaving bodily fluids to penetrate the earth. Many plant a tree over the body, which is fitting for a Druid.

This is an area in which people who are bereaved believe you have to play by the rules. Most of the rules do not exist; you just need permission to do certain DIY funerals. This includes being buried in your garden. Your family will have to tell local authorities if you intend this in order to ensure they comply with health and safety regulations. There is also the problem of the house being sold at a later date. People are not always keen to buy a house with a body beneath the flower beds!

It may be that you prefer cremation to burial, although there are environmental concerns. Most crematoria are happy to allow non-Christian services these days, although they often run to a tight schedule and there is very little time allowed for any sort of service or ritual. The ashes can be scattered more or less where you like although you still need permission from the appropriate local authorities to scatter them on the sea.

The actual funeral rites involve closing the circle of the life of the departed person, leaving them free to begin their new journey to the Blessed Isles. Most funeral ceremonies are held indoors. After the funeral, you could also have a passing ritual somewhere outside, as the ashes are scattered or the body laid to rest within the earth. The seashore as the Sun is setting makes a beautiful and appropriate location - easing the journey of the departed soul to the Summerlands in the West.

The Druid presiding over the funeral would need to speak beforehand with the family or friends of the loved one. This helps when the family are in shock from the death, at finding out that their loved one was not only a Druid, but also does not want a traditional funeral. It provides an opportunity to explain about the rites and the general outline of proceedings. It can also be explained that Druids believe in reincarnation, so the event, though sad, will also be a joyous one of rebirth.

Initiation
Initiation is a ritual of symbolic death and rebirth - a transformation during which the initiate affirms their faith or beliefs to themselves and the deities they hold dear. In some spiritual paths, this rite would also be the time when secrets of the group would be passed on. On the Druid Way, there are no such secrets. A Druid initiation is, or should be, between you and your deities.

When we think of initiations, we are inclined to imagine strange goings-on in magical communities, or bizarre rituals in the public school tradition of hierarchy. It is true that initiation has a certain aura of 'do you want to be in my gang' about it and if you do want to, then you must do the initiation first to prove your worth.

Druid initiations are very different from these examples. They are entirely personal, marking the movement from one cycle of understanding to the next. In most cases, they will be visited on a person - natural events with a clearly mystical element that make themselves known. They can be celebrated formally afterwards (we all enjoy a knees-up), but there is no element of proving the worth of one's self before others. No genuine Druid Order, Grove, or group will ask you to prove your worth, any more than they will expect you to swear allegiance to them.

Some Druid Orders have a three-grade system of Bard, Ovate, and Druid. They offer initiation into the three grades within the Druid Way, a ritual marking of acceptance into the grade and not the Order. You should be very wary of any Druid group that demands an initiation into the actual Order. You can, of course, develop a loyalty to your Grove or Order, but that is a different thing all together.

There are some people who collect initiations! They feel that the more they have, the more devout and enlightened they will become. It does not work like that. A person can be Druid and never become a formal initiate, yet still their being Druid comes from the heart. An initiation does not make you a better Druid. That does not mean that they are not an important part of the Druid Way. They are, of course, and for many people an initiation is a beautiful and very powerful way of connecting to spirit and marking a step forward.

An initiation is a very serious rite. It should never be taken lightly as they work on many levels of your psyche. They also stay with you *forever*. Of course, should you decide that the Druid Way is not your path in this life after all, no harm will come to you because you have decided to leave; the Druid Way is a path of freedom. Even though you may tread another Way, the initiation took place and is still there. Its meaning to you may change, but it will not leave you because it marks a change in you that cannot be undone. So, if you decide the time is right for initiation, make sure it is really what you want. And remember always that it is between you and your deities, not between you and other people.

The initiation itself can be a formal ritual presided over by a Druid and witnessed by others, or it can be done alone. Many people simply feel one day that they are stepping through the next gateway on the path, that it is now time to move on to a new phase. This might well be from one grade to another if the person feels they must tread separately all three aspects of Druidry. If, however, they feel that all three are intertwined like a triple knot, then it could well be a reaffirmation of their commitment to the Druid tradition. One thing is certain, whether it is done alone or with a dozen Druids, neither one is more important than the other for the great community of Druids is there in spirit to witness the event – blessing all who are true in heart and action.

Moments in your life

Sometimes in our lives, we undergo a rite of passage without any formal ritual. These are the moments when, deep inside, there are changes. They are not associated with any of the major events of our life; they may come to us in unexpected moments when we are engaged in the most mundane of tasks. Often, they are moments when we feel the essential unity of existence, when we become aware of the uniqueness of our self at the same time as we realize we are nothing more than the tiniest ripple on the surface of the greatest ocean.

There are also the small moments. These are no less satisfying and no less important - the moments when we realize we have mastered a small skill or completed a task, the moments of pure joy that visit us in the simplest things of life. All these are initiations, moments of rebirth into a new understanding. They do not need to be marked with ritual, but it is important that we learn to recognize them and acknowledge them with thanks to the Goddess.

ARTHUR - THE SUN KING

Of their finest he pierced more than three hundred
he slew in the van and the wings
most worthy to stand at the head of the host
in winter he gifted his horses.

Black ravens on the rampart were gorged
although he was no Arthur:
strong in battle
an alder fence was Gwawrddur.

from *The Gododdin* - Aneirin c. AD600

Druids do not have a sacred text. In common with other pagan religions, they derive their spiritual inspiration and instruction from the natural world. That is why the Druid Way remains constantly connected with the now and the here; that is why it is always relevant.

There is, however, a great body of written work - known as the Matter of Britain - which has within it many of the teachings and beliefs of ancestral Celts. This collection of writings has, at its heart, the epic tale of Arthur. Yet it is much more than that because Arthur is simply the most obvious strand in a much larger cycle of tales and myth, the Sun around which the rest orbits.

The earliest extant British texts consist of a number of tales and poems in some of which Arthur figures as a hero. Yet the majority of these tales and other fragments explore a much wider realm than the later Logres of medieval King Arthur. First collected in the fourteenth century into *The White Book of Rhydderch*, *The Red Book of Hergest*, and *The Black Book of Carmarthen*, these and other independent pieces have re-emerged in various forms along with collections of poems attributed to Myrddin and Taliesin. All originate in a much earlier oral tradition.

The very earliest mention of Arthur is that quoted above from *The Gododdin*, an epic poem by Aneirin. It relates the tale of the Battle of Catraeth in which Gwawrddur fought fiercely, but could not match the prowess of Arthur. This poem was composed almost within living memory of Arthur by a bard whose function was to attend the battle and record what happened. Whilst he tells us much of the warriors who perished, the mention of Arthur is tantalizing in its assumption that anyone who heard the poem would know all about him.

Best known of the early tales are to be found in the collection called *The Mabinogion*. Some collections contain eleven tales, others a twelfth – the story of Taliesin - that was written down later, but which shows signs of having been extant orally as early as the sixth century. All have their origins in the pre-Christian Celtic world of Britain.

The Mabinogion contains tales of the British Gods and Goddesses, of humans and beasts, of battles and quests, of great matters of state and the intimate matters of friendship and love. All of these tales are woven through with great mystery and tell us much of the culture and thought of ancestral Celts. They shine with the starlight of the Otherworld in which we are given our first and most distant glimpse of Arthur beyond his name and his prowess as a warrior.

In addition to these, there are many Irish and Breton tales, which have a remarkable underlying similarity. This suggests that all these tales have developed from a much earlier common source – a loose cycle of tales that helped to explain the world as well as provide entertainment during long winter evenings.

The earliest glimpses of Arthur show a figure very different from the exemplar of medieval chivalry that he later became. Through those Celtic mists that shroud much of distant myth we see, paradoxically, a much more realistic figure than later Christian interpretation has given us.

In early hagiographies, where Arthur is mentioned it is usually with little respect. He is considered a ravager of churches and an unpredictable, almost otherworldly character. Even in those early texts where he has been subsumed into Christian legend, there is very much a sense that he is a hard fighting warrior who dares to face the invader in this world and the denizens of the Otherworld that he himself has invaded with impunity.

Nowhere in the very earliest texts is there any mention of Arthur as a king. He was a warlord – fierce, proud, daring, and pagan. He was a man whose life was lived in both this world and the Otherworld – something he manages to do even today, for although he is a hero of myth, he may also have been a genuine historical figure.

The first time that Arthur appears as a coherent figure in a fully formed narrative text is in Geoffrey of Monmouth's glorious *History of the Kings of Britain*. Not only does this give Arthur a historical context, but it also sets out the bare bones of the tale that was to become the great and tragic epic that has enthralled people for a thousand years.

The Celtic Arthur who moved freely between the worlds, who went on magical quests and sought out a magic cauldron; the warrior of the wild forests whose tales were interwoven with those of gods and goddesses is loosely anchored in a world that seems almost real. The Roman Empire is collapsing, the Saxons are invading Britain, and the leader of battles becomes High King, creating for a single generation a period of peace and prosperity without foreign overlords. That is the historical legacy, the real world aspect of Arthur, but even that is suffused with the mystery that will always surround the whole story.

For whilst Arthur exists in a recognizable historical context, it is one in which magic still sends ripples through the landscape, in which Druids still walk, in which dragons fight. It is a place and a time in which we find the likes of Myrddin still holding sway – a place and a time before the muddying and ignorant hand of Christianity begins to confuse the story beyond easy recognition.

Two further versions and developments of the tale were to appear during this early phase of Arthur's journey. That by Wace was a rendering into French verse which follows the substance of Geoffrey, but which also presents us with a vibrant new version based on a number of sources. Perhaps most importantly, at the beginning of the period of chivalry we find the Round Table introduced to the tale. Layamon told the tale again, this time in Old English, elaborating the story and returning some of the more magical elements that had begun to fade – the presence of faeries at Arthur's birth and his journey to Avalon to be healed of his wounds.

Much of this earlier writing is dismissed simply because it is largely mythical. Arthur could not have existed, we are told, because these are made up stories. Yet that is to impose a modern view of the world on a people who saw things differently. They did not separate various aspects of their existence and call them history, myth, entertainment and so on. The factual deeds of people did not occur in isolation from their spiritual or mythical resonance in the world. What the characters and the themes represent and convey are as important as the narrative structure;

the spiritual and psychological elements are as important as historical fact – whatever that, in itself, may be.

Of course, the real flowering of Arthurian literature was yet to follow. From Chrétien de Troyes right through to Sir Thomas Malory a whole host of tales have been told and retold with much else besides becoming attached to the great canon of work.

What binds them all is an underlying recognition of their pagan Celtic origins, which are evident in the most Christianized of the texts. Even Malory's tale of jousting knights, which brings most of the tales together into a narrative whole, does not emerge wholly from the deep forests in which Arthur had his Celtic genesis.

In the end, the debate as to whether Arthur was a real person or 'just' a myth is irrelevant. The legacy of the tales is still with us. Moreover, embedded within them is an endless wealth of learning that has been passed to us from a time and a place when the world was understood in a way that acknowledged its whole, complex, and unified being – a way that we must learn anew to understand.

Sovereignty and the Goddess

It is impossible to separate the various aspects of the Matter of Britain, as they are merely the same things seen from different perspectives. However, to begin to understand the importance of what is embedded within these texts, it is necessary to follow specific threads of the tapestry. All the time we do this, however, it is important to remember that what we explore is just one aspect of the pattern and that each time we have followed a thread we must step back to see how it relates to the whole.

For all that, we can say that the unifying pattern, the warp on which the weft is woven, is the notion of sovereignty. The word sovereign has today a different emphasis in its meaning, connected as it is with a hereditary monarchy. Yet not only was the way in which leaders came to power different in ancestral times, sovereignty itself was not the preserve or concern of an elite.

Unlike many of the characters that are associated with Arthur, he does not actually appear to have an overt encounter with the sovereign Goddess. This is partly because the earliest sources that might have given us a more complete and accurate outline of Arthur's life are now lost to us. Fragments survive embedded in other tales, yet even they are enough to show that Arthur had no one encounter with Sovereignty. This is not because he did not have such an encounter, but simply because his whole existence is a multi-faceted reflection of the notion.

Arthur's conception and birth are overseen by Myrddin, whose role we will consider a little later. Suffice it to say for now that Myrddin is also intimately entwined with the Goddess and with the land over which he has watched until the return of the king. To the outside world, the identity of Arthur's father is uncertain as the conception occurred at a threshold time in a threshold place.

In Christianized versions of Arthurian tales, the women take a passive role. Ygerna is fought over by two men. They go to war. As Gorlois dies, he seems also to be with his wife in a place that is not truly part of the mainland, not quite of the sea. Yet this scene is contrived by Myrddin and by Ygerna, for Ygerna is the Goddess and she has the right to bestow sovereignty upon whom she sees fit. Hers is a difficult role for she is deprived of her son the moment he is born and will know nothing of him again until he steps forward to claim the throne.

At his birth, Arthur is removed from his mother and placed in the care of a foster-mother, an important part of Celtic life that helped to form bonds between tribes and peoples. In this case, however, it is an unusual form of fosterage for the real parents know nothing of the child's whereabouts. To all intents and purposes, the child who was conceived in a border world is kept there. He is not dead, but no one knows that he is alive. It is little wonder that some tales have the denizens of Faerie attend his birth.

Conceived during a struggle for national sovereignty, Arthur is then raised in a way that conveys upon him a sovereignty that is just as important. Free of the knowledge of his lineage, he is raised to be himself, rather than a fragmented reflection of what others expect him to become. Personal sovereignty and social sovereignty are aspects of a single form. A person who does not have personal sovereignty cannot possibly win social sovereignty.

Although later tales have his education directed by Ector, in Celtic magical tradition the young warrior is trained in all arts by women – with the implication that not all the arts a warrior must learn are martial. We know next to nothing of Arthur's foster mother, yet it is likely that it was she who directed his education whilst he lived isolated from the world.

A parallel (one of many) can be found in the life of Cúchulainn. He was taught the martial arts by Scáthach nUanaind who ran a military academy where many of the Irish heroes learned their skills. Scáthach means shadow and it is perhaps a fitting name for one who, in the Arthurian tales at least, is insubstantial.

Born and raised in terms of sovereignty, Arthur then returns to the ordinary world where his training is put to the test in his encounters with three more aspects of the Goddess, the three who shape the rest of his story.

The first of these is Gwenhwyfar. Later tales do her a terrible disservice, making her out to be a weak-willed and fickle person who eventually betrays everyone about her. Nothing could be further from the truth. It is Gwenhwyfar – a flower bride - who represents the land, for Arthur must marry the land if he is to become king. This is a sacred marriage bringing with it the Round Table as dowry, a hugely symbolic element within the Matter of Britain. Marriage to Gwenhwyfar brings with it the world.

Where later redactors became confused was in the fact that Gwenhwyfar bore no children and that she apparently bestowed her favours elsewhere – in later tales upon Lancelot. Yet this is to mistake Gwenhwyfar for a merely mortal woman and her marriage for a Christian ceremony. She was, in fact, daughter of the king of the Summer Lands. This is not Somerset as some would have us believe, but the Otherworld – where Arthur later ventures in search of the sacred Cauldron.

We know that Gwenhwyfar is a goddess because Arthur marries her three times. The Welsh Triads interpret this as Arthur marrying three different women of the same name. It would seem, however, that this is a corruption of Arthur marrying all three aspects of a Goddess. She may have been represented by a priestess in sacred ceremonies, but she was not necessarily Arthur's loved one in a conventional sense any more than either was bound to the other in the conventional terms of marriage. Indeed, early texts suggest that Arthur had a wife, Eleirch, and that they had at least four children.

Arthur's sacred marriage established his right to take the throne of the realm of Logres. Yet taking the throne and keeping it are two very distinct things. The notion of the Quest for the Cauldron of Life, which was later Christianized as the Quest for the Grail, is central to the Matter of Britain. Arthur stemmed the tide of Saxon invasion so that there was time for this quest.

Often portrayed as a physical quest for a material object (no matter how spiritual its connection) there is much more to it than that. The quest itself will be looked it in more detail in the next section. For the moment, we must consider it in terms of sovereignty and its connection with the Goddess.

Although Cerridwen is not mentioned in connection with the journey that Arthur takes in search of the Cauldron, her presence is unmistakable. In *Preiddeu Annwn*, the poem attributed to Taliesin that relates the hazardous journey into the Otherworld, we learn that nine maidens tend the Cauldron - no doubt the sisterhood of Morgan. Taliesin, of course, knows the Cauldron well as in it he had his rebirth, passing through the many forms of initiation.

That is the major key to understanding the quest. Arthur seeks not so much the physical object, but the transformation it has the power to bestow on one ready to undergo the tasks required of them. Arthur's legacy was not just for his lifetime, it was his role to show the way to a spiritual autonomy that could be found within the Cauldron.

He established a realm that would transcend the material world and allow others prepared to undertake the quest to find not only spiritual sovereignty, but a way into the Otherworld – an Avalon of the heart where will be found the most enigmatic of all the forms of the Goddess that are to be encountered in his tale.

Morgan's role is the most complex of all, as she has undergone the most dramatic of changes of all characters in Arthurian literature. Those who preserved the tales in Christian times found it difficult to understand who she was, for she has always changed her own appearance of her own volition, moving through many realms in many forms. Yet although her outward shape has changed, the importance of her role has always been acknowledged, if not properly understood.

In her earliest incarnations, she is introduced as one of nine sisters (although Geoffrey of Monmouth who first mentions her only gives us eight names). They all dwell together on the Isle of Avalon. The parallel with the nine maidens who tend the Cauldron of Annwn is immediately obvious, as are parallels with other sisterhoods of nine to be found in early Celtic tales. The connection with the Cauldron of Annwn is reinforced by the fact that Morgan is known as a learned woman, a shapeshifter, and a healer – all attributes associated with the Cauldron of Annwn and the Cauldron of Cerridwen.

Other texts stress that Morgan has an independent nature as well as strong connections with Faerie and the Otherworld. Medieval writers had problems in believing such a woman could exist unless she was using evil powers to confound the 'natural order'. Things became further complicated with the introduction of Lancelot into the tales and his gradual usurping of Gawain as the central knightly figure.

Lancelot is a hero raised and taught by the Lady of the Lake. It is possible that 'Lancelot of the Lake' is in fact a title, which rightly belongs to Gawain. Whatever the truth of that may be, Lancelot owed his allegiance to Morgan, for she is a Lady of Avalon, which lies in the Lake. When Lancelot becomes involved with Gwenhwyfar, it was assumed there would be conflict between the two women. Malory completed the subversion of Morgan's character, presenting the autonomous and learned healer as a malevolent witch intent on the destruction of Arthur and all that he had achieved.

We cannot deny that one of the aspects of the original Morgan is that of the raven of the battlefield, picking at the flesh of the dead. However, it is not she who brings about the destruction. War is a folly of mortal men whose lives are, in any case, limited in length. This dark aspect of Morgan is simply a reflection of the realities of this world. There is no more malevolence in it than there is in old age.

Morgan does preside over the downfall of Arthur, but in fact she does all she can in her power to hold back the dissolution of the man and his kingdom – knowing his worth to the world and the importance of his role. And when she can do no more in this world, she removes Arthur to Avalon where she will heal him of all the hurts he has endured on behalf of the Land and for the Goddess.

The raven aspect has been conflated with a quite distinct role in which Morgan is a motivating force – a force that arranges tests to ensure that those who seem destined for positions of power and authority are suited for them, tests to ensure that they are worthy to represent the Goddess in the world. When characters sit down to play 'chess' (in fact a game called *gwyddbwyll*) at a board on which the pieces move themselves, it is Morgan's invisible hand at work.

Arthur passes his early tests, but the world changes and the hero of one generation cannot be the hero of another. The cycles must turn and regenerate. Yet even as his power wanes, Arthur carries forward a legacy that has created a sacred place in both space and time where the heart of Logres can be held in safety. Arthur has bought life for the Land and all who dwell there. The price he pays is great.

So it is to Avalon, the Isle of Apples, that Morgan carries Arthur. In Celtic tradition, the apple is the fruit of healing. It is associated also with the Druid tradition as orchards are often cited as places where learning takes place. But most importantly, it is the fruit of the Otherworld for Avalon is a place in the waters on the borders. It is perhaps more of the Otherworld than this, but it is accessible from both.

In taking Arthur there, Morgan completes the cycle of Arthur's life – a life with which she has been intimately associated at all stages. She completes that cycle by bestowing upon Arthur one final form of sovereignty – sovereignty over death. For Arthur is the once and future king, ready now to return to us in our need.

The strength of Morgan's powers is confirmed to us in *The Mabinogion*. In a vision recounted in the tale called *The Dream of Rhonabwy*, we are told of Arthur sitting on an island in a river just downstream of a ford playing 'chess'. He waits on the borders at a place where we can find him if we look hard enough.

And the point of all this? Sovereignty is central to the Matter of Britain, even in those tales that do not feature Arthur directly. Sovereignty is also central to being Druid. To function properly as a Druid, one's respect and work for the Land forms part of the sacred marriage. Our Service, if it is true, brings with it spiritual sovereignty. At what stage we earn sovereignty over death - the right to stand aside from the cycle of rebirth and return when we choose - is in the hands of the Goddess.

The Wasteland and the Quest for the Cauldron of Life
In order to maintain the integrity of this world, Arthur uses the powers bestowed upon him by the circumstance of his birth along with the skills he is taught as he grows. He was conceived on a threshold, grew in a hidden midway land, and later travelled freely between the worlds. Such enterprise is not without cost. In the

greatest of his quests, Arthur went with three shiploads of men to attain the Cauldron of Life from the Otherworld. Of this host, only seven returned.

Yet the quest for the Cauldron of Life was not the only one undertaken by Arthur. His marriage to the Land brought with it obligations that he had to fulfil in this world. Logres was under attack. In historical terms, we recognize this as the Saxon incursions that began in the early fifth century. After a series of battles (the names of which are preserved for us in a poem, even if the locations are now frustratingly uncertain), the Saxons were confined to the south and east of Britain. The Celtic realms, newly emerged from 400 years of Roman rule, were given time to reassert themselves.

Without this period of grace, it is entirely possible that the Celtic peoples of Britain would have been completely overrun and subsequent history would have been very different. However, there is another dimension to this for the twelve battles of Arthur can also be interpreted as a series of spiritual struggles, stages in the establishment of a kingdom that had material and spiritual integrity. Arthur could not have achieved all that he did, had he not been able to win his inner struggles.

What was so important that he should fight so fiercely for a generation of peace? Certainly, it was important that Celtic identity should be preserved as it has an important place in the world. However, the peace was important in itself as it allowed a generation to come forward whose talents could be devoted to a quest in which Arthur took the lead.

This is because Logres is also a land of myth, which is constantly dying and being reborn, not through a process of nature, but through the efforts of people. Logres is the mythical projection of what we have elsewhere called the World, the social construct of humanity. The World, at its best, is a construct that works by the rules that govern the universe. It is a healthy, creative, life-giving place in which people may flourish without causing harm to one another or the rest of the world. Nevertheless, it can become a cancerous burden, destroying people and poisoning the Land.

Without a constant check on the way in which Logres is governed, the sensitive and living entity becomes a dead weight. It needs constant tending to keep it viable and healthy. In mythical terms, this is accomplished through the sacred marriage with the

Land. This empowers those who participate with the ability to search out those sacred items that will enable Logres to be governed wisely and in accordance with the ways of the Goddess.

This quest was for the four hallows and the thirteen sacred treasures of Britain, which are once again in the safekeeping of Myrddin. Of the hallows, it is the Cauldron or Grail we hear most about, simply because of the way in which the story was Christianized. However, the other hallows were originally of equal importance. Indeed, it was in the four together which lay the real power to renew the life of the Land.

The four hallows vary slightly depending on the tradition, but they fulfil the same basic functions and are objects that a king must win in order to claim and maintain his stewardship of the Land. These four hallows are the Cauldron (or cup or grail), Shield (or dish or stone of destiny), Sword (which has no variations), and the Spear (or wand). Each of these has many correspondences and may be familiar to some as the suits of the Tarot.

It is the hallows that allow for spiritual regeneration of the Land through each of its cycles under the stewardship of successive guardians. The thirteen treasures are objects of power that allow those who undertake the quest for the four hallows to complete their tasks. Each of these material objects is itself an object of power, a key to release the vital energies within the world. They are also the means of enlightenment, paths through the Forest along which travellers will learn how to tread softly and with respect.

This is because for all the complexity of the Matter of Britain, at the heart of it all is the health of the Land and the health of those whose task it is to keep the Land. Without this, the Land would fail and become waste. This is evident on a material level as we look about us now. The World is a Wasteland. The wells are poisoned or dry, the very food we eat is tainted, children starve to death every day, wars rage, and spirit withers.

We each have a quest before us in order to do what we can to restore the Land – that is part of the Service a Druid must perform. Yet this quest must also be undertaken on a spiritual level for we all carry with us the potential of an inner wasteland and we must work at all times to enshrine the hallows within us. That, too, is Service. For without the life and the strength that the hallows can bestow within, our quest in the outer world will not succeed.

Myrddin

Kyntaf henv a uu ar yr Ynys Hon, kyn no'e chael na'e chyuanhedu:
Clas Merdin.

The first name that was on this Island, before it was taken or settled:
Clas Myrddin.

from *The White Book of Rhydderch* (fo. 600)

No account of the Matter of Britain would be complete without Myrddin. Indeed, there would be no Matter of Britain were it not for this enigmatic figure. He is the agent of the Goddess, an ancient guardian of the Land – in some respects so close to the Land that he is a living embodiment of the soil and all that lives in, on, and above it.

The quotation above tells us this in no uncertain terms - and it tells us a great deal more. Clas Myrddin is usually interpreted as the Enclosure of Myrddin, yet this is just one, specialized meaning that does little to convey to the modern mind the full impact of what is meant.

In modern Welsh, *clas* means 'a monastic community, cloister, college'. It is, therefore, an enclosure within which learning and the sacred are important. This further broadens the scope because 'enclosure' has an association with the god Lug, one of a number of links between Myrddin and the god.

Lug (who has cognates throughout the Celtic world) is a solar deity, a god of all arts and crafts. One of his outstanding accomplishments was the invention of the game *fidchell* (cognate with *gwyddbwyll*). Lug gained his place amongst the Tuatha Dé Danaan by defeating them at this game using a move known as 'Lug's enclosure', which repelled the enemies of the Land and its King. This has enormous symbolic resonance as the game board represents the Land and the pieces are the key characters whose task it is to preserve the Land from harm.

The name 'Clas Myrddin' therefore takes on a completely new meaning, especially as Myrddin's patron Gwenddolau possessed a magical *gwyddbwyll* board – one of the Thirteen Treasures of Britain. This is not to say that Myrddin is Lug, simply that there is a strong connection between them and that Myrddin's role is as a guardian of the Land. This role could not be bestowed by any but the Goddess.

Whilst the role of the Goddess and the women who represent her various aspects have diminished in importance in successive retellings of the Matter of Britain (with one or two notable modern exceptions), the role of Myrddin has increased. This is not to say that it was insignificant to begin with, simply that it has been given a more overt form as his importance has been understood. Yet even with Myrddin, the Christians distorted his character until he ended his life a dotard, seduced by the wiles of a young enchantress.

One reason for the growth of the outward role of Myrddin is that there are a number of distinct traditions in which he features. This is not surprising. He is an archetype, ever present as the Land is ever present, a figure who moves in and out of the story like the shadows between the trees of the deep forest – the shadow of the deer, the shadow of the wolf. He is found in Ireland and different regions of Britain, as well as in Celtic regions of mainland Europe.

Valuable and interesting as diverse and later interpretations of Myrddin are, we must go back to his earliest appearances to understand his role, and his importance. It is in Britain that the heart of Myrddin lies, for he is the Guardian of this Land that once held his name. And it is in the Matter of Britain that we find the essence of this elementally powerful and compassionate figure.

His position as guardian of the Land needs consideration, as it would seem that the Matter of Britain contains an overabundance of such figures. The relationship of Arthur and the Goddess has already been explored – albeit briefly. Myrddin stands between not only as a conduit, but also as an ever-present representative of the Land, distilling the wisdom to be found therein and ensuring that those in need of such wisdom are trained to see it – or have it pressed upon them in forms they cannot ignore.

In terms of the Celtic world that Myrddin and Arthur inhabit, this makes Myrddin a Druid. His role is very much the traditional role of the Druid, extended into its elemental realm. For whereas a Druid must learn about the world and the Land, Myrddin is the Land and must learn about the mortal humans who take refuge within his sacred enclosure.

Despite appearances to the contrary, he cannot interfere directly in the lives of people. He will intervene if asked (or coerced) and he will guide by prophecy. However, the Celtic metaphysic is based firmly on the principle that we all have free will. We must do as we see fit and we may not coerce others. We can guide when asked, but each of us must take responsibility for our actions. Myrddin was at work in Britain long before Arthur appeared, and others carry his work forward now Arthur has gone. Yet he was most active during that short dynasty of the Red Dragon Kings.

For this, Myrddin will always be associated with the dragon. His earliest overt appearance in the world was when he was taken before Vortigern. This king had been building a stronghold, yet every night the ground would shake and the previous day's work would be tumbled. His magicians advised that the only way for the fortress to be completed would be to sprinkle the blood of a male child who had no father on the foundations.

Vortigern sent messengers out and eventually they found such a lad – Myrddin. When taken before Vortigern he asked the reason and was told. He asked Vortigern to bring the magicians before him where he would prove that they lied. Once they had been summoned, Myrddin told Vortigern of a pool beneath the earth. Vortigern's men dug and found the pool. Myrddin then told of the dragons that slept in two hollow stones. The dragons, one white and one red, were released and fought. Myrddin then burst into tears and fell into a prophetic trance, giving forth many prophecies that end with the dissolution of the stars.

Myrddin's time in the outer world has come. He has foretold the coming of the Pendragons and of the turmoil that Vortigern has unleashed. By doing so, he has also announced his own presence and his place in what is to be.

That work, despite the love he may have for individuals who help carry it forward, is the Land and its protection. It is why Myrddin has always been central to the Druid Way. He still teaches and guides, although his role is no longer overt. Nor is the guardianship of the Land left solely in the hands of a male. Myrddin, in earliest tradition has a twin sister, Gwendydd, to whom he relinquishes his role after Arthur has gone to Avalon.

These two were originally seen as inseparable, in some traditions as the morning star and the evening star (which are both, of course, the planet Venus). Over the centuries, their story has become confused, not least because the notion that they were lovers would have been repugnant to Christian storytellers who were unable to see the mystical element of the story. Indeed, and as always, Gwendydd becomes seen as the wicked seductress and evolves into the figure of Nimuë.

It is clear on close reading that Myrddin is no dotard and she no evil maiden intent on stealing his powers. In fact, she and Myrddin are engaged in the same task, each helping the other in their own way, each protecting the other when necessary. They are guardians of the Land and spring directly from it. Myrddin is the embodiment of the Land; Nimuë is the Doorkeeper, the Lady of the Margins who guards both the Enclosure and the routes to the Otherworld.

The earliest British tales of Myrddin and his sister to have survived are in the form of poems, and the works of Geoffrey of Monmouth. His *History of the Kings of Britain* introduces us to Myrddin and his prophecies. More importantly, he later produced the *Vita Merlini*, which appears to make use of early Celtic sources to tell the full life of Myrddin and his work. Although Arthur is mentioned in this text, it has a much broader context and blends the great elemental being of the land with the life of the Bard of the same name.

It is a truly astonishing tale of madness and prophecy, of learning, and of magic. Myrddin is seen in his true form as shaman and Druid and as the very Land itself. It follows him through a period of 'madness' when the horrors of war (the ultimate sickness of the World) unbalance his mind and he retreats to the forest where he lives wild with his wolf through the harshest of weather.

This 'madness' is, in effect, Myrddin's final withdrawal from the World after Arthur and the other pagan kings have gone. He has returned to his elemental form, become once more the swift shadows between the trees of the deep forest. There he eventually finds his true form and retreats to his personal enclosure, passing on his role as prophet to his sister.

There he remains to this day, watching over the Land, guarding the Hallows and the Treasures of Britain, and studying the stars. If you wish to find him and his sister, they are willing to be found. It is a long and difficult journey into the forest where they dwell. However, if you are prepared, you will succeed, and they will welcome you to Clas Myrddin with open arms and warm hearts.

The Sun King
Arthur is the King who does not die. His power waxes and wanes, but it never disappears. At its lowest ebb, when the world is a

winter wilderness, he finds redemption in the cauldron of plenty and is restored to growing strength. Being sovereign, his strength is the strength of the Land. As his power waxes, the Land becomes fruitful.

In this, there are many parallels between Arthur and the Mabon. The Mabon (which means the Son) was a living god to ancestral Celts, reborn each winter solstice to Modron (the Mother). This Divine Youth was a solar deity whose story is now largely lost, but fragments still survive within *The Mabinogion* and other early Welsh texts.

From those fragments, we know that the Mabon was a champion of his mother, the Goddess; that he disappeared during his childhood and was 'imprisoned' before emerging into the world; that his strength grew in the summer and nourished the Land. It is also clear that much of what relates to the Mabon also relates to Arthur and to Myrddin.

This is important because if we look at the Matter of Britain from a solar perspective, we find rites associated with the solar stations of the year embedded within the tales. Although Christianized, the texts are clear that the major events in the Matter of Britain occur on both the solar and lunar quarters of the year. This cycle of events has some gaps, but the relationship between the quarters and the cross-quarters would suggest that where gaps appear it is not because these were not marked, simply that the events have not been recorded, or that the records have been lost.

A few examples will serve to illustrate this. Arthur becomes king when he draws the sword from the stone. This nascent act takes place, appropriately, on the winter solstice, the most mystical and important moment of the year when all is withdrawn into the cold and dark waiting for the moment of rebirth. This point on the cycle also marks the beginning of that other great mystery of the Matter of Britain, told in the tale of Gawain and the Green Knight.

Another beheading occurs at Easter with Lancelot's father being decapitated. Easter is also the time most associated with the Grail, but it also marks the crowning of Uther and his first sight of Ygrane. Easter, of course, is a Christian festival and is a movable feast, but the fixed point from which it was calculated and on which it was probably originally celebrated is the spring equinox.

The summer solstice (or St John's Day in most texts) plays host to innumerable events – appropriate, as the day is the longest. Most significant of these and the most easily overlooked in all the battles and portents, however, is that the Mabon invites Arthur to a feast and that Myrddin meets with the Lady of the Lake.

It is the autumn equinox that is apparently devoid of any significant event. Given that the other seven stations of the year are crammed with incident, it is unlikely that this solar quarter is without significance. It is possible that whatever originally occurred on this date has been drawn to the powerful festival of Samhain (All Hallows). It may just be that the equinoctial festival is appropriately given over to a time of rest.

These examples have barely scratched the surface of the ritual year and a more detailed consideration is given in *Arianrhod's Dance*. The important thing is to realize that the Matter of Britain is a vast repository of Celtic and druidic lore. In some cases, this is distorted by distance in time and place, but it is there nonetheless. And the only way truly to appreciate the depth and complexity of what is there is to read these tales for yourself.

Just as Arthur is the once and future king, so the Matter of Britain is an endless cycle with an ever changing perspective. There are many places to enter the cycle, but the best is where the texts are oldest as that brings us closest to the rough magic at the untamed heart of the tale.

SIMPLICITY

The notion of simplicity is related to the Celtic metaphysic and may best be described as the practical application of the Celtic vision of the world to everyday life. Simplicity is complex. But all things are relative. Simplicity is the art of finding the least complex route.

The world is complex. The World is complicated. The natural order of things where life is involved is toward increasingly complex systems. Yet no matter how complex they become, none of it is unnecessary. The same cannot be said of human endeavour in the world for much of that is unnecessary. It has taken what is complex and elegant and complicated it for no apparent reason.

When things become complicated, they all too easily obscure what is needful. This is true at all levels from the most basic of material requirements to the highest of spiritual aspirations. In order to support the complicated structures that are erected, the World tells lies, creates problems to solve that never existed, avoids or ignores the problems that do exist, destroys life, and promulgates war. Indeed, deceit, violence, and war are supreme expressions of the complications upon which the World is built.

Simplicity is a search for the complex. It is a search for the most natural way in which to express one's self, to live, to conduct the everyday and mundane activities of one's life. It means learning to see through the complications of the World and managing one's life in a way that sidesteps those entanglements.

There are those that would call this opting out. In a sense, this is true. One is opting out of a system that is materialistic, violent, and destructive, that has abjured the Truth, and has no moral basis. If you are to be Druid, then you must minimize your support of such a system. In the first instance, this involves looking at every aspect of how you live your day-to-day life and embracing that which is simple. After all, any fool can complicate things; it takes awen to be straightforward.

Simplicity requires trust. Much of what is complicated about the World derives from the fact that we live in a system based on a lack of trust - not just between individuals, but also in the world about us. And the more complicated the World becomes, the easier it is for people to exploit any trust that does exist and to foster doubt in what is merely complex. It is a cycle of abuse.

Truth is a supreme quality for Druids. It is the expression of what the world consists in. With that expression comes trust. Trust in the land, trust in the sea, trust in the sky. Trust that these can and will provide for all our genuine needs.

To rekindle the faith we must have in the world, we each need to assess our lives to remove all the complicated clutter that has built up around us like a dead weight. And this is not simply a matter of throwing away all those material things we do not actually need. Every last part of our lives must come under scrutiny so that our whole approach to life – material and spiritual – is simplified and attuned with the way in which the world works.

Much of this involves nurturing our intuitive faculties and learning that a transrational apprehension of the world is far less likely to accrete the unnecessary and the unneeded. Our instincts are far more reliable than we have been allowed to believe. They tend to cut through great swathes of unnecessary rational thought that we have learned to manipulate and which, paradoxically, manipulates us. Besides which, rational thought looks at all possibilities and ties us up with all the ifs and might-bes and just-in-cases that lead to us accumulating clutter.

Simplicity is, of course, relative. There are no absolutes, not least because we each have our own relationship with the world. We cannot make hard and fast rules about what is simple, because such hard and fast rules belong to the domain of the World. They complicate matters. To cover all eventualities, they are endlessly long and can wrap people up in arguments about what is and what is not appropriate, removing responsibility from the person and placing it in some nebulous elsewhere.

Balance is the key and begins within each of us. Whether we like it or not, we are part of the material world. We have jobs, watch television, buy food, wear clothes, own cars and houses, and go on holiday. Unfortunately, many people are caught in the material trap. They become so unbalanced by the merry-go-round of a money-orientated material life that all other forms of thought and action are off limits.

The Druid Way is a spiritual path that accepts we have a material existence, accepts that the material is essential to our well-being. It is not a path of deprivation, where one must give up all possessions and become parasitic on others in order to find personal salvation. Indeed, it is not even a path of personal salvation.

The Druid Way is a path of balance between and integration of the material and the spiritual in order to effect healing. If we fail to integrate the material and the spiritual, we cannot ever hope to keep them in balance. Without balance, we face very great dangers. Go too far down the material road and the spirit withers along with compassion and love. Go too far or too obsessively with the spiritual and the spectre of fundamentalism rears its ugly head. A 'fundie' Druid is every bit as unpleasant and dangerous as a 'fundie' from any other religion.

Acknowledging the relative nature of simplicity means that we must trust our intuition. This is not easy. We are taught from a very early age that there is something not quite right about this. Yet this is because rational minds cannot distinguish between intuitive decision-making and a purely egotistical and emotional response to one's surroundings.

Each decision about life has to be taken on its merits. It has to be done openly and with total acceptance of one's responsibility for what one does, says, and thinks. Taking such responsibility is another aspect of simplicity that many find difficult to accommodate. The World has so complicated things that we are taught to go to the experts and we are taught that someone else is always responsible for what happens – be that the state, a deity, or whatever. Whilst some experts are necessary, for even simple lives are complex, acting responsibly and in full knowledge of what we do and what effect that has is part and parcel of what we are as self-aware beings. We cannot claim self-awareness as part of what makes us human and then just turn our backs on what that implies.

Inherent in this is a rejection of conventional ideas of 'progress'. This is a term that is invariably used to mean increased material complication and it rarely coincides with any true improvement in our lives – materially or spiritually. It is also tied inexorably to the linear view of the world, which polarizes all things.

Yet we know from observation that although the World may be constructed in linear form, the world is not. What people have created over the last few centuries is largely an aberration. The world is cyclical. Improvement in our lives is achieved by lessening the complications and realizing that each point on the cycle (just as each season of the year and each time of the day) will provide for what is needed in our lives.

It is, after all, the complications in life that allow people to starve when the planet produces more food than we all need. It is the complications that prevent equitable distribution of water and reforestation of what we have destroyed. It is the complications that prevent everyone from having a decent education and a roof over their heads and gainful employment and a chance to sit in the sun without fear.

Rejection of progress and the linear allows a different relationship with time to be forged. Many of the complications in our lives and in the World as a whole come from the distorted vision we have of time and of our lives. A simple life is based in the now. That does not mean it has no regard for the past or the future. Indeed, those who live simply pay more heed to those things than do those who live linear lives. However, those who live linear lives are always trying to live their lives in the future – and it cannot be done. Tomorrow never comes. It is always today. Live it. Do not regret it when it has gone.

Simplicity is also an acceptance that we cannot control the natural world. Accepting that, is part of the trust we must have; accepting that, is saying that you do not adhere to the philosophy of nature as red in tooth and claw. What we can do is understand the natural world and work with it. We do not have to give up the things we have become comfortable with because we can produce them in ways that are benign. Any other course of action is nothing more than destruction.

Stepping back from the notion of control also means accepting that humans are not superior beings with an innate right to do as they wish with the planet. Humans represent a great deal less than one per cent of animal life on the planet and a much tinier fraction of all life. We do not own the world any more than we control it. We have a place in the world and our particular form of intelligence may have a role in its preservation. We may even be arrogant enough to call ourselves stewards. However, we are no more than that and we can never be more than that.

To find our place, we must act appropriately. In the things we do and the things we make, we should always try for the minimum level of refinement. Materials that we use should be as close to natural as possible and should be biodegradable or, at the least, recyclable.

Our actions should accord with systems that use the least energy most efficiently, which do not waste materials, and which do not tie us up in meaningless activity.

All of this requires that we become aware of the true cost of things. Not just the price on the ticket stuck to the box, but the social and environmental costs of production, as well as the miles travelled between sourcing raw material, getting the finished product into your home, and disposing of all the waste material the product produces. The same is true of your relationships and all the other non-material aspects of your life. Look at them all carefully. There are invariably simpler, truer, and less destructive ways of doing things.

It is obvious that there is a high degree of ambiguity and paradox within the notion of simplicity being found by embracing the complex. However, ambiguity and paradox are part of the world. They belong in life and are great teachers for they provide us a timeless means by which to explore the mysteries of the world and human existence within it.

To embrace simplicity is to embrace the complexity of the world and recognize that it is not in any way alien. Rather, it is to recognize that we are but a part of that complexity and that the complications of the World are unnecessary. It is a declaration that in our everyday lives, in our thoughts and actions, in our whole being, in the material and the spiritual, we are a part of the whole.

WISDOM

There is a great deal of debate about what Druids once were and no less of a debate about what they now are. The answer is exceedingly complex and will no doubt continue to evolve. There has been a great deal of historical and archaeological research done in recent years and much that is new has come to light.

It is a sad reflection of modern academic life, however, as well as of many modern Druids, that much of this work is blighted by two maladies. The first is the need to build an academic career or gain academic credibility. Neither of these is, in itself, necessarily a bad thing - as long they are not seen as ends in themselves, but rather as means by which to search out the truth. Knowledge may lead us to truth, but it is not its sole constituent.

The second of these maladies is a modern unwillingness to tackle issues that go beyond the rational. Whilst this might be understandable in academics, it is also too often true of those who seek the Light. Both these maladies make it impossible for a true understanding of druidic practice to emerge and evolve from a purely academic direction. They also make it impossible to understand the essence of the Druid Way, because that essence lies not in knowledge, but in understanding, in Truth, in Wisdom.

Ancestral Druids inherited and were guardians of a wisdom tradition that was once known as the True Religion but is now more commonly referred to as the 'ancient wisdom'. Augustine of Hippo (AD354-430), not noted for his tolerance of non-Christian religions or of druidic teachings that were adopted into Christianity (which he considered heretical), made the following observation:

> What is now called the Christian religion existed among the ancients and was not lacking from the beginning of the human race. When Christ appeared in the flesh, the true religion, already in existence, received the name of Christian.

His antipathy to pagan religions makes this statement all the more powerful, although it is not a reference, as some Druid revivalists believed, to a connection between the Ark of the Covenant and the cauldron of Cerridwen.

The origins of this 'true religion' are lost to us. They predate written records by many thousands of years. It is possible, however, to piece certain elements of the tradition together and explore the earliest of understandings of some of the great mysteries of being - the perception of natural law, the mystery of life, the divine origin of the universe, and the relation of human beings to these things.

These principles remain an immutable depth, no matter how much the surface of life may alter. They apply to all people at all times and they have been the theme of the teachings of all great teachers. They are a common thread running through all religions.

This statement is often questioned. If it is so, why do we have so many different religions? If it is so, why are there such things as religious conflicts and wars? The answers are simple.

The conflict and the wars may be conducted in the *name* of this, that, or some other religion, but that is merely a pretext. No conflict, no matter how just it may seem, can be termed religious. It is a contradiction in terms. Religion is to do with the *uni-versum*, the becoming one. Conflict is to do with fragmenting the one. The pretext is made by those who do not understand what religion is, most often those blinded by a fanatical adherence to something that gives them a feeling of power over others. These are souls in torment who wish to inflict their own pain on others.

As to why there are so many religions when they are all derived from a common source - it is simply because people are different. We each understand the world in different ways, as individual persons and as groups of people shaped by their environment. The journey of the spirit may derive from a common source and be toward the same goal, but we each start from a different place and must travel, therefore, by a different route. To those brought up in cultures in which reincarnation is an accepted fact, there is no difficulty in accepting this. Each life will give us the opportunity to explore a different route, and each route is explored from many perspectives.

The body of inner knowledge, the 'ancient wisdom', is retained by us all at an unconscious level. It cannot be retrieved by intellectual effort alone, although we can go a long way to uncovering it by that route - laying the foundations, as it were, for what will follow. Access to this wisdom is through intuitive processes that have to be nurtured within those who are receptive. This takes it beyond the rational and beyond the grasp of the intellect - which is why the very notion of its existence is often dismissed by academics and rationalists.

There are a few, in each generation, who carry this wisdom at a conscious level and who guide those of us who seek to unlock it from within ourselves. They function beyond the confines of time and space, are ageless and deathless, are human and more. Once in every thousand years or so, one of them will step forward and make their presence known in order to remind us of our greater destiny and illuminate our path, which may have grown dark.

As with any tradition that passes from generation to generation, some is lost, some is corrupted. However, we can recover enough to keep it renewed. It is hard work, but that is part of the task. The wisdom, in its ultimate form, may be simple, but the getting of that wisdom must be difficult so that when we finally reach the goal, we are mature enough to handle what we have earned.

Each people has its own way of entering into the search for this wisdom. The Celtic peoples inherited and refined a way that has a stronger continuity than do many others. Much has happened to dilute it over the years, but that has also acted to strengthen it - one of the many paradoxes we face. For the Celts, it was *wood-sense*, tree knowledge, forest lore, an understanding of the natural world that provided a surface system with which to train the mind to the point where the mystical apprehension of the wisdom was possible. That is the way you have chosen as a Druid.

Although details of this 'ancient wisdom' are obscure, there is little doubt about the basic tenets. It is comprised of a deep understanding of natural law, of the patterns that underlie and bind together all life and all spirit. Moreover, the natural law is a reflection of the divine. Through an understanding of the world about us, we come to an understanding of what is hallowed.

This does not happen in one great leap. There are many stages and levels of understanding, each contingent upon the one before. We are many steps away from being one. Our goal is always the next step, not the final one.

The principle of reflection - in which the divine is reflected in the natural world - applies also to the way in which we come to win our wisdom. The wisdom is within us as much as it is around us. We must understand ourselves as much as we must understand all that is about us. Everything is connected. The whole is to be found in each part. Therefore, your search must begin within and begin without at the same time.

This is succinctly symbolized by the spiral maze that has come to us from prehistoric times. Sometimes known as a septenary spiral, this form (and its variations) can be found in many places, including St Nectan's Kieve near Tintagel in Cornwall. Carved onto megaliths, laid out on cathedral floors (and claimed by Christianity), even cut into turf - it takes you inward and leads you out. It traces a journey of mystical death into the dark centre that is the womb from which you will be reborn.

Many treat this as a form of temple, concentrating only on its material aspect. Although it is satisfying to create it in physical form and to walk the path, all such forms are symbols and must be understood in this light. They are the entrance to the mystery that lies beyond.

The only true temple is Life. From our own perspective, this resides in the form of our bodies. Yet it must be remembered that our bodies, our selves, our being - all have many aspects. It must also be remembered that our self is not isolated from the rest of Life. We are an integral part of the universe. One of our quests is to overcome the deficiencies of our material senses in order to understand this. It is one of the wisdoms we must win.

It is easy to accept this on an intellectual level. It is harder to accept it emotionally; harder still to absorb it into the core of our selves so that it becomes instinctive. The entrance to this innermost mystery is in the narrowest confine of our being. The spiral must be followed to its centre before one can return, reborn.

In this journey, the consciousness must be put aside. This is conditioned by our many environments. And today these bear little or no resemblance to early times when the wisdom was more fully appreciated. Not only has the physical world changed, but so too has the very psychological make-up of humanity. This is one of the things we work to change within ourselves, as we become Druid.

In this journey, we must also put aside our intellect. There are dire limitations to our knowledge, conditioned by centuries of thought based on materialistic and analytical patterns. Knowledge is delivered using the alphabet, an invention that hinders the activity of the right side of the brain.

In this journey, we must go forward with our eyes closed. We must leave behind all the maps we know. We must forget everything we thought we knew about the world. It is a frightening experience. It involves a great leap of faith, the step from the edge of what seems to be a precipice into nothingness. This is the leap of The Fool in the Tarot deck, the leap of Gloucester in Shakespeare's *King Lear* (a masterpiece of spiritual insight).

It is, of course, a leap that is no leap. It only seems a step off the edge into nothingness because of the way we are conditioned to think about and see the world. However, in taking the step, in leaving the old ways behind, in making our way to the centre of the spiral, we emerge into a new world. And in that world we are open to the guidance of those who keep the 'ancient wisdom' alive.

Along with the many accomplishments of Druids was the ability of their adepts to understand, evolve, and make use of the 'ancient wisdom' that they had inherited. Not all Druids worked directly on this. Many were content to be healers or lawyers, singers and seers, but even their skills were derived from and attuned to the natural laws that form part of the wisdom tradition.

It is this role, as seekers after wisdom, which modern Druids have in common with their ancestors. Nevertheless, there is more to it than just a search. There is a purpose in the search itself, a purpose in the goal. The goal is just the beginning. We seek this wisdom, this Grail, so that we might use it in the world.

If you read between the lines of even the most Christianized of the Grail stories, you will see that attaining the Grail is not the ultimate purpose of the quest. The Grail is sought so that it can serve, heal, and bring fruitfulness to the Wasteland.

In that, we see the purpose. We must make ourselves fit for the journey - which is where most seekers stop. They have improved themselves and that, as far as they and the teachers they have found are concerned, is the whole purpose. It is a step in the right direction, but it is only a step. Having made ourselves fit, we must use that to seek out our Grail, seek out the Light.

For many others, the journey ends there. Once more, they have satisfied their own ends and feel they may bask in the light they have discovered. But there is more. There is a third part to the journey in which we let go of our own desires and ends and make ourselves a vessel for the Light that we may carry it back and radiate it for the benefit of others.

For all that we have talked here of 'ancient wisdom', it is important to remember that it is ancient only inasmuch as it has been with us for a great length of time. It is not ancient in the sense of being out of date. It is timeless, dynamic, evolving.

It is also important to remember that the wisdom is not 'hidden' or 'secret'. It is there for all who are prepared to look for it. The discipline involved in seeking it out and making sense of it once we have learned to apprehend it is what is difficult. That is often mistaken as a way of hiding things. However, as we seek, we learn the one real secret – that there is no secret and that nothing is hidden.

The 'ancient wisdom' is alive, it is vibrant, it is right in front of our eyes. Indeed, the 'ancient wisdom', the 'timeless wisdom', the 'great wisdom' is to be found in every blade of grass, every flower, every tree, every mouse, dog, cat, cow, hawk, and fish, in every cloud and star, in every human being. It is written in huge letters in the world about us.

What we finally apprehend, no matter how profound it is in one sense, is exceedingly simple in another. What we seek is not the wisdom itself because it is ever changing, but the wherewithal to recognize it where it is, the wherewithal to recognize the great simplicity, the wherewithal to understand the profundity within the simplicity.

SERVICE

The Druid Way is an espousal of a set of values, which are derived from the Celtic metaphysic. Many people are drawn to this instinctively as they feel it is the most comfortable way of expressing their inner nature and of coming to understand the world. It feels very much like a coming home, a return to the hearth that they have been seeking. And there, for them, the journey ends.

However, there is much more to being Druid than simply finding what is comfortable. That is what much of new-age thinking consists in - self-development with no other end in mind. Yet this is nothing more than a turning of one's back on the world. Having found the hearth, having satisfied one's self, it is a closing of the door and a settling into the comfortable chair. It is a lonely and sterile thing to do.

It is quite understandable that this happens. For many, the search for the hearth and the heart, the search for what we are, is long and arduous. Yet that search is simply the starting point, the journey inward. Having rested, it is important that the search resumes, this time taking the journey outward. If it does not, then the spiritual element withers.

Finding one's self and coming to know that self are exceedingly important elements of any spiritual Way. However, that does not constitute the whole of the Way. It is merely a preparation. To follow the Way requires discipline, strength, and perseverance. It also requires a solid and dependable base from which to explore - hence the emphasis on the use of 'hearth' as an image.

Most religions and spiritual Ways will then say there is a second stage. Having trained one's self for the search, one then has to set out on the search. And what is it that is sought? Enlightenment. To many who get beyond the self-improvement stage, seeking the Light is the goal. Ultimately, however, this is just as self-serving as self-improvement. It is what has divorced most religions from the real world and led to the sanctioning of such great destruction in the name of this, that, or some other god.

The emphasis on simply seeking the Light is centred in the person who seeks. Their goal is entirely selfish - salvation of the self. Not all Ways believe this. Some teach that we must seek the Light through many lifetimes until we fully understand it, but the goal is always a final entry into some other place, be it paradise or nirvana.

For Druids and most others whose religion is based in nature, Enlightenment is not the goal. It is a step toward the goal. Druids do not aspire to some other state of existence, despising the material aspect of our being in the meantime. They know they will be reborn in the Summerlands.

Instead, they aspire to harmonizing the material and the spiritual in this existence. They work toward Enlightenment so that they may offer themselves as channels for the Light, working to maintain balance where it exists, working to heal where the balance has been disturbed.

The values inherent in the Celtic metaphysic form the framework that guides the way in which we use what we have come to understand of the universe. We might argue, between us, over the finer points of those values, but broadly speaking they are concerned with the maintenance of order. This is not a reactionary stance, for a true understanding of the universe will show that the one constant to be maintained is change.

Nothing is ever still; nothing remains fixed - no matter how things may appear to us in each of our relatively short lives. Service – that is, maintaining order - means understanding the ever-evolving underlying principles of things and ensuring that all we do in the universe adheres to these principles.

Ultimately, everything we are as Druids and do as a result (thinking, acting, relating, and so on) is woven about the framework of Service. We work to become channels of the Light, working with the Goddess to bring things into harmony. This is the ultimate magic. This is the ultimate Service.

The measure of this is Truth. Indeed, Truth and Service are inextricably linked - two sides of the one coin. In the past, ancestral Druids were ultimately concerned with maintaining a balance - materially, socially, spiritually. Their Service was to set the boundaries, listening to the voice of the universe, and guiding others. Now, Service must be about restoring that balance - showing that there are boundaries, showing that the universe has a voice that must be heard.

Of course, we can never hope to achieve these things fully in one lifetime. What we can do is work towards them. In addition, whilst we work towards them we must acknowledge a number of things.

We must accept that we do not know very much and that we understand even less. We must accept that we are a part - a small facet of the great jewel that is the universe. We must also accept that we cannot Serve until we each have some idea of the present state of the World. To do that, it must be measured against the Truth.

When the Truth is placed against the World (that is, when the conscious creations of humanity are measured against what we know of the underlying principles of the universe), the World fails miserably. If Truth really is told, the World is an unmitigated and bloody mess. Humanity has little or no integrity. It constantly ignores the real cost of its actions. No longer listening to the voice of the universe, it has lost control of its own actions.

We know that sounds gloom laden. We know many of you reading this will think to themselves, 'What of all the progress we have made?' What progress? Do not be too quick to judge humanity by the best it might achieve. Look carefully and judge it by the worst it has already done.

This is not to say there is no hope. Just that there is much to do. Which is why we must know what we are doing and why. Without such guidance and such goals, we could spend our lives floundering about making lots of noise and accomplishing nothing.

We are capable of changing things, each in our own way. Finding that way is one of the quests we undertake as we learn the basic teachings of our tradition. The overall aim is to bring about a lasting spiritual impression and no hint of a material impression, to make the work easier for future generations and leave no scar. Such work is hard and at times a burden almost too heavy to bear. However, we are part of a tradition that has ancient roots and will flourish for millennia yet to come. We hold the line. As we work, ripples flow across the surface and currents run in the deeps of our lives and relationships with others and the planet.

AWEN

The Lord God will give me the sweet Awen,
as from the cauldron of Cerridwen.

Llywarch ap Llywelyn (12th century poet)

In the next section of this book, there is a chapter on circle casting, where it is suggested that the 'awen' is chanted or intoned three times. You are unlikely to have this word before now if you are new to the Druid Way. It is one of those mystical words that means as many things to as many Druids as you care to ask. For many people, the first time they hear it intoned is at a public Druid Gorsedd where, depending on the amount of Druids in the circle, it can cause quite a vibration. It is usually intoned three times, but some groups chant it in multiples of three. It is pronounced 'ah-oo-en'.

The awen has a very long history and dates back beyond the Druid revival of the seventeenth and eighteenth centuries. In fact, the earliest extant mention of it is in a Latin text from AD796 by Nennius. This work, *Historia Brittonum*, was itself based on an earlier text by a Welsh monk called Gildas. The mention is in reference to King Ida of Northumberland and although no meaning of the word is given, it does prove that the word was in existence before Britain became completely Christianized.

There are later and very interesting references by Giraldus Cambrensis (Gerald of Wales) who wrote in his *Description of Wales* c1188:

Among the Welsh there are certain individuals called Awenyddion who behave as if they are possessed by devils. You will not find them anywhere else. When you consult them about a problem, they immediately go into a trance and lose control of their sense, as if they are possessed. They do not answer the question put to them in any logical way. Words stream from their mouths, incoherently and apparently meaningless without any sense at all, but all the same well expressed: and if you listen carefully to what they say you will receive the solution to your problem. When it is all over, they will recover from their trance, as if they were ordinary people waking from a heavy sleep, but you have to give them a good shake before they regain control of themselves.

[trans. Lewis Thorpe]

A modern Druid's use of the awen is likely to be somewhat different from the above, with the twelfth century Awenyddion seeing it as an 'oracular spirit'. Texts later than that of Gerald of Wales (such as the *Book of Taliesin* from the thirteenth century AD) also include the word 'awen'. For all that, we still do not really know how it was perceived or used in the past.

Today it is not only used in a number of different contexts, but also has a number of different, related meanings. For example, a Druid today may think of awen as inspiration or divine power - an energy flow or communion. It is also the poetic muse, the breath of creativity, even the reins that bind us to the source of all inspiration. All these meanings derive from the root, *awen*, still in use in the Welsh language and meaning, 'poetic gift', making it bardic in nature – the gift of Cerridwen's cauldron.

This difficulty in apprehending its meaning lies partly in the way we tend to view the world and partly in the nature of the word itself. What it names is an elusive and mysterious essence, which cannot be understood simply by naming it. Unfortunately, most of us are brought up to believe that we understand things by taking them apart. Awen is, in itself, the very opposite of this. The more we try to explain such a word, the less it wishes to be understood. We have to accept that it is simply awen.

The closest we can get to a proper understanding is to use it as a meditative focus. Druids in ceremony chant it, mantra style. This is probably a long way from its original use or meaning, but who can tell? Ancestral Druids were well aware of the power of sound and the spoken word. The sound of awen is very like the Indian mantra Om when chanted or intoned.

Some Druids use it when working alone. It is said softly and silently in the head - very good as a daily centring meditation and for healing at a soul level. Others will chant it to obtain inspiration at a sacred or trance-like level. To understand the flow of this sound into spirit and back out again is to understand the divine flow of energy that underlies all things in this life. It is not the only divine flow, of course, for all religions of the world have some form of mantra, word, or prayers that do the same, connecting to the same source.

Awen, this little mysterious Welsh word, that would take many lifetimes to understand fully is well worth working with if you wish to tread the Druid Way. It has always been linked with inspiration, spirit, and the creative principle. All of these are found in awen. This does not mean that awen will necessarily help you write poetry (although it might), but it will help you understand where the Bard's inspiration came from and lead you to ways of understanding how you can tap that creative energy in other ways.

PART THREE

WORKING IN THE WORLD

TOOLS OF THE TRADE

As Druids, it is important to understand that there is no real need to use magical tools for ritual or any other purpose. We are enough within ourselves and we can work creatively with what nature provides. Most Druids use something, however, even if it is just a candle although some have been known to turn up at rituals and Gorseddau with bagfuls!

So why do we have them? The answer is that for many Druids they are a way of focusing the mind on the task ahead. They contain, through ritual use, the symbolical and psychological triggers that allow a shift in consciousness – moving from ordinary space and time into a sacred realm that is deep within us as well as on the borders of this world and the other.

If you feel the need for magical tools there are a few ground rules worth observing. To begin with, make your own using natural products if it is at all possible. Not only is it more satisfying, but it also imbues the tools with your personal essence. It is also cheaper. Do not be slavish about this - we are not all highly skilled artisans - but always do as much as you can.

The next thing to remember is that all paraphernalia you use for your Druid work should be kept solely for that purpose. Using tools and other bits and pieces for other purposes dissipates their effectiveness and can have a distorting effect on the work you do. For the same reason you should not work with other people's tools or allow them to borrow yours.

Finally, take it with you when you go. Make provision in your will for your paraphernalia to be disposed of in a responsible fashion. If it is composed of natural products then it can be buried with you or cremated.

Robes

The public's vision of the Druid is often that of the white-clad, cowled figures in a circle at Stonehenge. This is far from the reality of what most Druids actually wear (or do). Many do not bother with robes, especially Hedge Druids. It is usually people who belong to a Grove or an Order who feel robes are something they must have, especially when they see everyone else wearing them.

It is always interesting to hear the comments from a Druid who wears their robes for the first time. The very act of putting on a special set of clothing, let alone the clothes themselves, makes a person feel different. Inevitably, a set of robes becomes a treasured item and important to your Druid work. Remember, though, that robes do not a Druid make, even though as a tool they are very powerful and help you to connect quickly.

If you do decide that robes are for you, what should they be like? There are many styles from which to choose. Many Druid Orders choose to wear the eighteenth century revivalist, white robe with hood or cowl. Over this is worn either a tabard of blue (to designate a Bard) or green (for an Ovate), or a belt in these colours. Those in the Druid grade wear plain white.

There is, however, no long tradition of Druids wearing white, and it is up to the individual if this is the colour they wish to wear. There is, in fact, no genuine tradition of any colours. The Romans wrote that the Druids in Britain wore dark robes, which is probably more realistic, but it is one of those things we will never know for sure.

Your robes could be white or black, or you might prefer a woodland green or a deep sky blue, maybe even an elaborately embroidered affair. You might even decide that a robe is not for you, but a certain T-shirt is. Whatever you decide, keep it special, and when you change into your garment, know that you are stepping into the sacred and leaving behind the ordinary.

As with other tools, it is good to try to make your own robes. A number of patterns are available. However, if you are not good at sewing or cutting out patterns, do not attempt it. Appropriate cloth is expensive and it would be a shame to waste it. Of course, if you do make your own, they become *very* special.

Whether you make your own or buy something ready made, make sure it is not a synthetic material. Many rituals are conducted near fire. Natural materials (cotton or wool) smoulder rather than melt to your skin or burst into flames, if you should have an accident. Fire accidents can also happen with long, flowing wizard-like sleeves and cloaks.

The length of robes and cloaks is also a factor. As Druids, we spend much of our time out in the woods where it is muddy and often very wet underfoot. Wet grass and mud soon creep up a floor length garment. Cut them short or have belts handy so that you can kilt them up. Your robes also need to be large enough to wear something warm underneath in the depths of winter!

If you don't feel up to making your own, pagan magazines often have advertisements for robe makers or you might even find something suitable in a High Street shop. When you get them, conduct a small ceremony to dedicate them to ritual use. If you buy anything from a second hand or charity shop, cleanse it of its last owner. A small cleansing ritual of your own devising and the washing machine will do.

Altars
The work of a Druid is focused on the land, the sea, and the sky and much of what they do in ritual terms takes place outside in the natural world. In one sense, this makes the idea of an altar redundant. On the other hand, it is nice to have a corner of a room or garden as a focal point for your Druid work or for honouring the Goddess and God.

Many people are discouraged from making an altar because of the cost. A lot of books say you must have certain items, but this is nonsense. An altar need not cost anything. You only need what you want and what feels right for you. Indeed, most Druids create an altar to display the gifts that have already come to them from and through the Goddess.

There are a million ways one can make an altar and each one is special to the individual who made it. It could be a shelf on the wall, a table or dresser top, a windowsill, or a tree surrounded by stones in the garden. If you have young children, a high shelf is a good idea. The more you study and practice the Druid Way the easier it will be to decide the most appropriate location and form.

What do we put on the altar once we have made one? Druids are great collectors. They gather the gifts they are offered such as stones, leaves, feathers, candles, and any other items that depict the Druid Way. These can be displayed along with wands, chalices, and anything else that is used on a regular basis in ritual work. If your altar is very elaborate and in a public room, be prepared for visitors to your home asking you what it is.

You might like an altar dedicated to one particular deity, especially if you work closely with them, or you might wish to honour the whole Celtic pantheon. An altar dedicated to Arianrhod might have a cloth with silver stars or wheels on it. One in honour of the Triple Goddess could have a stone with a triple knot carved into it. The examples are endless.

On Julie's main altar is a model of a hare to represent the Goddess and a stag to represent Herne. There are several stones, pine cones, and normally a sprig of something from the last Grove ritual. There is also a pentacle-shaped candleholder that her aunt gave her mother for Christmas one year, for which Julie begged. Along with these, there is a goblet bought in a charity shop for £1.20 and a small bowl for water. She often adds the odd shell or feather.

On a second altar, Julie has a candlestick holder in a Goddess shape surrounded by stones with holes in them. Over this hangs a wicker pentacle, which was given away in a magazine. The garden is, of course, one big altar, but there are little corners specifically dedicated to her Druid path.

Graeme's altar is in his study. A wooden box contains cards and small treasures. On this is a carving of an oak tree. He also keeps a bowl and chalice (of wood) along with several wands. A carving of a hare suckling two young has pride of place.

If you create an altar, keep it dust free and tend it at least once a week. This is a simple act of reverence, although it is important to remember that the objects on the altar are symbols. It is not the symbols we revere, but that which they symbolize.

Other pagan paths such as the Craft have a tradition of creating an altar within the ritual circle. Druids do not normally do this as they like to focus on where they are rather than on what they are doing, but if you like the idea there is nothing to stop you. This can be decorated appropriately for the season and the rite. You can find different colour altar cloths, flowers, pictures of your ancestors and loved ones; the list is endless. Bear in mind, however, that it will need to be portable and weatherproof.

Candles
Most Druids do not work with other people in a Grove and so elaborate ceremonies or rituals are seldom, if ever attended. The lighting of a specially bought candle for a festival is a lovely way of honouring the wheel of the year. They create an ambience that is extremely conducive to ritual work. They also represent fire and are especially useful in this respect when a real fire is not appropriate.

We can create a sacred space with light from candles when they are placed at the four quarters of our ritual circle. One large candle in the middle can represent the central fire. Many rituals, however, are performed outside. Unless you are good at digging a fire-pit and lighting a fire, a candle in a lantern or a jam-jar is a good idea. It causes no damage to the environment, no wax is spilt, no holes are dug, and it is much safer than lighting a bonfire.

Much has been written about what colour candles should be used for what ritual. It does not matter. White ones are fine for everything although if you want to buy special candles it is up to you. Beeswax candles have a lovely honey aroma and are free from paraffin, as are those that are made from vegetable waxes. There are also perfumed candles that can be chosen to fit the season, enfolding the ritual with their delicious aroma. As with all forms of fire, be careful of flowing clothes, curtains, pets, and children.

Incense
Whether working outside or indoors, most Druids use incense. It represents air and fire and is mainly used for the consecration of a circle. It can also be an aid in meditation.

There are two main types of incense - joss sticks and loose incense. Sticks are useful for indoor workings or for meditation, without smoking the room out. They can be bought in hundreds of different perfumes, and are often easier to obtain than the loose incense. You will need a holder to keep the stick upright while it smoulders and somewhere safe for the ash to fall. These, too, are easy to obtain.

Loose incense dates back into prehistory and was probably one of the earliest magical tools humanity used after fire. This type of incense is made up of herbs, gums, and resins to suit either the type of working or individual. They are sold already blended in specialist shops or you can blend your own.

This type of incense can be difficult to light, and you need one or two other implements to do so, but it is worth the effort. The first of these items is a bowl or censer in which to burn your incense. A metal one with feet is ideal. This helps to protect any surface that the censer stands on. A cork mat is also a good idea. These containers get *very* hot, so it is advisable not to attempt to pick them up once lit, unless there is a safe way, such as a handle.

Place some sand in the container to help keep it cooler. This is also a safer surface for the charcoal to burn on. The charcoal is sold in tubes of ten or so discs, and once opened it needs to be kept in an airtight tin. You will also need some tweezers or tongs to hold the charcoal while you light it. When one side is alight, it may well spark and spit briefly. Place the lighted charcoal in your dish and wait until the heat has spread across the whole disc before putting a pinch or two of your blended incense on top. You can add more as and when needed. Let everything cool down before removing. Some water nearby is an ideal safety precaution.

There are many lists in books and many blends in shops that will suit all sorts of workings and correspondences. They often smell different when burning from when they are in the jar, so you may have to experiment. If you are working indoors and you have pets, remember that their noses are far more sensitive than yours are. Loose incense can be unbelievably powerful for them and make them sick. Joss sticks are not as powerful.

Wands and Staffs

Most Druids own a wand, normally made from wood. Wands are used for directing energies when casting a circle or as symbols during specific rituals. They are a continuation of a Druid's relationship with tree spirits.

When looking for a wand, it is a far better to enter a wood and seek for a fallen branch, than to cut one from a living tree. If you decide that it must come from the tree, you will need to converse with the tree spirits to show that you honour the live tree. The tree will let you know in some way if all is well. The same goes for a fallen twig. Let the tree know your intention and please leave a gift or offering to say thank you.

A wand is normally about eighteen inches in length – that is, from your elbow to your fingertips. It can be of any kind of wood, although each type has its own energies, so you might decide to have more than one. Certain woods are more appropriate than others depending on the occasion. You will need to study the properties of trees and their relation to such things as ogham before you decide.

Once you have your wand, you can leave it exactly as you found it, or you can change it. Most wood will lose its bark when it dries out. Your wand can be stripped back to the heartwood, smoothed with glasspaper, and polished with beeswax. If you have the skill, you might even wish to carve the wood with appropriate designs. Whilst you are doing this, find a cloth or make a bag in which to keep your wand when it is not in use.

Some shops sell wands made of precious stones and metals, which might be your desire, but working with the mineral kingdom requires a great deal of specialized knowledge and power and is not strictly druidic. A tool made by you or especially for you is far more potent. Of course, you can just use your finger. It is the intention and the direction that is important, not what the wand is made of.

The above also applies to athames, blades, or sickles. In the Craft, an athame is a black-handled, double-edged knife. It is never used to cut anything in the material plane and the blade should be kept blunt. In Druidry today, those who choose an athame or blade, whether it be a small knife or a large sword, will select one that feels right whatever the colour of the handle.

A word of warning about blades. The Police can consider these offensive weapons, even if they are blunt. Being caught in possession of them can lead to prosecution. If you intend to use them in public ritual, it is best to seek legal advice.

Not really a wand, but in the same vein, is the Druid's staff. These come in all sorts of wood and lengths. The same applies to collecting the wood as for wands. Most Druids do not use their staff for any particular ritual intention, although it could be used for directing energies if needed. Many Druids have beautifully carved and ornate staffs, but they can be a bother when in a circle and you need to link hands, or when getting to a ritual using public transport!

The Journal
A journal kept over the years provides a history of your development along the Druid Way, as well as being a handy place to keep information and references. In the Craft there is a tradition (albeit a recent one) of a journal called a *Book of Shadows*, in which the witch keeps a record of spells, dreams, and other workings. Some covens have a book passed down that coven members copy into their own Book of Shadows.

The journal of a Druid is more like a diary and will include meditations, dreams, poetry, drawings, divinations, reports on rituals attended and things spotted in nature. Although it is similar to a Book of Shadows, they are rarely passed down to other Grove members. Not all Druids keep journals and some use them less as time passes, but they are extremely useful when you first start along the Way.

Any type of notebook will do, including ring binders. There are many beautiful hand-made journals in the shops these days if you fancy something extra special. You may even prefer to put your journal on computer, but you are working with the mineral kingdom again.

Other items

A few other items need to be mentioned in addition to those above. During some ceremonies, mead is offered to the Land and the Gods. The libation is often poured first into a goblet. This can be one bought especially for this purpose, or it can be something you already have. Ensure that it is robust. Glass is beautiful, but if it broken outside you have to make sure every piece is removed so that it does not damage wildlife. As with all other items, if you start to use it for rituals, keep it solely for that purpose.

A small bowl to consecrate your sacred circle with water is another item that can be found quite easily. This bowl could be kept in a special box along with the goblet.

You will often see Druids wearing amber and other magical jewellery. This is not a necessity, but special pieces worn only during ceremonies or rituals can add an extra dimension to your own personal preparation.

The use of a cauldron is probably borrowed from Witchcraft, although there are links with Cerridwen, the Tuatha Dé Danaan, and the womb of the Goddess. Cauldrons can be very heavy to carry around, especially when working outside. They are useful for burning offerings in rather than lighting a bonfire. If you fancy a cauldron, size does not matter. The symbology is the same whether it is a tiny model or a huge cast iron pot.

Most Druid workings are done outside and with this in mind, there are a few other necessary items that all Druids should have. To begin with, wellingtons and wet weather gear for those not so sunny days. Good quality walking boots are also important if you have to hike to your destination - you can always go barefoot when you get there. You will also need a good torch for working at night and a compass to find the quarters. One other important item is sunblock. Many Gorseddau are held on high places in the 'eye of the Sun', and if the ceremony is a long one you can get badly burnt, even on overcast days.

Sacred objects

Sacred objects are those things that we collect, normally from nature, and into which we breathe our spirit for use in our work as

Druids. They can be such things as a crystal or a hawk's feather, a shell or a sprig of yew to place on our altar. These are all gifts from the Goddess and should be revered as such.

The use of animal skins is not necessary - we are twenty-first century Druids, not fifth century ones. Some Druids buy skins of deer and wolf. They are supporting a cruel trade that endangers these animals. Finding a dead animal or its bones is a different matter if you really feel you must have such things. A much nicer exercise would be to bury the creature and wish it a safe journey into the Otherworld. This is, by far, the best way to honour the creature's spirit.

As we progress along the Druid Way, we find that we learn to direct our energies without the use of tools. Our confidence in what we are doing allows us to dispense with much of the paraphernalia we have collected. People who have been Druid for a long time tend to work with one or two mundane, but treasured items with which they feel comfortable. However, to dispense with things we must, first, have collected them and experienced them.

CASTING A CIRCLE AND CIRCLE WORKING

The importance of the circle

To cast a circle is to create sacred space - a place between the worlds and beyond the boundaries of time and space. When we cast a circle, we build an energy circuit with which to work. It contains certain forces and keeps others out.

The act of casting a circle resounds far beyond the two-dimensional figure that is traced upon the ground. In fact, we actually create a multi-dimensional sphere, one that encloses us entirely in all the worlds and which, as a result, provides access to those worlds. Whilst we might consider the necessary complexity of this in meditation, it is far easier in practice to refer to this space as a circle.

Within such a circle, different rules apply from those of the everyday world. We are in meta-time, working at nature's pace. We are in a place that borders all the worlds where we can perform our rituals and enact our meditations – channelling energies from all sources and working with them on physical, mental, and psychic levels. It is where we meet the Goddess and God.

Our pre-Celtic ancestors who built the great stone circles probably did not cast as we do today. The priesthood at the time would presumably have enacted rituals at these sites, and the energies would have built up over hundreds of years, stored within the structure, so getting rid of the need to cast each circle anew.

The content and practice of ancestral Druid ritual is equally obscure. There is, of course, clear evidence that Druids worked in a circle, or an oval shape. They used circular groves of oak and yew, and maybe even built some stone circles of their own. Whatever the case, the circle was important to them at a symbolic, ritual, and magical level.

They saw the universe as a circle and the circle as the universe. The sky was round as they studied the stars, the Earth was round as they studied the horizon. The Sun and the Moon were not only circles of light, but also travelled on a circular route through the cosmos, which in turn brought about day and night, light and dark, heat and cold. Indeed, the circle symbolized life and death and life itself.

Today we work in a slightly different way to our ancestors. The world is a different place. Although we still create sacred space, commune with nature and the Goddess, and do our Grove workings in a circle, we try to leave no trace of where we have been. We still visit stone circles and groves of trees like our Celtic ancestors, but we tend to make use of what is already there, connecting and working with the spirit of a place as it already exists.

Preparation

Before you begin to think about casting a circle for your working, you need to prepare yourself and a few items. As an example, we will discuss casting a circle for a solo Druid to do a working. You do not always need to cast a circle. Certain rituals and most meditations do not require it. Indeed, there are times when the casting of a circle is entirely inappropriate.

To begin with, you need to consider the location of your circle. This depends, in part, on the number of people involved. Some Druids work in large, open Gorseddau. These are meetings of Druids from several or many Orders and Groves, generally (though not always) held in public places. The Druid presiding over the ceremony will generally walk the circle outside of those attending, casting as they go. Other Druids work just with the Grove they belong to or on their own.

Outdoors is the ideal place. We call upon the spirits of the natural world to aid us in our work and it is simple politeness to meet them on their home ground. They are far more likely to respond. However, circumstances can dictate against working outside and it is very much up to the individuals involved to decide which location is best at a given time.

That said, for our walk-through we will use a room indoors. When you are beginning, you need to be able to concentrate on what you are doing. Choose familiar surroundings in which you know you will not be disturbed by people, the elements, or curious creatures. Once you know the content of the ritual, you can take it outside and apply it to a more open environment.

Decide what room you will use. You will need space to walk around a small circle as well as room to sit in the centre. Try to have this room uncluttered, as well as clean and tidy. Preparing the site of any ritual is as important as the ritual itself and helps you achieve the correct frame of mind for the work you are about to undertake.

If you decide on candles – which provide a kinder and subtler form of illumination than electric light - do be careful of where you place them. Keep them well away from curtains and fabrics. And remember that you will be moving around (perhaps in robes) which can cause drafts. Sturdy candleholders with wide bases – for stability and to catch running wax – are highly recommended.

Decide what you will need in the centre of your circle. You might want nothing. Alternatively, you might like a cushion to sit on, a central flame (candle), a stone you are fond of, some flowers, anything you wish that is appropriate to the ritual or working you are about to undertake. For the example that follows, you will need a small bowl of water, some incense (either loose or a stick) and matches, and your athame or wand. Put all of these items in the room before you start.

You next need to work out where north is, so you can accurately call the quarters. A compass is always useful to have (especially when you start working outside), but if you know, for example, that the window faces north, that will do. If using loose incense, light the charcoal in advance of the ritual, as it takes a while to get hot enough to melt the incense.

How it is done, step by step.
Turn off the phone. You will be amazed at how many people decide to call you the minute you sit down to work or meditate. Ask anyone else in the house not to disturb you until you have finished (unless, of course, the place is on fire). This is very important. You will not be harmed if you are disturbed, but you cannot work properly unless you are confident that others are respecting your space.

A bath is a good way to prepare for your Druid work. A symbolic cleansing, using scented oils, is an excellent way to focus your thoughts and attain an appropriate state of mind in readiness for entering your sacred space. You can then put on your robes (if you use them) and go straight through to the room that you have prepared.

When you are ready, move the water to the west of centre on the floor, and the incense to the south, again on the floor. You then need to walk deiseal (sunwise or clockwise) around to the gateway at the west (do not forget your wand or athame if using one) and stand there for a moment, facing east.

All your movements should be deiseal, even when turning on the spot. This keeps the energies flowing in the same direction. To walk the circle anticlockwise is known as going tuathal, and it is for taking down energies and banishing, especially at the end of rituals.

We do not want to banish energies just yet, so keep everything flowing the same way.

You will not come to any harm if you walk in the wrong direction; it simply dilutes your hard work and disperses the flow. Try to get into the habit of doing everything deiseal, even stirring drinks.

As you stand in the west, facing the east, you are on the threshold of what will be your circle. Wait until you feel it is right to enter. When you first start to cast circles, it is difficult to believe you will feel this, but there will be a definite moment when you know all is ready.

Walk through the gateway and move deiseal around to the opposite side, the east. Face outwards and give a salute to the spirit of the east, the Guardians of the circle, the spirits of place. How you salute them is up to you. Some raise one hand, whilst others hold up both arms. Some simply make contact. This salutation is best done with your eyes closed.

If you are working alone, walk the complete circle again, finishing back in the east. Turn to face inwards. You then make a statement of intent, whilst asking for guidance from the Goddess. This tells the spirits of place why you are there so they may respond appropriately. After this is done, turn and face the south. You are now ready to cast the circle.

Take your wand/athame in you right hand (if you are using your finger, it is still the right hand) and hold your arm out straight across your body and below shoulder height so that you make the circle outside of you as you walk. Visualize energy coming up from the Earth and down from the stars, meeting within you and travelling along your arm into the wand or finger.

Start to walk slowly round from east to east, the path of the Sun. As you do so, feel and see the energy flowing from your arm, forming a circle of light. When you reach the east, and the circle of light is complete, turn and face the centre.

You will now consecrate the circle with fire and water. It must be pointed out here that some traditions (particularly within witchcraft) use salted water. Do not use this outside as salt kills plants and the small creatures that live in the soil.

From the east, walk the circle to the south, pick up the incense holder and walk from south to south with it. Place it in the centre. Walk to the west, pick up the water and walk from west to west. You can sprinkle some water around the circle as you go if you wish.

These two acts consecrate and secure the circle. You are now in protective space. Whatever you do inside the circle will stay there until you disperse it, use it (as in a healing ritual), or close everything down. Undesirable influences will not penetrate it while you work. You have created a centre to your own universe.

When you have put the water in the centre, step straight back, and then walk round to the east. You will now give peace to the quarters, something that is done in most Druid circles worldwide. You move to each of the cardinal points, starting in the north and then moving to the south, west, and east. It may seem an odd order, but the quarters are worked as opposites so that the energies running between them establish a central point within the circle.

In many Druid rituals, a prayer is now said. This is a supplication for those gifts and qualities we most associate with being Druid. In open circles it is often the Universal Druid Prayer. This first appears during the eighteenth century revival and is neither Celtic nor pagan. You could write your own, or you could use the example below.

Grove Prayer
Over the turning tides
The silver stars glide
Above the fish that swims
And the green Earth that spins

Between the soil and the skies
The majestic Hawk flies
From the Oak tree that grows
Above the one who knows

Before the Goddess immortal
We stand before the portal
Of the wild wood so dark
With a hunter at its heart

And here within the spiral
We celebrate the cycles
And to the Earth and Sky above
We send forth light and love

Next, come the invocations. These are to invite those from other planes that you would like to enter your circle. Normally it is the

Goddess and God, but it could also be a particular deity such as Brigid for an Imbolc or healing ritual. Invocations do not need to be complicated. Simply ask politely for the presence of those that you wish to be in your circle.

A word of warning here. Be very sure of who or what you are inviting in, and why you want them there. If it is a deity, make sure you know their history. Some are difficult to work with. All bring particular energies that should be appropriate to the occasion.

It is also important that you do not mix rays. If, for example, you invite the Dagda into your circle, remember he is Irish and teaming him up with Isis, who is Egyptian, just will not work. Stay with the Celtic pantheon, which is enormous, but also do your research, as even within this there are deities and spirits whose energies will clash.

The same warning goes for inviting faerie folk. This has become something of a fashion and it sounds wonderful, but not all faeries are friendly and they can be very hard to get rid of afterwards. Celtic faeries are not the pretty little flimsies with wings that we see in picture books any more than they are elementals or elves.

Following the invocations, you will open the gateways at the four quarters (which we give capital letters to differentiate them from the cardinal points). This allows power and energy from each of the quarters to enter your circle; it also gives added protection. Starting with the East, the place of air, the dawn, birds, and spring, you do what is known as 'calling the quarter'. You then move around deiseal to the south, west, and north, before returning to the east. Calling the quarters is done facing outwards.

When you get back to the east, you turn to face the centre and declare the completion of the circle and the opening of the ritual. You may now do your central working. This could be a meditation, an Inner Grove working, a ritual celebration, a healing, anything at all to do with your Druid work.

When you have finished the central section, it is very important that the circle be closed down properly. No trace should be left on any plane of existence, physical or astral. Time and space should be allowed to return as they were before. All gateways to the quarters must be closed. All visitors to your circle must depart back to their own worlds. This is known as the 'closing'.

You should start this process by stating that the ritual has ended and that you have finished your work. The Oath of Peace is often said three times, followed by the awen. This is intoned or chanted as many times as you wish, normally in multiples of three.

You will then need to thank the four quarters for their help and let them depart. This begins with the North, and then moves to the West, South, and East. You still walk sunwise at this point. If there is a Druid in each quarter, they would each face outwards and close the gateways in turn, but working solo, you need to walk around.

When you have visualized the gateways closing, turn inwards and thank all those who have come to your circle, seen and unseen, and ask them politely to leave. Try not to forget anyone. Then, finally, declare that the ritual has finished.

Take up your wand with your right hand and walk from east to east. This time walk tuathal, seeing the circle of light draw back into your wand/athame/finger, down your body into the Earth and back up to the stars.

Turn to face the east and salute it, before walking deiseal to the place of the ancestors, the west. This is your gateway by which to leave. When you feel ready, step out and know that you have returned to this world. Quietly clear your things away and finish with a drink and something to eat which helps to ground you in this reality.

Try to avoid leaving a circle during a working. If it becomes necessary, go to the west and cut a doorway (psychically) tuathal, step through, and turn to face the circle. Close the doorway by pulling the circle back deiseal so it joins. When you go back in do the same, but walk a complete circle deiseal when you re-enter to get the energies flowing again.

This all seems very long and difficult to begin with. We hope that by explaining it, you have come to understand the structure and the reasons why you do certain things. This in turn should make the whole thing easier to remember. In addition, the more you perform such rituals, the easier they become, leaving you free to concentrate on the working within.

No harm will come to you if you make mistakes, as there is no real right or wrong way to do things as you travel the Druid Way. The Goddess does not expect us to be perfect beings and no one is watching in judgement over you. It is the intention behind your workings that is important, hence the need to become conversant with the Celtic metaphysic.

143

The Ritual
The ritual that follows is just an example with which you can practice. You can walk around holding the book to follow it if that makes it easier for you. Later you can either write your own or adapt this one. Like ancestral Druids, you should try to commit your rituals and other workings to memory.

If you write your own rituals, you will need to work out what corresponds with the quarters. There are many books with tables of correspondences in them, but it is so much better to meditate and find your own. It empowers your Druidry.

<u>The Opening</u>
Enter from the west and walk deiseal to salute the east. Walk a circuit back to the east and turn outwards. Open by saying:

Oh Great Goddess, I ask for your blessing, guidance, and protection on this my Sacred Inner Grove ritual.

Cast your circle from east to east. Walk to the south and take the incense round the circle. Walk to the west and do the same with the water. Return to the east. Walk to the north and turn outwards. As you salute the quarter, say:

May there be peace in the North.

Walk to the south and turn outwards. As you salute the quarter, say:

May there be peace in the South.

Walk to the west and turn outwards. As you salute the quarter, say:

May there be peace in the West.

Walk to the east and turn outwards. As you salute the quarter, say:

May there be peace in the East.

Turn to face the centre. Say:

May there be peace above and peace below. May there be peace throughout the worlds.

Say the prayer:

May I be blessed with the cauldron's gift,
May the breath of inspiration touch me,
May my voice always sing clear,
May the light reach within me,
May I learn from the land,
May the seeds I plant be fruit for all children,
May calm be my mantle,
May wisdom blaze out from the depths of my soul,
May truth be in my heart.

Say the Invocations:

O Great Goddess,
Bringer of life,
Queen of the Stars,
Mother of the Earth and Seas,
Be present now within this place.

O Great God,
Lord of the Land,
Guardian of the Wild Wood,
Walker of the silent ways,
Be present now within this place.

Turn outwards and say:

In the name of the spirit of Hawk, the springtime breeze, and the element of Air, I open this eastern gateway.

Walk to the south. Turn outwards and say:

In the name of the spirit of Adder, the power of the Sun, and the element of Fire, I open this southern gateway.

Walk to the west. Turn outwards and say:

In the name of the spirit of the Sacred Salmon, mighty oceans, and the element of Water, I open this western gateway.

Walk to the north. Turn outwards and say:

In the name of the spirit of Wolf, dark, deep forests, and the element of Earth, I open this northern gateway.

Walk to the east. Turn inwards and say:

This circle is complete. In this sacred place, I declare the opening of this ritual of my Sacred Inner Grove.

<u>Central working</u>
(For this example, you would undertake the Sacred Inner Grove meditation to be found in the following chapter.)

<u>The Closing</u>
When you have completed your central working, say:

I declare that my work is done within this circle this day. May my memory and my heart hold its sacredness.

Swear the Oath of Peace three times.

I swear by peace and love to stand, heart to heart and hand in hand, mark O spirit and hear me now, confirming this my sacred vow.

Intone the Awen as many times as you like.

Walk to the north. Turn outwards and say:

Spirits of the midnight cold, of crystal, and stones, I thank the element of Earth and close this northern gateway.

Walk to the west. Turn outwards and say:

Spirits of evening light, of sacred spring and well, I thank the element of Water and close this western gateway.

Walk to the south. Turn outwards and say:

Spirits of the Sun at noon, of mighty Oak, and the sacred flame, I thank the element of Fire and close this southern gateway.

Walk to the east. Turn outwards and say:

Spirits of the dawn, of lofty hill, and mighty gales, I thank the element of Air and close this eastern gateway.

Face the centre and say:

I thank the Goddess and the God, and all those seen and unseen who have joined this circle today.

Depart in peace. Hail and Farewell.

I send healing and love to the animal, plant, and mineral kingdoms. May they always be protected from harm.

I declare this ritual is now ended. It ends in peace, as in peace it began.

Close your circle tuathal, grounding it back into the Earth and up to the Stars. When you reach the east again, turn outwards and salute it, before walking deiseal to the west and leaving.

*

A comprehensive exploration of ritual, along with examples for the eightfold year and rites of passage can be found in *Arianrhod's Dance*.

MEDITATION

An area that causes many problems for those following the Druid Way is the practice of meditation. People find every excuse to avoid it. They say it is too difficult, that they do not know how, that it is eastern and has nothing to do with Druidry, that they have not the time or the place to practice. The excuses are endless and take up more time and energy than would the meditation itself.

Meditation is an essential part of any spiritual path and is practised worldwide. The earliest known mention of 'meditative ecstasy' is in the *Rig Veda*, which is thought to have been composed a thousand years BC in northern India. Siddhãrtha Gautama (the Buddha) found enlightenment whilst meditating under a Bodhi tree and so the Buddhist path of deliverance is via meditation.

It was in the fourth century BC, however, that formalized meditation became known through the Taoist work *Tao Te Ching*, which emphasized the importance of breath control within meditation.

Because of the popularity of certain forms, meditation has become best known as an eastern spiritual discipline. Many eastern techniques involve attempts at mental control allowing the meditator to move beyond normal experience into a void that has absence of all thought.

In the west, we only usually hear of the Christian custom of silent prayer and reflection. All this leads people to believe that meditation is primarily an eastern discipline. However, there is a long and well-established tradition of meditation within pre-Christian Celtic religious and spiritual practice.

Druid Meditation

Druid meditation is different from many other forms, as it is primarily visual. Rather than clearing the mind of all thought and imagery to achieve a higher state of consciousness, a clarity of vision, and a peace of mind, the Druid will use carefully chosen visual narratives. Nor will a Druid consider such states of mind as the goal of meditation. They are the means to a further end.

Druids do not meditate in order to transcend this world; they do it in order to become more in tune with it. Rather than divorcing their self from the universe, they seek higher states of consciousness in order to open their self to the world and better integrate it with the matrix of existence from which we have become divorced.

Noticing the sunset colours across the sky, feeling the grass between your toes when it has been raining, holding a peach coloured shell, or sitting on a windy hilltop, are all states of meditation – best described in the later poems attributed to Taliesin. Although you need a clear and settled mind for this, the belief that *all* meditation is done in an uncomfortable full-lotus yoga position while trying to think of nothing is unfounded.

There are several techniques practised by Druids today, which may or may not have a long history. We cannot deny, however, that ancestral Druids practised certain forms of meditation. This is partly because they believed in an inner and outer world as we do today. But it is also because we know that the training of Bards and Druids involved techniques that cut them off from trivial distractions of the World to enable them to concentrate on their inner being in order to open them up to their awen. We also know that ancestral Druids had the ability to travel between the three worlds.

These and other activities suggestive of meditative and trance states are found in many of the old tales. Whether these states were achieved with the aid of hallucinogenic substances is a matter of debate. Modern Druids, however, do not use them and it is better to practise meditation when one's system is clear of all pollutants - including alcohol.

A good way to start meditating is to find a few minutes every day to sit and concentrate on your breathing. Choose a place where you will not be disturbed. You might like to light a candle and burn a light incense to enhance the occasion. It does not, however, have to be in the dark or even indoors. There are wonderful places outdoors to sit and meditate such as the seashore or a woodland glade. Remember, though, that these can be busy and noisy places and are probably best left until you have developed your technique.

With this type of short meditation, it is not too uncomfortable to sit on the floor with a straight back. If you are unable to do that, a straight-backed chair is fine. If you lie down on a bed, it is difficult to feel the rise and fall of your breathing and you will, in any case, probably fall asleep. This meditation could easily be done at sunrise or sunset, or even midday. You could even do it during a break at work.

When you are comfortable, simply close your eyes and follow the flow of air in through your nostrils, down into your lungs, and then back out through your mouth. Try not to exaggerate your breathing. If you are relaxed, it will settle into a steady rhythm of its own accord and you will probably find yourself breathing more deeply. Just close your eyes and feel the gentle ebb and flow of air as it connects you with the world. Do not worry if thoughts pop into your head whilst you are doing this. When you become aware of them, just imagine them gently sailing out on your breath as you exhale and go back to concentrating on the flow of air.

Eventually, by letting your body follow its own rhythm and by concentrating on that alone, you will achieve two rare things. The first is that your body will be at rest whilst you are awake. The second is that your thoughts will be still and you will be able to experience a high degree of calm.

Practise this until it becomes second nature. When your body and mind get used to tuning into meditation mode, you will find it easier to become proficient in the other Druid techniques.

Visualization and pathworking
Visualization and pathworking are forms of meditation practised by most Druids in which journeys, scenes, and encounters are worked through on an inner level. Visualization in general involves working with images. We use our inner eye to see the spiritual landscape we inhabit. Pathworking is a specialized form of this in which someone either reads or tells of a journey and the person listening imagines the landscapes, peoples, and animals mentioned. This is one of the safest methods of journeying in the inner realms. The reader will guide the meditator into and through the landscape, returning them safely to their starting point.

There is, however, a type of visualization technique that is a cornerstone of all Druid practice - the Sacred Inner Grove. This is when the Druid accesses a special place within their inner realm and returns to it whenever they wish. It is, in effect, an inner sanctuary. The nature of the sanctuary varies. Sometimes it is a stone circle or a forest grove, a cave or a hilltop, a roundhouse or a spring. We do not know what it will be until we first go there.

Within this Sacred Grove, the Druid will meet people and animals that act as guides within this inner landscape. They will remain with you for a very long time, if not forever, teaching things not found in books or the material world we normally inhabit. The lessons they offer are not always obvious or immediately relevant, but they are lessons nonetheless.

Many people, when they start to work at this level, wonder why they see extinct British animals (such as the bear or the wolf), or ancient Celtic archetypes and old Druid characters. They are all part of the spirit of the Land from which we are born and in which we practise. Our connection with them is deep-seated and immediate. They can travel in all realms and it is no wonder that as we take our first steps beyond this physical realm, they are there to welcome us back home.

Now and again, you might encounter someone or something with whom you feel uncomfortable. If this happens, all you need to do is tell them to go away. Be firm and all will be well.

Your Inner Grove is your domain. It is a place of rest, a calm centre in a hectic world, a spiritual hearth where we can centre ourselves when we are working on the inner planes. From this place, we can make journeys into the deeper reaches of the Forest, knowing there is somewhere secure to which we can return.

Over the years in which we visit our Inner Grove and work within it, it develops a richness with which we are intimately attuned. It is a place in which we can be completely secure and to which we can gain access with increasing ease.

Some Druids find it difficult to work in their Sacred Grove because they do not visualize very easily. Rather than see it, they may just feel, hear, or sense this place. That is fine. Inner visual acuity comes with practice. It is a sense we are not normally encouraged to exercise in any meaningful way.

As humans we are inclined to believe only what we see with our physical eyes – as long as that accords with what we have been taught is possible. We have to learn that there is more to the world than what we see, just as there is more to it than we can hear, smell, taste, and touch.

Many people dismiss the notion of other dimensions to our life as mere imagination. However, as those who do not have the conventional five senses can testify, there are many more ways of understanding the world. Imagination is one of them, a faculty we should not dismiss as mere fantasy. It is much more than that. Imagination is the ability to experience the world other than by our five senses; it is the ability to experience aspects of the world we would not normally be able to encounter. Without imagination, we cannot have compassion. Without imagination, we cannot transcend our material existence.

A true realization of this comes when our Sacred Inner Grove begins to grow. There comes a point when we realize that the place is real and has an independent existence. We might gain access to it through our thoughts, but it is not something we have created.

Having realized that, we can accept that not only is it part of us, but also that we are part of it. Our discovery of it is, in fact, a rediscovery of something with which we have always been linked. As young children, we did not question our journeys to such places. It is only as we grew that we were told over and again that such places are mere fantasy that do not really exist, causing our non-material sensory perception to wither.

When you have completed an Inner Grove meditation, write it up in your journal. Put in as much detail as you can and think carefully about your experiences. As you do this, try to avoid embellishing your account. You are not writing a novel, but keeping a diary of your travels.

There now follows a Sacred Inner Grove meditation to enable you to find you own Inner Grove or sanctuary. You might like to record it so that you can play it back, or get a friend to read it while you make your first forays into this new world. There is a lot to remember, and it is difficult to read and meditate at the same time.

Do not do this meditation if you have been drinking alcohol or using drugs. All drugs, whether prescribed or otherwise, can distort our material and psychic abilities. If you have a history of mental illness, you should also be extremely careful. Mental health problems do not preclude you from becoming Druid, but you should be aware that visualization techniques could have very powerful effects on your mental processes. If you are uncertain, read the meditation instead of actually doing it.

Sacred Inner Grove Meditation
Make sure you will not be disturbed for about an hour (it need not take that long later on). Find a comfortable place to sit, either on the floor or in a straight-backed chair. You might wish to light a candle or a lamp, or burn some incense. Be careful. You will not be watching over these things. Keep all flame well away from curtains and fabrics.

153

You may feel you would like to cast a circle to sit in, or visualize a blue circle of protection around you. Once that is done, close your eyes and concentrate on your breathing. Allow your body and mind to settle. When you are ready, begin your journey.

You find yourself on the edge of a meadow, which is on a slight hill. You notice how the tall grasses are forming waves in the gentle breeze. Rest a moment here...

Before you is a narrow path through the long grass. It leads up the hill to a wood at the very top. The wood looks dark from where you stand, but there is an aura surrounding it, just visible from where you are.

When you feel ready, you start to walk towards the wood. This might take some time. Choose your own pace and enjoy the walk. Look out for any creatures or people on the path.

Near the top of the slope is a hedge in which is set a wooden gateway. You open the gate and step through, closing it behind you. There is the wood, dark and green. At first sight, you wonder how on earth you will get inside, as there seems no way in. Pause here, and wait until your eyes see an opening within the trees...

When you see the opening, there may be someone waiting for you. This might be the Guardian of the Grove or it could be your Druid guide. It might be human, faerie, or animal. Introduce yourself and then ask their name. They may tell you now or at another time.

As you walk on (either alone or with your guide), you start to notice the ground beneath your feet has changed from grass to a soft earthy layer of leaves. You can still make out a path leading towards the heart of the wood. Notice the types of trees in the wood.

It is not long before you find yourself in a clearing, a small inner circle of trees within the wood. There are gentle beams of light pouring in from the sky above the treetops. They might be moonbeams, sunbeams, or even starlight. Stand and look around the circle for a moment to take it all in...

In the centre of the grove, you notice three standing stones. You notice how tall they are and if they have symbols carved on them. They are far enough apart for you to sit down between them, which you do in silent meditation. After a while, you become aware of the energy from the land beneath you and sky above meeting within this place. You feel very safe and feel you belong here.

When you are ready, you may leave. If you met your guide, they may take you back to the woodland edge or you may go alone. Thank the Guardian of your Grove, even if you have not yet met, and thank anyone else you may have met at this time.

You walk back along the leafy path to the way out of the wood and there in front of you is the gate in the hedge. You walk to the gate, open it, and step through. Close it behind you and follow the path through the tall grass down the hill. Step into this reality when you reach the boundary between the meadow and your outer world. Spend a few moments in meditation, before slowly opening your eyes.

*

After you have finished your meditation, unwind your circle if you have cast one or allow the blue circle to fade and spread out away from you. It is important to ground yourself by having something to eat and drink. Another important task is to write up your experiences in your journal. This also helps with the grounding process.

This is a short meditation in order that you may enter your Sacred Inner Grove. From now on, you can go there anytime you want and over the years, you will be taken on journeys, given teachings and guidance by your Druid guides. The place you first go to may just be a staging post, a place to orientate yourself before moving on to other sites that become your permanent home within the Forest.

The place you have visited is one of healing and security, a place of knowledge and learning. With this in mind, it must be noted that sometimes someone that you meet there might tell you to do something in the Outworld. Use your own judgement about this. Wait until you have grounded yourself and think things through carefully for yourself.

Because we live most of our waking lives in an outer world where we are bombarded by stimuli from many sources, it takes a meditation or a working to open us up to thoughts, ideas, and messages that are otherwise drowned out. You know what is right and wrong.

If you feel unhappy working in an inner landscape, you do not have to do so. People become Druid on many different levels, it is a multilayered path, and not everything suits everyone. One of the many things we learn is to develop the gifts the Goddess has entailed and not hanker after or worry about those things She has not.

ETHICS

Celtic Ethics

Diogenes Laertius recorded that the chief maxim of the Druids was that everyone should 'worship the gods, do no evil, and exercise courage'. Its triadic form is good evidence that it is a genuine teaching. Yet there was one thing more important to the Druids than honouring the gods and being good and brave - and that was the Truth.

Truth is the very foundation of existence. For Celts in general and Druids in particular, Truth was the very sustaining power of all creation and the central tenet of their metaphysic. This is not simply the linguistic Truth of logicians, but a much broader concept that encompasses all thought, all action, all dreams, all work, all play - the whole of the universe. Truth is the right way of things, the natural order, and the closer one comes to this right way in one's life, the closer one is to the Truth.

As such, it was recognized as a dynamic and evolving matrix - alive and vibrant in the world, if increasingly lacking in the World. It was the task of the Druid to divine the Truth in all things and to guide people in such a way that all aspects of their lives accorded with the Truth.

It is one of the essentials of the Druid Way that links us with our ancestors, for all that we do today is also governed by the Truth. We have to learn to divine it, we have to learn to live by it, and we have to learn how to teach it to others.

Druids Today

Working ethically as a Druid in the twenty-first century can be summed up like this: we should only work for the good and the happiness of all beings on this planet. This includes the animal, plant, and mineral kingdoms. We should harm nothing – including ourselves. We should respect all life and live in the Truth, as did our Celtic ancestors. We must learn to respect our brothers and sisters once more, whether they are Druid or not. There is enough intolerance in the world. We should never add to it.

Working with others

When working with others in a group or Grove we need to be very aware of their needs within that group. We also each have to take responsibility for our own actions and thoughts. What happens during work together is part of a sacred act and should not become the subject of gossip. Problems should be faced openly and resolved openly.

The Druid that presides over a working or a meeting is not the 'all knowing one' or 'wise one', even though they may be highly trained and knowledgeable. They should always come from a place of love and peace, leaving all ego at home. There are those who go off on an Arch-Druid trip, but this sort of behaviour is not acceptable in circle (or anywhere else) and it can be very intimidating for others.

Most Druids in a position of responsibility, such as running a Grove or an Order, are very aware of the ethics involved. They will not be there for themselves, but to help others. Nor would they expect anyone to partake in anything with which they feel uncomfortable.

This extends to dealings with people outwith the Grove or Order. Druids may make their presence known, but they never actively recruit people on to the Druid Way. It is just not done. If people ask questions about the Way, then a truthful answer is given, but Druids have never tried to convert. The Druid Way is one of freedom. You come to it in freedom and you may leave in freedom.

The Ethics of Magic
Druids do not have a tradition of spell casting like other pagan belief systems. They do, however, work magic – seeking out the underlying patterns of the universe and using that understanding with care to restore balance and heal the world.

Druid magic is found in nature - in the land, the stars, and the mighty oceans. We have to care for these just as we have to care for the life that is to be found embraced by them. Aligning ourselves with fundamental forces and acting in concord with them empowers us all. That is true magic. Deep magic.

What is more, magic should always and only be worked with purpose and for the benefit of others out of a sense of compassion and for healing. That, too, is the true magic. Healing magic. Balance. Everything else is a glittering sham and harmful.

Magic is a strange area. It means many different things to as many different people. Some people are englamoured by the idea of 'magical powers'. These immature souls have much to learn. True Druid power is in truth and love given to all whether they are human, beast, or plant.

Sacred sites

Many of the sites that Druids hold sacred and make use of are also sites of archaeological importance, sites of splendour, sites that others enjoy visiting. Some are also on 'private' land. Whatever we may feel about archaeology, tourists, and the idea of ownership, these things are realities in the present day world, and we must take cognizance of them.

All sacred sites (be they of archaeological importance or not) must be treated with care and respect. Unintentional damage can be caused, for example, simply by there being too many people clambering about. We should be aware of our numbers and choose sites accordingly. Moving anything or taking anything away (even just stones lying on the surface) can reduce the integrity of or completely destroy the site at many levels on inner and outer planes. The first principle of work on a sacred site, therefore, is that when we leave at the end of our work it should be, physically, as if we had not been there. Only love should be left behind.

We should avoid any activity that could damage the site. Do not pick flowers or break branches from trees, do not try to raise fallen stones, do not dig, and do not mark the surface of the earth. All these activities can alter energy flows and destroy what others may enjoy of the site.

Be aware of who 'owns' or has responsibility for the site. They may be willing to allow you to use it. Access to the site may be along established pathways. Stick to these. Always follow the Country Code. If you have to clear litter and rubbish left by others, use thick rubber gloves (for your own protection) and put all such rubbish into a bag. Make a gift of it to those who should have ensured the site stayed tidy.

Many ceremonies, festivals, and acts of worship make use of candles. Aside from the fire risk, great care must be taken with them. Never use paraffin wax candles (unless you are prepared to keep your candles enclosed within lanterns) as the grease can stain and damage stonework and will not fully degrade within your lifetime. Do not fix candles or lanterns (or anything else for that matter) to stonework. Make lantern poles or lantern stands.

Fires lit regularly on the same spot will damage and alter soil chemistry. If you require a fire, choose a spot where the impact on plant and animal life will be minimal. Always build a hearth to keep material in one place and keep the fire under the watchful eye of someone responsible. Bring water to make sure it is thoroughly doused when you have finished or to put it out if it gets out of control. Never use an accelerant to light the fire. If you think this excessive, then consider how much damage is caused by fire to the countryside and its inhabitants each year.

Sacred sites are inhabited. Many creatures and beings on inner and outer planes, as well as plant life, call that site their home. Many creatures and birds are especially vulnerable in the spring and early summer when they are bringing their young into the world and trying to raise them. The less they are disturbed in this, the better. They have far greater claim to the site than you.

Offerings should be suitable for the children of the Goddess. Leave fruit, grain, nuts, and the like. Never leave large amounts. A handful is sufficient. The Goddess knows. Do not leave bread as young birds can choke on this. Do not leave sweets and chocolate, much as they may be precious to you. Consider who comes after. If you leave sweets, who knows what child may later come along and help themselves to what may, by then, be contaminated. Do not scatter salt, as it is poisonous to many life forms (including us) if it is sufficiently concentrated. A few grains can kill an earthworm.

If you are having a celebration and wish to decorate the site, use only natural materials and clear up after you have finished. Never take anything from the wild. Never use balloons, attractive as they may be. Balloons that escape (and some seem to have a determined will of their own) can maim and kill wildlife and domestic animals.

We have not mentioned these things because we want you to stop having candles, fires, and making offerings. It is just that we have to be aware of the fact that what we see as an act of worship may also be an act of vandalism if we are not sufficiently careful of how we go about things. All our work must be done with care, with love, and in order to enhance the world in which we live.

LANDSCAPE

Ancestral Celtic society was almost entirely rural. They were a people that lived in direct communion with the land on a day-to-day basis. Their connection was personal and vital, for if they could not understand and live with the land, their very survival was at risk.

This is not to say that every person was a farmer, but virtually all life revolved around agriculture and virtually all raw materials were derived from agricultural activity. We should not interpret this in a narrow sense. The practice of growing plants and rearing animals was far more widespread and fluid in its approach, everyone recognizing the need to work with nature in order to maximize the crop.

Working with nature was not just a case of learning the facts in the matter. Nature was recognized as a spiritual force in all life and that, too, had to be worked with. Our ancestors recognized that everything we have as a people is derived from the land. If the land is abused, materially or spiritually, it will withdraw its cooperation and its bounty.

This is as true today as it has always been, although our largely urban and highly complicated social existence tends to obscure the fact – in more ways than one. For while we are prepared, if we give it some thought, to accept that all material goods are ultimately derived from the land, most people would find it difficult to acknowledge that what we are as spiritual beings is also derived from the land.

There are a number of levels to this that are not easily separated, for in reality they are inextricably intertwined. Here we are concerned with the very deepest level that affects our everyday lives. It is, indeed, so deep that most people have forgotten to pay it any heed.

As we have said, when pushed, people will acknowledge that all raw materials derive from the land. Yet their only concern is with those materials – the minerals, the plants, the animals - and with the products that are refined from them. They rarely think back to the land itself. Yet the land has been instrumental in shaping those materials that, in turn, shape us.

The land about us has been shaped over aeons by forces we can little comprehend. Pressures that have pushed up vast mountain ranges that extend for thousand of miles and reach altitudes where the air is almost too thin to support life. Temperatures that have deposited layers of ice miles thick over millions of square miles - ice that has ground mountains down to powder and carved out vast trenches, later to be filled by the sea. Huge explosions of volcanoes, earthquakes, tectonic drift, the endless wearing away as raindrops fall and find their way to the sea.

It goes on all around us on a scale so vast that we rarely witness any but the most explosive of events. Our lives are gone in the blink of eye by comparison, yet these forces have shaped the world where we live. They have created the environments into which we are born, environments that shape our material form and our spirit.

We may learn all this in our geography lessons at school, but they are the facts we need to pass our tests. It is important, if we are to fully explore our spiritual nature as Druids, that we go beyond that and make an emotional connection with the land – not just as a form, but as the spirit within the form.

Ancestral Celts, as a people that lived in the world, would each have known their own landscape in intimate detail and with personal connection. This connection was with life, with the tribe who inhabited a specific area, with the spirits and denizens of the Otherworld (which is a reflection of this), and with the Goddess.

It is important that we learn to connect with the land in which we live. To do this we must shrink our expectations. We think on too large a scale because we are used to hearing of things happening at a great distance. It is good to know where places are in the world, but it should not be at the expense of the intimate detail of what is, in some cases literally, to be found in our own back yard.

For urban dwellers, this can be particularly difficult. The presence of so many buildings and roads can easily obscure the shape of the land on which they are built. Indeed, towns and cities have often altered the underlying landscape so that space is not wasted. Rivers and streams in particular are made to fit the plans of humanity, diverted into culverts and longer tunnels, hidden away and used to carry our waste. Hills and valleys are altered to provide easier gradients and vegetation is confined to the cages we call parks.

Animals too are largely banished, although not to the degree to which some would have us believe. Indeed, some animals are so persecuted in the rural environment that they have become urban creatures and flourish on a perilous fringe.

Yet even beneath all the concrete and steel it is still possible to trace the shape of the land and to explore it. In fact, it is essential that we do so as it enables us to understand the shape of the urban environment in which the majority of us live. It might also help us to understand how we can make our urban spaces more attractive and safer.

Rural dwellers should not be complacent. It is not just concrete and steel that hides the landscape from our eyes. It is the way in which we view the world as a whole. Rural dwellers are, these days, often as ignorant of the land about them as urban dwellers. After all, most people do not encounter a river unless they are going over it via a bridge. Most people do not know where the footpaths lead.

If we are to reconnect with the Goddess, however, it is truly vital that we become intimate with the land in which we live. We need to get out and explore and this can only be done by walking. Commercially produced maps can help, as they will provide the starting points. However, they should not become the be-all and end-all of exploration. That is simply to introduce another filter that prevents us from seeing the land, touching the land, smelling the land, hearing the land, and, with care, tasting it as well.

Having used a commercial map to become familiar with the general shape of what is about you, it is a useful idea to start making a map of your own. It does not have to be to scale or graphically accurate, the important thing is that it is your map. Each time you explore, you can add more detail including the sort of things you would not find on a map in any shop.

If you see an animal or bird, you can mark it on your map. If you stop for a chat with someone, add it to the map. If places seem strange, mark it down. If you do not know the names of places, make up your own that accord with your experience. In this way, you lay claim to the land about you whilst the land shapes your experience.

As you do this sort of thing, you can use your local library to explore the history and folklore associated with the place where you live. Look also for the ways in which our ancestors have worked with the land. Not only will you find everyday signs of agricultural and other use, but also hints and whispers of a mystical understanding that reaches way back into the distant past. Not all these mysteries are as open to us as some practitioners of Earth

Mysteries would have us believe, but the Earth will sing you a song if you take the time to listen.

Bring the land alive and learn to become one with it. Care for it and discuss what you discover with other local people. You do not have to share all your thoughts, but there are times when very simple things can be done to improve the environment in which you live. And these are all things for which the Goddess will bless you.

In engaging in this sort of activity, you open your own spirit to that which inhabits the land. You will become aware that the land, although shaped by the forces of nature, has been shaped in ways that the human eye will recognize. Sometimes humans have, in the past, carefully worked the landscape to enhance that of which they were aware. For, if you look carefully and with an eye for the larger picture, you will see the Goddess in the landscape and you will know that She keeps you safely protected in her arms just as long as you are prepared to protect her.

At this point, the landscape about you begins to merge with your inner landscape. This results from a shift in perspective that is part and parcel of subsuming the Celtic metaphysic into one's being. The barriers that we have been taught exist between ourselves and the rest of the world are false. We inhabit a landscape that exists without *and* within, flowing in a continuum such that we can inhabit both at the same time.

The inner landscape of the Druid is centred on their Sacred Inner Grove. Although this stems from a communion with the Otherworld and with the Goddess, it also has roots in the landscape about us. We are, after all, a product of that landscape. We carry it within us at an elemental level. When we search for our Sacred Inner Grove, we explore a landscape that is nascent within us. The exploration awakens the awen within us, brings sunlight on the first day, and sings the inner world into creation.

Many Druids are content with their Sacred Inner Grove and explore no further than that. Within that, there is much with which to be at peace. However, there is a whole inner world beyond it and with careful exploration, its secrets can begin to unfold.

It does require careful exploration because it is a wild realm. One should not blunder into it without preparation or without becoming familiar with home territory. It is also the case that one should not go where one is not invited. Despite the fact that it is an inner world, it does not belong to you or any other person. The right to be present, the right to explore, brings with it great responsibilities. These rights have to be earned and bestowed by She who holds sway. The responsibilities have to be discharged.

We are moving here into territory (literal and metaphorical) that is steeped in mystery. This is the very heart of the Forest, the very heart of the inner landscape, the very heart of our relationship with the landscape. For it is here that we encounter the nature of sovereignty.

Understanding the nature of sovereignty is crucial. As we have seen, it was a central theme in the Matter of Britain and much misunderstood by later Christian redactors who were unable to understand the pivotal role of Gwenhwyfar.

Sovereignty is the right to rule. It is the right to control. However, this right is not absolute. It is a gift bestowed by the Goddess upon those who have earned the right. If the gift is denied or withdrawn, the Goddess will destroy those who try to abuse her.

Often portrayed in terms of kingship (to a people who elected their kings in full knowledge of the need for the candidates to be approved of by the Goddess), sovereignty is Service – Service to the land and to the people. Yet sovereignty also has a personal dimension. Our life is a gift from the Goddess. The degree to which we can exercise an autonomous existence depends on how well we treat her and abide by the natural order that she represents. If we follow her precepts, our landscapes will be green and flowing with clear water. If we turn our back on the Goddess and abuse her gifts, our landscapes will be a deadly waste.

TREES

Trees have always been an integral part of humanity, but few peoples have held them in such high regard as the Celts and their Druids. Today, one would have to look to the indigenous peoples of the Amazon to gain any idea of the closeness that our ancestors felt for trees. This is not and was not a blind and primitive worship, but a genuine veneration based on an understanding of the importance of trees to human existence, both materially and spiritually.

Although most people no longer recognize this bond, it is still there and there are times when it makes itself known. The Great Storm that tore across southern England in October of 1987 uprooted 15 million trees in a few short hours. The storm wrought great damage on houses and other constructs of humanity, it killed people, but it was the loss of all those trees that left many people in a state of shock. Even now, the landscape is so altered that it can be disorientating.

Mythologically, we are descended from trees, the sacred oak Bíle in particular, sprung like fruit from the branches. In popular evolutionary terminology, we 'came down from the trees'. Our earliest ancestors dwelt within the forests and up within the protective branches. There, we were provided with shelter and food, nurtured, allowed the opportunity to become aware of the universe.

Even when we became creatures of the plains, we never wandered far from the great beings with which our evolution has been so intimately entwined. Indeed, until very recent times, trees have continued to be a major source of materials and food, a major source of understanding.

So deeply embedded is this relationship between humanity and trees that they are to be found at the heart of many mysteries as sources of wisdom. The cosmic tree stands at the centre of the world, which it supports and nurtures. All the great and momentous occasions of our lives occur through the medium of the tree. We are born from it, it feeds and shelters us, gives us wisdom, we make sacrifice to it.

Even today, we are heavily dependent on trees, although as with much else, they have become commodified – shattered and torn from the earth faster than they are replaced, processed through factories with no regard for the properties that lie in the timber after the tree is felled. We use them without respecting their spirits and without realizing that they are far more important to us alive than they are dead. What use a roof over our heads and a daily newspaper if the soils have been washed away, the rain has stopped falling, and the air is foul with carbon dioxide?

The importance of the tree to ancestral Celts and to Druids past and present is enormous. Nor should we think only of individual trees, important as each one and each species most certainly is. Woodland and the deep forest – the tribes and nations of trees with which we share the land – have also informed the metaphysic of the Celts, providing a model by which to understand the world and our life within it.

This is readily apparent in Celtic art. The first recognizable appearance of the tree motif in illuminated manuscripts is late, some time in the mid eighth century AD. Yet there, it appears fully formed as if it had long been in the collective mind. It may also be that it had appeared much earlier but in a more abstract form. It was not until the early Christian period that more naturalistic forms began to appear in decorative work.

Those representations that do appear are not of any particular tree. The symbolic quality of the tree is so strong that it cannot be tied down to any specific species. Indeed, the tree form that appears in this period resembles mistletoe in its structure far more than it resembles any other plant form.

This is unlikely to be accidental. Mistletoe was regarded as the spirit of the tree. Moreover, the many branches and the fruit are just part of the hugely complex web of symbolism that is woven from the presence of the tree and the life of the forest.

The form of the tree presents itself readily for contemplation of our self and our relationship with the tree and the rest of the world. Roots deep in the soil speak of the past that has nurtured us and of the environment in which we live. If soil, environment, and roots are healthy, then the tree will be well nurtured and will grow true.

The trunk is the soul, the self, the great centre, which must stand steadfast in the world. Into this are fed the nutrients that come from the soil. Yet that is only part of the story, for the trunk puts out branches that spread outward to the sky and the sun. There, too, is nourishment, but of a lighter form. For the soil represents the material world whilst the sky and the sun represent the worlds of mind and spirit. Nourishment from the material flows upward through the trunk to build the branches and leaves, nourishment flows down from the spirit to build strong roots into Mother Earth.

The branches, too, are the means by which the tree touches the rest of the world, growing outward, forming leaf and dying back with the seasons, fruiting and giving forth to the world that which has been formed by the meeting of matter and spirit.

That the tree does this at a slow pace is a great lesson for us all. We cannot hope to emulate the great yews, some of which may have stood with us for as many as five thousand years, but we can learn of what is important to us and what is dross. We can learn to flow with the seasons of our lives and the seasons of the world in order to be simpler and wealthier people.

The forest, too, is a rich symbol that is worth contemplation. Much of Arthurian quest and adventure takes place within the forest, which is populated with all nature of beings and spirits. It was the forest that covered the land before the dusts of the wasteland came as a punishment for the greed and brutality of humanity. It will be forest that returns when the Grail quest is truly completed.

The forest is also the great symbol of the Druid Way, for the forest is within us as well as without. Finding our way into and through the forest, coming to know its glades and groves, its springs and flowers, the high places and shady dells, the cultivated areas and wilder reaches, learning the paths between these things, and the ways of all who inhabit this forest - all this is the life journey of the Druid.

There are many other ways in which trees and forests can reveal their teachings, but as Druids, we should always be aware that trees and forest are far more than just symbols. They are living creatures who have given to us without cease and without question. They have fed us and clothed us, sheltered us and provided us with all manner of things including medicines. They have given us life. The least they deserve in return is our respect and our protection.

Working with Sacred Trees

All trees are sacred to Druids, especially the 33 native trees of Britain and Ireland and the 20 trees that are represented by the Celtic ogham. It is possible to work with these trees, and indeed all trees, in many different ways. We know that many of them are mentioned in the poems and stories of the Bards, where they intermingle with mythology, teachings, healing, and magic. Trees have so much to offer, if we would just spend the time to look and listen.

Today one of the best ways for the would-be Druid to work magically with a sacred tree is to make contact with its spirit. This can be done in their Inner Grove or they could go to a wood or park and make contact 'face to face'.

If working internally, it is possible to go inside a tree and explore other realms. Working outside you will be able to visit the tree regularly throughout the yearly cycle, building a relationship with the tree, its animals, and spirits. Go to a wood and explore until you find a tree that draws you towards it.

The list offered below gives a tiny amount of information on six selected trees. This information is gleaned from Celtic writings, ogham, arboreal biology, everyday experience, and, just as importantly, intuitive meditations on the actual tree. Although we can find out more than enough on trees from books, the real essence is in intuitive work, or actually contacting the tree spirit for guidance and teaching. Creating a small journal of tree meditations and journeys would be most useful in your Druid studies. Although you might agree with all that is written below, it is not written in stone. You need to add your own interpretations, for they may be different. The relationships you build with individual trees will be unique. There is, of course, one other very important way of working with trees, which not only aids your path, but also the planet - plant some of your own.

Six Sacred Druid Trees
Birch (Beith)

The silver birch, *Betula pendula,* is one of the prettiest trees in the northern hemisphere. It is also one of the hardiest, growing as far north as Greenland where it has to cope with icy winds and snow. It is distinguished by its silver and white coloured bark and its delicate tooth edged leaves.

Throughout Britain and northern Europe, it has become known as 'Lady of the Woods', an apt name as this tree is very feminine and Goddess like. Many Goddesses have birch linked with them, including Frigga from the northern tradition and Grainne from the Celtic pantheon.

Birch dispels negativity from our lives and has been used traditionally by witches for making brooms to sweep this away. This connects it with new beginnings and gateways, the most prominent being the winter solstice, the 'cold time'. Sometimes, the Yule log was birch wood.

It is connected with air and water because of the ice and snow, and with the deep cold earth of the north. The first sparks of spring and the warm sun bring it into bud, to add a touch of fire. In the depths of winter, birch is there dormant, waiting for a new start. Remember that she will also protect you through those long dark days with a halo of light.

Oak (Duir)

The English oak, *Quercus robur*, is a deciduous tree that is very long lived, sometimes exceeding 600 years. To many, the oak is the most sacred of all the trees in the forest, connected fast and true to Druids. Oak forests once covered these lands with their dense foliage. Now the oaks are mainly seen growing in woods and parklands, or in our Inner Groves. Ancestral Druids used great oak groves for rituals and worship. Myrddin also worked magic from a grove of oaks.

Oak belongs to the time of the summer solstice, but is used at all Druid celebrations as it one of the most magical of trees. The energy of oak is fire. It is associated also with the Sun, the little wren, and the battle with the Holly King for the favour of the Goddess. Celtic tradition has it that we are all descended in a spiritual sense from the great oak Bíle.

Oaks (in common with all trees) are inhabited by dryads. These have been called faerie Druids and Druidesses. They are happy with human contact, provided it is courteous and honest, and it has been said that it was the oak dryads that gave the secrets of tree magic to the Druids. The Welsh goddess Blodeuwedd was created from oak, broom, and meadowsweet. The oak attracts lightning and the thunder god Taranis, so do not stand beneath one for shelter in a storm. Carry oak wood for protection or an acorn to help rid yourself of pain. An oak wand would be full of Sun energies.

Holly (Tinne)

We all love the bright red-berried holly, *Ilex aquifolium*, around our hearth at Mistletime. Its glossy, dark green leaves with their sharp spikes bring with them a reminder of the sharpness of the season. Its associated ogham, 'tinne' offers a more comforting aspect as it is the Gaelic word for fire. The Holly King rules the dark half of the year and vies continually with the Oak King.

Holly is a tree of transition, when changes take place in the season and our lives. The holly tree was extremely sacred to the Celts and it was used as a powerful herb for pneumonia and rheumatism, from which ancestral Celts must have suffered a great deal. We don't use it medicinally today because the berries are poisonous and could cause death in the young and weak, but the presence of holly is thought to protect us from just about everything harmful, including thunder and lightning.

Hazel (Coll)

In spring, the woods are brightened by the glowing yellow catkins of hazel, *Corylus avellana*. They grow all over Britain and much of the world. In the autumn, these large shrubs provide hazelnuts for tiny creatures to eat. The hazel is a magical tree that features in many wondrous Celtic tales, none more so than the story of the nine hazelnuts containing wisdom that drop into the sacred pool, to be eaten by the salmon that lives there. The salmon then becomes the repository of all wisdom and knowledge.

Hazel, because it grows so straight, has been used to make staves and wands. This tree holds much quicksilver energy and is often linked with the snake, making it very druidic. Find some hazel and meditate there. You might see faeries for they are attracted to hazel.

A forked twig is traditionally used to divine for water. It will help you to connect with silvery water and air energies. Hazel wands are very powerful, coming into their own in spring and autumn, where they have the air and water to govern them. Hazel is also known for inspiration, sometimes called the 'poet's tree'.

Apple (Quert)

The apple tree, *Malus sylvestris*, is associated with the Gods throughout world mythologies, not just the Celtic. Greek and Roman myths are full of sacred apple symbology. In Celtic Druid lore, the 'silver bough' was cut from the apple tree. This branch bore nine magical apples that played music to induce trances.

The fruit of the apple tree is not only used for healing and immortality, but its sweet wood allows the sacred mistletoe to grow. The apple belongs to all seasons and to all the elements, but especially water. This leads us to its association with Avalon and the Isle of Apples, that magical place just across the water of the borderlands, the place of Morgan and Myrddin, of Arthur healed and sleeping, of orchards full of apple blossom, sunny days, and bees.

The apple also provides for us on freezing cold days with mulled cider, or at Samhain giving russet coloured apples to the Goddess at our last harvest celebration. Apple also reminds us of our ancestors, immortality, and the Otherworld. Cut an apple in half horizontally and there is a pentagram - a truly magical fruit.

Yew (Ido)

The tree that symbolizes transformation like no other is the yew, *Taxus baccata*. It shows us the cycle of death and rebirth. Many churchyards throughout Britain have ancient yews growing in them, such as the one at Wilmington in East Sussex – a venerable tree that is 1600 years old. These ancient churchyard yews were often *in situ* long before the church, Christians often building on a Druid site or Grove.

The yew tree grows outwards, so getting wider and wider. Many ancient trees have hollow hearts of great size. They also grow down and it is said that they are as large under the ground as they are above, an ancient teaching made manifest - as above so below. All parts of the living yew can be poisonous. The timber of some yews is much favoured for the making of longbows, adding to its symbology of death.

The yew is very slow growing and takes on all the earth and sky energies. With its greeny-black leaves and red berries with a five-pointed star inside it is a truly magical tree. Use yew to meditate with for long winter journeys within your Inner Grove. They have seen so much and will impart it to you if you approach them with the reverence they deserve. They are the great historians of all the sacred trees and the great keepers of magical secrets and time itself.

Use sticks of yew on which to carve your ogham for divination. Do not cut them from the tree, there is no need as the yew gives us plenty of gifts beneath its branches. When we contemplate the yew tree, it reminds us of Samhain, the Dark Goddess, the ancestors, the beginning of the new Celtic year and the leaving of the old. Wands and staves of yew are particularly powerful.

Conclusion

This book would need to be many times its size to cover all the lore of trees sacred to Druids. The six above are just to give the reader an idea of some aspects with which they can work. Do buy a good book on trees, one that gives full details of what parts of the tree are poisonous or irritant.

As a Druid, it is extremely important to incorporate trees into your life on all levels. Druids love trees, and trees love Druids! Meditate about them, around them, and in them. Journey with your guides to meet new ones that will heal or teach. Grow them in your garden or in a pot on you patio. Sponsor the planting of trees. Honour them, for it is the tree that is keeping you alive.

PLANTS AND HERBS

The Irish god of medicine, Dian Cécht, killed his son, Miach, in a fit of jealousy, envious of his superior healing powers. After he buried him, 365 herbs grew on the grave. Miach's sister, Airmid, collected them all and placed them on her cloak in the shape of a human - each herb connected to an illness in the area of the body depicted.

Blodeuwedd was the Welsh flower maiden made from the blooms of oak, broom, and meadowsweet. She was conjured out of flowers by Math mab Mathonwy and Gwydion mab Don, when Arianrhod put a curse on her son, Lleu Llaw Gyffes, saying he would never marry a mortal wife.

These are just two of the many Celtic stories that mention the use of plants and herbs. Both demonstrate that they were considered to be extremely powerful in healing and magic - these being pretty much one and the same thing to ancestral Celts.

We must remember that in the past all people (not just Druids) relied on plants and herbs far more than we do now. In Iron Age Britain, we have a people whose lives were connected entirely with the land. They planted crops, grazed their cattle, built and thatched their roundhouses, made their furniture, painted their faces and bodies, dyed their clothes, seasoned their food, and healed themselves – all with plants and herbs.

It is unfortunate that so little is written about the use of plants and herbs by ancestral Druids. There are, however, many texts that refer to ancient herbal lore and medical practice throughout Celtic history, so we can safely assume that our ancestors used those same herbs and plants for magic, medicine and healing, cooking, and cosmetics.

Today, many of the materials we use are heavily processed and synthesized from petrochemicals. This is particularly true of our foods and medicines. We no longer connect them with the Earth Goddess, the Moon Goddess, or even the Sun. A few people may still plant to the Moon cycle, but on the whole, we have allowed this vast area of wonderful magic to slip away.

Sacred Druid plants

There are a number of plants that are mentioned more frequently in connection with Druids than others. They would have been in common use in the past, but Druids in their more mystical and magical role would perhaps have used them in slightly different ways from the ordinary person.

Druids would have used herbal concoctions to induce trances and visions, for astral journeys, and for connecting with the spirit world. This is no longer necessary and would, indeed, be dangerous, as our material bodies are different from those of our ancestors.

The following five plants are mentioned for information only. Several of them are highly toxic if not handled correctly. Please be sensible and refrain from trying them. All use of plants should be on the advice and under the supervision of a qualified and experienced herbalist or homoeopathist.

Mistletoe - *Viscum album*

This is the most famous of all druidic plants, along with the oak. Translations of Pliny have Druids wearing white robes to gather the herb on the sixth day of the Moon, or at midsummer. They also say that a golden sickle was used to cut the branches. This, of course, is not true. Gold is far too soft a metal to carry an edge sharp enough to cut the tough mistletoe stalk. It is also unlikely that Druids wore white. Other, more reasonable translations exist. For some reason, however, the image of white robes is that the general public envisages when thinking of Druids.

Mistletoe was considered magical because it did not grow in the ground and remained green when its host tree had shed its leaves. It is a partially parasitic plant that favours sweet woods on which to grow, such as apple and hawthorn. It very rarely grows on oak, as the birds that disperse the seed (notably the mistle thrush) prefer the hedgerows and small trees of open land to the oak and other trees of the forest.

As well as its magical appearance, it was noted as a potent fertility symbol with its splayed legs and berry sacs containing sticky white fluid. Modern kissing rituals are a direct descendant of the powerful influence of this aspect. We also use mistletoe in our winter solstice rituals as the combination of its attributes has strongly associated it with the Mabon and the rebirth of the Sun.

Medicinally it was known as a heal-all to ancestral Druids, which merely confirmed it as truly magical and a gift from the Gods. They probably also used it for seeking visions and trance. The twigs and leaves are still used in medicines today. The berries should *never* be taken internally. Large doses will cause convulsions.

Vervain - *Verbena officinalis*
Known as the 'Enchanter's Herb', the spiky, mauve-flowered vervain is probably the most sacred of druidic plants. It was (and still is) used to counter rheumatism and infections. Altars were brushed with a bunch of vervain, and Druidesses were supposed to have worn a crown of the plant on initiation although this is probably poetic licence rather than fact.

It is another plant that was gathered at midsummer, when neither the Moon nor the Sun was in the sky. It was used to help with visualizing the future. It was also used for invoking spirits and seeing them off, protecting one from lightning, calming the emotions, and for dulling sexual desire. However, it was also said to be an aphrodisiac!

Druids still use it in ritual today, mainly to sprinkle on the bonfire, or in incense. It is not poisonous, but best avoided unless prescribed.

Mandrake - *Mandragora autumnalis*
The history surrounding this plant is both extensive and ancient. Mainly used in fertility magic throughout Europe and the Middle East (where it mainly grows and is still used), it was also used to induce trances. It is supposed to ward off evil possession and was used as an early form of anaesthesia as far back as the first century AD, if not earlier. The modern hypnotic drug 'Mandrax' is derived from mandrake. The plant was actually cultivated as a crop as late as the 1560s. Ingestion of any part of the plant can cause acute poisoning and death!

There are two old beliefs about the digging up of the mandrake roots. These are that the digger must be aware of 'contrary winds', and that they must keep digging for it until sunset. It was also said that the plant would scream when pulled from the ground. The roots of the mandrake often take on human form, which adds to its mystery and use in the magical arts.

Meadowsweet – *Filipendula (spirea) ulmaria*
This beautiful, white-flowered plant grows in meadows and on hillsides. The whole plant was used magically and medicinally in ancient times. It is still used today for water retention, infections, rheumatic conditions, colds, and fevers. It must have been invaluable to our ancestors living in damp roundhouses.

Meadowsweet was also spread on floors to help sweeten the air, as the flower has the most exquisite of perfumes. It is one of the plants that went into the creation of Blodeuwedd. This plant is worth growing in your own garden if you are lucky enough to have one.

Aconite - *Aconitum napellus*
Ancient peoples used this plant quite widely, for it had many properties. Most importantly, it was a strong painkiller as well as being used as a cure for pneumonia and fevers. Extreme care had to be taken in the collection and processing of the plant as it is extremely toxic. Tips of arrows were dipped into a mixture containing aconite to poison prey; hence, one of its folk names 'Wolfsbane'.

Aconite was also known throughout the ancient world as an ingredient of 'flying ointment', along with henbane, briony, and hemlock. This mixture must have killed quite a few people as it is a highly toxic combination - all these plants are deadly. Indeed, aconite is so poisonous that even handling the plant can cause numbness, extreme lethargy, and a feeling of suffocation.

*

Other herbs and plants used by ancestral Celts and Druids are likely to have been belladonna, agaric mushrooms, periwinkle, tansy, foxglove, and wormwood. Although most of these plants have been used in medicines in the past and form the basis of modern treatments, it is not a good idea to use them yourself, as they are all toxic.

Our ancestors lived different lives to us and it is even possible that the everyday use of these plants gave them a degree of immunity from their toxicity that we no longer possess. What is certain is that the use of these plants in the practice of magic and medicine is far removed from anything we do today.

Druid herbs today
The herbs we use today tend to be very different from the ones used by our Druid ancestors, although meadowsweet and vervain are still to be found in incense and some herbal medicines. You will notice that the old herbs are all indigenous to these shores. Ancestral Druids may well have used herbs and plants that are more exotic, such as frankincense, myrrh, and sandalwood as trade routes with the Middle- and Far East were well established in the

Iron Age. Wines, pottery, glass, and other luxury goods were traded for metals and cloth. It is not beyond the realms of possibility that exotic herbs and gums found their way to Britain very early on.

Druids no longer take herbal mixtures to produce trances or to seek visions. In fact, a Druid today will use self-discipline in the art of meditation and journeying and not take any drugs other than for medical conditions. Nowadays we are inclined to use plants and herbs for more subtle purposes in incense mixtures or by evaporating the oil derived from them in burners.

Because we can now go into our nearest town and purchase just about any herb, plant, or resin, we have many hundreds to choose from – most of them exotic. It is better to use native plants where possible, especially when creating a garden or decorating our altars.

Herb and spice scented candles and incense can be particularly potent and, as mentioned in 'Tools of the Trade', we can make our own loose mix incense to fit a given ritual or magical working. The plants mentioned below are just a few that you might like to use. You will notice the different accent on the plants used now from those used in the past. Ours are much lighter and used for pleasure as much as for healing.

Lavender - *Lavandula angustifolia*
A truly ancient plant loved by everyone throughout history. Every Druid should keep a bottle of lavender oil for its antiseptic, antibiotic, and antidepressant qualities. The oil is very safe and can be used on burns and scalds leaving no scars. It does nothing but promote healing on all levels and can even help to alleviate migraine headaches.

All parts of the plant can be used in incense formulas, or stuffed into cushions to make your home smell wonderful. It is one of the most popular plant oils used in aromatherapy. You can try growing it in your garden or in a pot by the front door so that every time you brush by you are greeted by its purple flowers and sweet perfume. It is also wonderful for meditation, but too much will have you sound asleep.

Frankincense - *Boswellia thurifera*
Loved by Druids everywhere, it is used for protection and purification during ritual. It has been used throughout history in

many different cultures, especially in the Middle East where it originates. It is also still used in the Christian Church, which is of course a Middle Eastern religion. Do remember - a little goes a *very* long way. This resin soon melts on charcoal to produce masses of strong smelling smoke.

As a herb, it is an antiseptic, but should not be overused as it can cause kidney damage. Frankincense was once used for embalming bodies, but now it is more often used in anti-wrinkle creams. There is no written evidence of Celts using this resin, although it seems to have been available throughout Europe from very early times.

Sandalwood - *Santalum album*
This oil and incense comes from a small tree that grows in India. Sandalwood perfume is warm and heady, and it makes a wonderful massage oil on its own or mixed with lavender. It can be used to treat respiratory tract infections, but traditionally it was used as an aphrodisiac or for relaxing the brain.

The plant may have found its way to Britain with early traders from mainland Europe. If you buy thin strips of sandalwood from a good herbalist, they burn on a fire sending out their wonderful aroma. The best sandalwood comes from Mysore. Sandalwood beads are worn for protection and to promote spirituality.

*

These are just three from the vast array of plants and herbs available. Other popular ones include rose (do not use rose oil if you are pregnant), peppermint, ginseng, cinnamon, vanilla, and rosemary (do not use if you suffer from epilepsy).

As Druids, we still use mistletoe, vervain, and yew in our rituals and on our altars, but this is for their decorative and symbolic qualities. Most of our plant usage is very different from that employed by our ancestors and a whole lot safer. For all that, the impulse and the basic reasoning behind the use of plants has remained constant through the centuries – a recognition that we evolved in and are a part of the natural world; a recognition that all that we need is to be found in a form that renews itself each year, born of the Earth and nourished by the light of the Sun.

DRUID ANIMAL LORE

As Druids, it is traditional to look to the animal kingdom for guidance. Animals see the many worlds with different eyes and different sensibilities. They know things by instinct that we can never hope to grasp intellectually and they are naturally aware of things that our senses cannot detect. We can, therefore, work with animals in many different ways and on many different levels of consciousness.

It is a great honour to have animals as our allies in life and we must always remember that we work *with* them in a partnership, whether in the inner realms or the outer. A Druid should always treat an animal as an equal, if not a superior; always as a guide or teacher. They have much wisdom to show us.

Once we start to connect with the animal realm, in spirit or otherwise, we start to expand our experience and understanding of the reality of all worlds. It can be disorientating at first, especially as we must learn to strip away what is inconsequential in our thought and our action.

Working with animals dates far back into prehistory where they were interwoven into the very fabric of human existence. Given the holistic approach to existence by humans until recent times, that meant that animals were also at the heart of spiritual beliefs. This was a worldwide phenomenon, not just Celtic.

To the early Celts cattle, horses, and dogs were all highly prized creatures and indeed still are today by many peoples throughout the world. They provided food, transport, a means of hunting, and a whole host of other raw materials as well as companionship. Cattle were also a huge financial asset in Celtic Britain and their importance is reflected in the number of words in Celtic languages (particularly the names of colours) that refer to them.

The Celts of old did not think of the human race as superior to the animal kingdom. In fact, the opposite was true as there was an ingrained belief that most animals were teachers and guides between the other worlds. There is also a very long Celtic and pre-Celtic history of animal worship - our God has antlers after all. This continued in various degrees until the Christian Church stamped out the overt espousal of such beliefs. Much of the lore was lost, but by working with animals ourselves, it is there to be rediscovered.

Shapeshifting

The Druid's relationship with the animal kingdom encompasses much more than just the physical. Druids in the past had power or totem animals, as we can today. They also knew the art of shapeshifting, turning themselves into an animal and becoming at one with the creature. This is a technique lost to us although some psychics and sensitives can communicate with animals.

Shapeshifting could well have been a drug-induced state, although we have no way of knowing. Native Americans, north and south, certainly have a history of drug-induced journeys, either with or as an animal. Our ancestors' work with animals was very close to Native American shamanic teachings in the way that they perceived animals, so it is safe to assume that drug-induced trance states were practised.

This book, however, is about the Druid Way today and the use of any drug to induce such a state is not considered wise or necessary. Our way today is to learn meditation techniques to enable us to contact animals in our inner realm as well as become sensitive to the language and needs of animals in this world.

It is also important to remember that the tales our ancestors told should not necessarily be taken literally. Celts were a sophisticated people and their stories about animals and shapeshifting humans are highly symbolic, packed with layers of meaning which require an understanding of animal nature to comprehend. This is not to deny that an elemental magic was at work, simply to point out that there are many ways in which to see the world.

Power Animals and Totems

We all have an animal guide, sometimes many, acting as mentors as we tread through life. These guides are often called 'totems', 'power animals', or 'allies' and they are with us from birth. Most people are unaware that they exist and would think you crazy even to suggest such a thing.

Sometimes animals can be linked to whole family groups or clans. Certainly, a number of ancestral Celtic tribes were named for animals and had a number of strictly enforced *geasa* concerning their totemic creature.

There are, of course, human guides who also act as guardians and teachers on this path. The sad thing is that whilst it is quite acceptable for a Native American to admit having an inner bear guide (even if they live in New York City), someone from Surrey (or even the wilds of Scotland) saying they have a she wolf as a guide is considered quite mad.

These inner animals form part of our psyche. However, over lifetimes and centuries we have neglected these creatures of spirit. This is an enormous loss to us and to the animal kingdom as a whole. Animal totems not only guide us; they also teach and can heal us. In Native American tradition, the knowledge they impart is often called 'medicine'. We have forgotten this medicine.

There is much confusion around this subject with many books explaining the difference between a power animal and a totem animal, when really they are one and the same. The important thing is that we have to learn to find our animals and then work with them, allowing them to help us in the physical plane.

Now and again, you find a person whose power animal is the same as one of their companion animals in this life, but that is rare. What does often happen is that a Druid with, for example, a wolf as a guide will often take great interest in wolves, often belonging to an environmental group that helps them.

To start work with our animal guides we first have to find them. This is normally quite easy, as they are eager for you to make contact with them. Indeed, if you are open enough they will come looking for you and can be contacted during a pathworking or a guided meditation. Sometimes they show themselves in our dreams, so you must be careful not to dismiss it simply as a dream. As Druids, we should be aware of all animals whether in our inner landscapes or in the outer, just like we should be aware of all of nature. This awareness is what Druidry is.

Many Druids have animal guides that are native to the country in which they work. Here in Britain, many Druids have bears and wolves as guides. Although they are extinct now, their spirit is strong and lives on. It is the same when a Druid finds that their animal is from the South American rainforest. Somewhere in their past, maybe even in a past life, this spirit animal came through. Some people even find they make contact with so-called mythical animals such as the dragon, unicorn, or selkie. We cannot say they never existed, just because we do not see them on a day-to-day basis.

Often your animal guide will answer your questions. When talking to these animals we seem to have a common language on a soul level.

Sometimes we hear their voices slipping over into our daily life, offering us help and support. Learn to be in tune. Learn to pick up these messages, but think about them before acting on them. Trust your instincts, but never neglect the gift of your intellect.

We sometimes invite animals into our circles when we open the quarters. Do not try to confine a certain animal to a certain quarter. Many books give correspondences to where everything should go. It does not quite work that way. Animals should be free to roam as they will. Trust them. They will appear in the most appropriate place; they know no other way.

This does not mean you cannot invite them into a particular quarter. Circle work is always best and more powerful if your own intent comes through. Be confident. As with many aspects of being Druid, there is no wrong way, simply ways that are better ways than others. Let the animals be your guide.

As you read the list of animals given below, you will notice they are often linked either with Celtic myths or with deities. A little research will help attune you with these connections and their implications. For example, swans are linked to the Tuatha Dé Danaan, so in this instance it would be good to study a few things about the Tuatha Dé Danaan, the Sidhe, and where they fit into the Celtic mythos. We have to understand that all the worlds are interconnected. Animals, like faeries, can travel through and between the realms at will. However, so can we.

Working with Animal Energies

We can, of course, work with animal energies in many different ways. Not everyone is happy travelling the inner realms. One way to deepen our animal connection in our normal day-to-day reality is to listen and watch for signs from animals. Is that crow just 'cawing', or is it a message? Is the postcard of a bear from a friend trying to tell you something? Sometimes these messages and symbols expand the dimensions of consciousness deep within us, without even trying. All we need to do is become more aware of our animal brothers and sisters around us. Remember that this includes mammals, birds, amphibians, reptiles, fish, and insects.

Do you collect representations of a certain animal? Some people collect pig ornaments and trinkets, saying they are lucky. Are they lucky, or is there some deeper meaning for the collection? After all, within Celtic religion the pig is a sacred animal. Do you live with any animals? Understand what an honour it is to have a dog, cat, or anything else as a friend in this life. Think how much they care for you and the unconditional love they give. They will never lie to you or let you down. They walk in truth. How many humans can you say that about?

Even at this level, it soon becomes apparent that animals are at work in our lives. They are trying to make contact with you, so the next step must be yours. Before you go to sleep at night, ask your power animal to visit your dreams or when you next sit to meditate open yourself to the animal spirits that surround you.

When you have become aware of your own totem, find out all you can about your animal from books and films, or buy an animal card deck and start to work with them that way. Put a replica of your animal on your altar. It doesn't have to be a porcelain model. The plastic owl you got from a cereal packet is just as valid as an expensive item. It will still make you think 'owl'.

Compassion

Many people who work with animals feel they would rather not eat them, wear their skins, or contribute to cruel treatment, or their deaths. There is, however, a growing trend for Druids and other pagans to purchase skins and furs in the belief that wearing the skin will help in taking on the particular animal's spirit. Do not fool yourself. All this does is contribute to the barbaric trade of animal artefacts and furs. It is the same as buying a fur coat or purchasing a piece of ivory.

People who use animal skins often say they bought them as a 'road kill' or they died naturally. Unless you see the animal drop dead before you or killed on a road, there is no proof of where the animal came from. Wolves and bears certainly don't die on the road in any great number. There is, however, a huge industry of illegal slaughter of wild animals for their skins and body parts.

We are all outraged at the idea of mink and beaver farms. Quite rightly so, as they are cruel businesses that exist simply to enable the vain rich to dress in furs. The business of chasing a wolf halfway across Alaska or Canada in a helicopter to shoot it for its pelt is also just as cruel. These pelts can end up in the pagan market place. Not just wolves, but bear, deer, otter, in fact anything you want. They have the same right to life as you. It is a sad fact, however, that in the twenty-first century there are still people who would say 'it's just an animal' as they kill it.

To find a crow's feather on the grass is a gift; to find a creamy, peachy shell on the seashore is a gift; or to feed the sparrows outside your back door is a gift. We don't need to go on a pagan ego trip and prance about in the remains of a dead animal. Our ancestors cut off the heads of people to remove their spirits. It was their practice and we can respect them for that, but we would not countenance such a thing today. The world has changed and in this day and age having a wolf skin is just as distasteful as decapitation.

Not everyone feels that the inner world is where they want to work with animals. Very practical help can be given in this world. Many Druids work for, or contribute to animal rescue centres or other organizations that work to protect animals. Adopting a wolf, for example, and helping toward their preservation is a far better way of contacting the spirit of the wolf than wearing the skin of a dead one.

The Druid path is one of freedom and no one can tell you what to do or how to behave. It is up to you as an individual to search in your heart for what is right and what is wrong. However, we believe that if you accept we are all children of the Goddess, that spirit permeates all life, then you cannot in all conscience be truly Druid if you harm life.

The Power of Animals
Listed below are just a few animals drawn from Celtic tales and mythology, along with some insights into their characteristics. The description for each animal provides a signpost; pointing you in the right direction should you wish to delve more deeply. It is also only a modest list. There is a wealth of study waiting for those who are interested in working with the animal kingdom.

Within this list are links between certain Celtic deities and animals. This is because the three Celtic worlds are interwoven like knotwork with the human, plant, and animal kingdoms. Most Celtic tales include animals somewhere in their weavings, and it is well worth spending some time studying these stories for the teachings and the magic that they have to offer.

Use the list to give yourself ideas of what animal speaks to you on your inner levels, or use it to help with linking the Gods with animals within your workings. And, as you work, you can add your own findings and insights.

Stag

The stag has long been held in high regard, both materially and spiritually. Cave paintings from many sites depict Neolithic peoples hunting stags with the suggestion that there is more to the exercise than merely gathering meat. By the fifth century BC, depictions of hunting are replaced by images of men wearing antlers. In the Camonica valley of the Italian Alps, depictions of the stag are linked with solar imagery.

These later images may depict the idea of shapeshifting, which is an act of magic, or they may be representations of a horned god. Whatever they are, it is clear that the stag had achieved an extremely important status in the world view of the early Celts. Indeed, the portrayal of stags in all these early depictions is so prominent that he would seem to be a 'Lord of the Animals' or 'King of the Forest'.

This status is confirmed by the Gundestrup Cauldron, which depicts an antlered God believed to be Cernunnos – one of the principal and most widespread of Celtic deities. He sits in a lotus position surrounded by animals, grasping the serpent of wisdom in one hand and the torc of kingship in the other. The stag has stayed with his land for the English also have a stag deity - Herne, leader of the Wild Hunt.

Antlers were often linked with the Sun's rays, which is a very druidic symbol. They also represented the cycle of the seasons as they are shed in autumn and re-grow in spring. The hardness of the antler clearly evokes male sexuality and carved antlers were used to make phallic amulets.

The stag is one of the five Celtic power animals of the Welsh Mabon legend of Culhwch and Olwen from *The Mabinogion*. The other four animals are the blackbird, owl, eagle, and salmon. This story is also linked with Gwrhyr who could talk to the animals in their own tongue. Myrddin, too, is closely associated with the stag, riding one through the forest.

The stag often appears in the inner workings of Druids as it comes from deep ancestry within our Celtic being. Sometimes you may be honoured with a vision of a White Stag. These creatures are fay and truly magical.

Raven

Like the stag, the earliest depictions of the raven are to be found on the walls of caves. They were often shown as if talking to humans – messengers from the Otherworld, perhaps offering prophecy. These paintings are also found in the Italian Alps, and appear to be the art of Bronze and Iron Age Celts. The raven (indeed, the whole *corvus* family) appears throughout Celtic myth as a bird that foretells death and carnage on the battlefield.

There are two goddesses linked with the raven, and they are often confused. They are, however, very different. The first is the Welsh Druid goddess Morgan, who later became known as Morgan Le Fay because of her connection with Faerie. Morgan has also been written about over the centuries as a rather unsavoury person, when in truth she was a very powerful healer and guardian of the land. She is the true Raven Queen of legend, has the power to heal or harm, and is able to shapeshift into raven form and circle these isles.

Morgan is often mistaken for the Mórrígan (the Great Queen) who, apart from being Irish, is a completely different goddess. The Irish battle goddess is part of a triad of goddesses, the others being Macha and Badb. This dark Raven Goddess can be terrifying as she utilizes the powers of life, death, sexuality, and conflict all at once. When working with either of these two deities be cautious, as they are extremely powerful and can overwhelm you.

In the Northern Tradition the raven is also sacred - an image of constancy. The notion of the go-between is also still there, Odin having two ravens called Hugin and Munin (thought and memory) who were his messengers. The link with prediction also exists, as a raven stayed with Odin when he hung nine days and nine nights upon the sacred tree before learning the mystery of the Runes.

Today many people see the Raven as an evil bird, linked with destruction and death. The bird may have predicted it, but it was humans that caused it. It would be better to see this bird as a magical creature, who can give us messages if we learn to listen. A bird that offers us the chance to change.

Bee

Although the bee is the most commonly recognized of insects, few people realize just how many different species there are in the British Isles. Indeed, few realize that most species of bee lead solitary lives. Of the bees that lead communal lives, it is only honey bees that gather in any great number. Bumblebees, the ones you are most likely to see because of their size and coloration live in burrows in the ground or other convenient places such as compost heaps.

The bees that dance are honey bees. Their communal existence is extremely sophisticated and highly regulated - a strictly matriarchal society. They keep the temperature in their hives at a constant level, feed their young and tend them with great care, produce honey, royal jelly, and propolis all of which have highly beneficial properties for people, let alone the bees for whom they are originally produced.

In most cultures, the bee has been linked quite naturally with the Sun, and in Celtic culture, that association has linked the bee with Druids. In Welsh, they are 'gwenyn' which means 'blessed particles' or 'white particles', the bright spark of pale pollen which is what we often see first of the dowdy little honey bee as it works its way across the flowers of our gardens.

Without that work, pollination of most plants would come to an end. They would die. We would die. Bees, then, are worthy of great respect for their lives are one of great Service to the whole community of life.

In the past, to the living memory of most, this respect has been accorded them - and is still accorded them by those who know. For the bees must always be told the news otherwise they might swarm and go elsewhere. Wherever bees were kept, on farm or in garden, any news (family, local, or national) was always told to them.

The history of this folk tradition is obscure, but it is likely to be linked to the old saying (which has many variations): 'Ask the wild bee what the Druids knew'. This implies that bees shared the knowledge of Druids and that they were their equals in wisdom. Village based Druids were likely to have been beekeepers as honey and propolis were much treasured for their healing qualities.

Bear
The bear was once indigenous to the Celtic lands. It does not appear in Celtic literature, but it is found in their artwork. The bear is often linked to Arthur and the name Artio. This is unlikely, as Artio of Muri was the name of a Celtic bear Goddess of the Romano-Celtic period, worshipped in the Berne area. She was a Mother Goddess, a protectress of bears and other creatures, including humans.

Although we are inclined to think of large brown bears hunting for salmon and fighting each other, they are very insular creatures and prefer not to be seen by humans. As we have encroached on their hunting lands in the USA (we killed all ours off a long time ago) they are beginning to come closer and closer to towns and cities in their search for food. This can only put them in danger.

The bear often appears in the Druid inner world, an image of strength, motherhood, and a link with a wild time before Druids came to prominence.

Cattle

Cattle were vital to the Celtic economy and wealth was often measured in the number of cows possessed by an individual or a tribe. They produced milk, flesh, leather, horn, and many other raw materials. This accounts for a major pastime of some Celts - cattle raiding.

Given this importance, it is no wonder that cattle (both cows and bulls) came to be regarded as sacred creatures. Yet there is a deeper element to this as cattle were also important creatures for the gods – perhaps indicative of the Celtic view of the Otherworld as a reflection of this.

The Irish goddess Brigid was, at birth, washed in milk from an otherworldly cow and is strongly associated with cattle. In Wales, there are many stories of cows with a never-ending supply of milk, as well as faerie cattle that give birth to many calves every year. The bull was also sacred to Druids, symbolic of the thunder god Taranis and used in complex rituals associated with the choosing of Irish kings.

The importance of cattle in both the material and the spiritual worlds is reflected in the *Táin Bó Cuailnge* (the *Cattle Raid of Cooley*). This is perhaps the greatest work of classical Irish literature, a heroic epic full of magic and mystery, humour and great sadness. The two bulls that are central to the tale were once human pig-keepers who were forever arguing. Their conflict had been carried through into various shapeshifted forms all over Ireland before they were finally reborn as bulls and caught up in a much wider and magical conflict.

Horse

To ancestral Celtic peoples, the horse was probably their most important domestic animal, so much so that if anyone should harm a horse in any way it was punishable by death. In parts of the Celtic world, it was considered sacred. The word 'pony' is derived from the name Epona.

Epona means 'The Great Mare', and she was the goddess of a horse cult throughout Gaul, often depicted carrying the keys of the Otherworld. She was so widely honoured that three hundred images of her appear on stones in Gaul. The Epidii, a people who lived on the Kintyre peninsula, are thought to be named for her. She was even worshipped in Rome, the only Celtic deity ever cited in the Roman pantheon (her feast day on the 18 December).

In Wales, Rhiannon is closely associated with horses. In the First Branch of *The Mabinogion*, she is set a penance for the loss of her son, carrying people from a horse block into the hall. That she was a horse goddess as well seems in little doubt. Her connection with the bull and the crane – both sacred to Druids – and her betrothal to Pwyll also links her with the Otherworld.

In Ireland, Macha is the horse goddess. She too is treated cruelly. In the *Táin Bó Cuailnge*, she is made to race the King's horses despite being heavily pregnant. She wins, giving birth to twins at the finishing line, and then dies cursing the Ulster men for their cruelty.

Another spectacular feature of the horse in Celtic history is that of the giant chalk figures cut into the downland turf of the South of England. The oldest of these is the Uffington Horse in Oxfordshire. Archaeologists used to date it to around 100 BC because a horse of the same design is found on some Iron Age coins. A recent dating technique known as Optical Stimulated Luminescence (OSL) or 'silt-dating' has produced the much earlier dates of between 1400 and 600BC, making it a late Bronze Age carving. The hill fort on Whitehorse Hill was also originally constructed in the late Bronze Age.

The horse itself is some 360 feet long 130 feet in height. Many people have suggested it is a representation of the goddess Epona, but the new dating puts it well before the cult of Epona is known to have reached Britain. It is very interesting to note that the Uffington Horse is best viewed from a distance, and was never meant to be looked at close to.

Salmon

I am a salmon in a pool - a line from a poem chanted by Amairgin when the Milesians landed in Ireland. It refers partly to his shapeshifting into a salmon, but also to his deep identity with the land and all its creatures.

The salmon is associated with otherworldly wisdom, which it gains by eating the nuts of the sacred hazel. Certain salmon are prized and sought for as they have eaten the sacred nuts at particularly auspicious locations – one such being the Well of Segais from which rise, in myth, the Boyne and Shannon. In Ireland, the number of spots on the salmon's flesh is thought to denote the number of hazelnuts that it has eaten.

There are many tales in which people shapeshift to the form of a salmon. This may be a symbolic signification of initiation. Two tales in particular, with strong parallels, speak of the search for wisdom and the levels of experience involved. In Ireland, the Druid Finnéces spent seven long years looking for the Salmon of Wisdom. He knew that if he found this creature and ate it, he would gain all this wisdom. He entrusted the task of cooking the fish to a young pupil who burnt his thumb on the flesh. When he placed his thumb in his mouth he was gifted with the wisdom of the salmon – thus did Fionn mac Cumhaill become a great seer.

In Welsh tradition the tale is that of Cerridwen who was brewing a broth to endow her odiously ugly son Morfran with wisdom. The cauldron boiled over and three drops splashed onto the thumb of the servant Gwion Bach. He put his thumb in his mouth to soothe his hurt and was immediately endowed with the wisdom that had been meant for Morfran. Cerridwen chased Gwion Bach through many forms and eventually he was reborn as Taliesin – a Bard of great renown.

The salmon also appears in the story of Culhwch and Olwen where it becomes one of the five sacred animals of the Celtic realms. We can learn to swim with the salmon in our dreams and inner workings, eating of the hazelnuts of the Well of Segais to gain wisdom.

Hare
The hare features in mythologies throughout the world, from the Americas to the Orient. Often it is linked with the moon. Later tales paint this creature as ill-omened and it became persecuted as a result – a sad situation that still exists. Witches, for example, were supposed to be able to change into hares, and if a hare is seen running along the roadside it is meant to indicate a fire.

These 'old wives tales' did not always exist, for the hare once represented the Goddess and the Corn Spirit. Indeed, its connections with the Corn Goddess still live on in some areas of the world. After the last sheaf of corn is cut, the 'spirit of the Corn' lived on there until the following year. The person who cuts this final sheaf is known as the 'Hare'.

Hare is magical, and can bestow the powers of rebirth and a new life. It is linked with shapeshifting as Gwion turned himself into a hare in the *Hanes Taliesin*. It was also used for divination by ancestral Celts who held it in high regard. The most famous instance is the story of Queen Boudicca using a hare to divine the outcome of one of her battles. She did this by seeing which side a hare ran out from the folds of her dress.

Because of its link with the Goddess, as well as its divinatory power, the hare remains a sacred animal for Druids. Now rare in some parts of the country because of hunting and coursing, it deserves our protection. When working with the hare things can get very tricky and start to move very fast, but it is a wonderful creature, moving from this world to the other in the blink of an eye.

Spider
The spider is not often spoken of as a sacred animal; nor is it often included in lists of magical creatures. Too many people shrink away from this fascinating creature and forget the very important role it plays.

It certainly has a place here in a book on the Druid Way for the spider weaves a web and weaver goddesses are very much part of the Celtic Tradition. The spider also has many deities associated with it worldwide, including the Norse Wyrd Sisters, who are very similar to the triple goddesses of the Celtic pantheon.

Ariadne, who helped Theseus to escape from the Minotaur by using a thread, had her crown placed amongst the stars when she married Dionysus. The spider has also been linked symbolically with magic, fate, sex, death, and entrapment. Its web is used in healing.

Arianrhod of the 'Silver Wheel' is a Welsh stellar goddess who was able to weave the fates. She was the mother of Lleu Llaw Gyffes, a Sun god, as well as of his twin, Dylan, who is associated with the sea. These all speak of the great cycles of Star, Sun, and Moon into which our lives are woven and which help to give shape to our being.

The link between the stars and the fates is the very basis of astrology. Although we know very little of the workings of ancestral Celtic astrology, we do know it existed and was one of the skills attributed to Druids of old. The stars in the night sky and the dew that sparkles on the spider's web are one of the many reflections of form to be found in the universe.

Seal

Seals are found on the borderlands, where the sea meets the shore or hits the rocks. Borderlands have always been mystical places of transition for the Celtic people. Any creature that inhabits such a region, moving back and forth between worlds, will be seen as having magical powers and properties.

Interwoven with stories of seals are tales of the selkie, animals that shapeshift into humans. The selkie's land of origin is Scotland (in Ireland they are called roanes) and they belong to the element of water for they appear primarily as seals with some human characteristics. They are able to shed their skins and shapeshift into the most beautiful men and women, which makes them very alluring to humans. Selkies have a history of mating with humans, but leaving them once they tire of them, which they eventually do as they long for the open sea.

There is another side to the story as far as the selkie is concerned. Because these magical creatures are so beautiful, they have long been the victims of humans. Men have stolen the skins of female selkie so they are unable to return to their homelands. They have been forced to live on land and have children. There is a tale of one such selkie who, after many years of searching, found where the man had hidden her skin. She returned to seal form and slipped into the sea, leaving all her children behind, for they were not true selkie.

The selkie and the seal are both very difficult to work with for they have been treated cruelly by humanity, so are very wary of us. If one should enter your inner realms, it is a great honour and act of trust. You will be shown the wonders of the beautiful depths of the oceans and work closely with the whole element of water.

Wolf

Wolf seems to be very prolific in Druid Inner Groves, some people having whole packs! They did once roam the forests of these islands, and their spirit lives on in the land and in us. Indeed, they are one of those creatures that we are all fascinated by, even those of us who are frightened of them. Their appearance in folk tales and fairy tales is a testament to their importance to us in symbolic and spiritual terms.

Many great spiritual cultures have honoured them. The Egyptians had the wolf-god Wepwawet and associated Sirius with the wolf. Wolf deities remained in Egypt until the end of their self-rule. In the tales from the Norse and Germanic peoples wolves abound, but are usually feared as inhabitants of the darker reaches of the pine forests as well as harbingers of the final battle.

The Lakota of the Great Plains were also wary of the wolf. A horse chased by a wolf was said to be cursed and considered lame thereafter. However, the Ojibwe shamans had a different relationship with the wolf. They considered it such an important teacher that it was far too powerful to be adopted as a totem.

In Ireland, the story of Cormac mac Airt tells of how he was raised by wolves. Packs of wolves accompanied him, and he walked between two rows of wolves at his inauguration as king. Myrddin also had a wolf companion who looked after him while he wandered in the wildwood during his madness. Tradition states that Myrddin's teacher was called Blaise, which is very close to the Welsh word for wolf, 'blaidd'.

The wolf is a loyal and powerful teacher, a pathfinder in the wilds who will stay by your side through thick and thin. Wolf links us with the land and cold midnight skies, with northern winds and snow, with full moon howlings. The Druid who has a wolf as a guide will never walk alone or be lost.

Wren
The wren is the totem of the 'Oak King', and each year at the winter solstice is locked in battle with the robin or the 'Holly King'. It is likely that this tiny 'King of Birds' has been a part of ceremonies and rituals performed at the winter solstice since the megalithic age, for the wren represents the turning of the year from dark to light.

Its old name is Drui-en, so close to the word Druid, and its nest is known as the Druid's House. The Welsh for wren and seer are the same – *dryw*, so it can be seen that this little bird is most sacred. Druids would listen to the changes in its song and divine from what they heard.

Adder

The snake, and especially the adder, is known throughout the Celtic world. Because the adder can shed its skin, it has become a symbol of rebirth, either in the life and death cycle or as a changing of ways during one's life. As it lives under rocks and in the earth it has also become linked with the underworld, where it guards the secrets of life, death, and rebirth, which belong to the Goddess. Cúchulainn, Fionn mac Cumhaill, and Conall Cernach all had to overcome the trials of a snake.

As with the spider, we are uneasy in the presence of snakes. With the adder, a degree of caution is necessary. It is the only venomous snake in Britain and although you would have to be very young or very weak for a wound to be fatal, a bite can be extremely painful and should be treated immediately. However, they are shy creatures and only strike when threatened. Should you be lucky enough to see one, watch it from a distance and allow it its time in the sun.

The mystical symbology of the adder has direct links with Druids, so much so that in some texts the words 'Druid' and 'adder' are interchangeable. In particular, tales of St Patrick driving the adders from Ireland refer to the rise of Christianity – although Patrick had much more sympathy for the old ways than later hagiographers would have us believe.

Druids saw the adder as a symbol of conception, and this was depicted in carvings. Often the adder will have an egg in its mouth, so representing both male and female sexuality. It is also linked with the idea of an energy source, which flows up the spine. In the Orient, this is known as kundalini, where two snakes intertwining make the energy flow. This is also depicted in the Mercurial symbol of the caduceus, which is associated with healing.

Because the egg and the adder are as one in the Druid tradition, eggs have also been a prominent feature in Druid mystery teachings. The modern trend of calling Druid seers 'Ovates' reflects this. The adder is a powerful guide if you have one, dedicated to the sun, a source of wisdom, a sinuous form in which is contained both the God and the Goddess.

Hawk

There are many species of falcon and hawk in the British Isles, including the kestrel, merlin, goshawk, and sparrowhawk. They are all birds of prey, like the golden eagle.

In the story of Pwyll, Prince of Dyfed from *The Mabinogion*, Pwyll exchanges hawks, dogs, and horses with Annwn, ruler of the Otherworld. In other tales about Arthur, Gawain is known as the Hawk of May or Gwalchmai. In yet another shapeshifting story in the *Irish Book of Invasions*, we read how Fintan mac Bóchra becomes a salmon, an eagle, and a hawk.

The hawk is one of the 'old' animals of the Celtic Tradition, having witnessed the events of the world since the time of the flood. Working with the hawk is both perilous and rewarding. It is far seeing and extremely wise, but it is a wild and remote creature, and it is all too easy to become trapped in hawk form.

Otherworldly Animals

Some Druids have otherworldly creatures as their guides such as the dragon, unicorn, or other white animals such as stags and hinds. In Celtic mythology most white animals are said to be either sacred, otherworldly, or of the Sidhe. Unicorns are the most pure and magical beasts in the universe - only the pure in heart will ever see one.

There are many dragons in Celtic literature, and the ancestors understood their massive power by building their stone circles on the invisible power lines in the landscape. They named hills after them and told tales of sleeping dragons guarding treasure deep within. When Christians came and built churches on these sites, they dedicated them to the dragon fighting saints George and Michael. Yet the power of the dragons remains.

The dragon is also the symbolic image of the Celtic King or Chief, and is still seen today in the Red Dragon on the Cymric flag. Dragons were buried beneath the ancient earthworks at Dinys Emrys in Wales, released at the behest of Myrddin who, as we have already seen, made his first recorded prophesies in their presence.

Other Celtic Animals

The full description of Celtic animals would warrant another book, for there are many more that could have been written about. The whole animal world was of importance to Celtic peoples and to Druids past and present, who accept their affinity with it. No animal is more important than any other – and that includes humans.

Other creatures that also deserve a mention are pigs and boars, cats, badgers, bats, swans, butterflies, red squirrel, cranes and herons, dogs, foxes, hedgehogs, frogs, skylarks, owls, otters, toads... The list is endless and each has a story to tell and a lesson to teach. When you start to work in your inner realms, you will often be surprised at what turns up to talk to you.

Finding Your Animal Guide
The following pathworking is to enable you to make contact with your animal guide. This is done from the safety of your Sacred Inner Grove. Please make sure you have visited your Inner Grove a few times before doing this exercise.

While doing this working you will come to no harm, even if the animal you meet frightens you. If you are really unhappy with the creature, simply ask it to go away, and leave your Grove the same way you entered it. Do not be disappointed if the animal you expect is not the one that appears. Just because you have, for example, a passion for bears does not mean that your animal guide will be a bear. Often the species of animal is a complete surprise to us, but as we learn more about it, and from it, we come to understand why we have been chosen by that particular species.

Choose a time when you will not be disturbed. You will need to prepare your room, cast your circle, do the meditation, uncast the circle, ground yourself, and relax. Make sure you allow plenty of time to do all this. To create a suitable atmosphere, you might like to play some very soft music. As animals are sensitive and wary of fire, do not use incense or candles.

Start by casting a protective circle of light around yourself. Sit in the centre of your circle. If you find it uncomfortable to sit cross-legged on the floor, have a straight-backed chair in the centre. There is no text anywhere that says Druids must be uncomfortable in the circle! Some people like to lie down. This is not always a good idea as there is a tendency to fall asleep.

Become aware of your breathing. Concentrate on that for a while. Feel the energies coming up from deep in the Earth and down from the stars to meet in your being. Stay there awhile, and breathe this way for a few more heartbeats. When you are ready, you may start your journey to your Inner Grove, where you will meet up with the guide that you met before.

Rest a moment or two in the centre of your Grove. Notice any changes. Is it day or night? What time of year is it? Can you hear the birds singing? Does your guide have any messages or teaching for you?

On the breeze, you hear the faint sound of some pipes. You are not sure whether it is the wind in the trees, or someone playing a long way off. Your guide starts to walk you out of your Grove and towards a path with trees and bushes on either side making a tunnel of foliage. You follow your guide through into the tunnel. It soon becomes very dark and quite narrow.

If the tunnel disturbs you, do not worry. You are quite safe.

It does not take long to pass through to the other side. Your guide says they will wait for you by the tunnel, for you must now go on alone.

If you still feel uncomfortable, ask your guide to take you back to your Grove and finish the working.

This side of the tunnel is another grove, one you have never seen before. All around are huge trees, great and ancient oaks. The grass under your feet is damp with morning dew, and there is a mist laying low across the ground. In the distance, there is a small mound, and through the mist, you can just make out the outline of a man sitting cross-legged on the top. As the mist clears slightly, you notice for the first time that this man has an antlered head. You look again and there is just the mist. Look around you and find a suitable place to sit down. Rest here awhile.

As you sit in this grove, ask the spirit of the wildwood to help you meet with your animal guide. Be patient. Concentrate on your breathing and focus on the mist ahead of you. As you do so, the mist will start to lift and there, on the borderland of the grove, shafts of sunlight will break through and your animal will appear.

At this first meeting, it is best simply to get to know each other. Your animal might talk to you, or tell you its name, or simply sit long enough for you to get to know its individual form. When you have finished and it is time to go, offer your thanks, and tell your animal that you will be back.

Thank the spirit of the wildwood and start to walk towards the tunnel of trees and bushes by which you entered. There, you will find your guide waiting to take you back through the tunnel to your own Grove. When you reach your Inner Grove, thank your guide, sit down, and start to breathe comfortably as you gradually make your return to your room.

*

Do not forget to close your circle when you have finished – this is a powerful working and should be properly rounded off for the sake of all involved. Afterwards, ground yourself by eating and drinking something light, before writing about your journey and your encounter in your journal.

As you meditate in your grove over the years, you will meet many animals. Once they are aware of your presence and your visits, they will be drawn to you out of curiosity. Your chosen animal guide will always be nearby in your Inner Grove and you will have no need to undertake this particular meditation again. Simply ask and it will usually appear. Remember, though, that your animal guide is an autonomous being who is also a teacher. If you call, it may not choose to come. It may sometimes appear when you have not called. This is animal nature and even in this, there is a lesson.

DEITY

Ancestral Celts were and many modern Druids are polytheistic. Of those Druids today who eschew polytheism, most still honour different expressions of an overarching divinity – manifesting as or referred to by the names of ancestral Celtic deities. Irrespective of how Celtic deities are interpreted, however, they still play an important role in the lives of Druids.

It has been suggested that the main Celtic pantheon actually consisted of thirty-three deities. Thirty-three was a significant number to the Celts, and other cultures with Indo-European roots have pantheons of thirty-three. It seems unlikely that we will ever know for certain. As Christianity spread and the Celtic peoples nucleated into distinct nations subject to different influences, combined with the Celts abiding sense of place, the pantheon took on local aspects and the deities gained variant names and attributes.

Several things are certain. The first is that Celts did not always depict their deities pictorially or as statues. Indeed, early Celts were known to find the idea absurd. It was not until after contact with the classical world that they began to produce formal imagery. The second is that the Celtic pantheon is very much like an extended family or tribe with all the same concerns and conflicts experienced by humans. The third is that Celts considered their deities to be ancestors rather than creators. The difference is subtle, but important, as it explains a great deal about the relationship that Druids today have with them.

The principal deity of the main pantheon, now as then, is the mother goddess Danu (sometimes given as Anu) whose name is associated with the river Danube, along with many other similar river names throughout Europe. In Irish mythology, her children are known as the Tuatha Dé Danaan. The Welsh equivalent of Danu is Don whose children also form a central pantheon. The similarity of name and the fact that both are considered to represent the 'waters of the sky' suggests an origin common to all Celts.

The children of Danu are locked in conflict with the children of Domnu (in Irish mythology) and the children of Llŷr (in Welsh mythology) who have connections with the deeps of the sea. The waters of heaven and the deeps of the sea are, of course, different aspects of a single cycle. Their natures, therefore, are also completely different and bound to lead to what seems like conflict, which takes place on the Land. That the conflict is never fully resolved, going through cycles of its own, indicates that both aspects are essential to the world we all share.

This conflict is often portrayed as a battle between light and dark with the implication that they are forces of good and evil. Druids do not see the world in quite this way. Indeed, modern Druids are as likely to be found working with or attracted to the children of the deeps of the sea, as they are the children of the waters of heaven.

Of all the examples and variations of the Celtic pantheon that must have existed, only two have survived in anything more than fragments. The Welsh version can be pieced together from various sources, especially the fourth branch of the *Mabinogi*. The story of the Tuatha Dé Danaan is to be found in the *Lebor Gabála Érenn* (Book of the Taking of Ireland). They are one of several peoples who arrive on Irish shores in successive waves from the Otherworld to displace their predecessors.

The Tuatha Dé Danaan brought with them four magical treasures, one from each of the great cities they had previously inhabited. From Falias they brought the Lia Fáil, the stone of destiny. From Findias came the sword of Nuada, a fearsome weapon for all wounds inflicted by the blade were fatal. The third treasure, from Gorias, is the spear Gáe Assail. This is used with devastating effect by Lug Lámfhota. Finally, from Murias, is the cauldron of the Dagda, which provided food (and possibly much more) for all of the Dagda's faithful followers.

These treasures have been listed as they are of enormous significance to Druids and will often be found mentioned in ritual, if not actually represented by physical objects. They will certainly be well known as symbols and objects to anyone who is familiar with Arthurian literature, which suggests that they also had a place in British mythology from an early period.

The leading figures of the Tuatha Dé Danaan include the Dagda who was the Druid of the tribe and sometimes also known as the Good God (in the sense that he was highly skilled rather than an exemplar of rectitude); Manannán mac Lir, a god associated with dominion of the Irish Sea; Dian Cécht, a healer who could restore to good health all but those who had been decapitated; Lug Lámfhota, a great warrior who was also a master of all arts and all crafts; Brigid, a goddess of fire and inspiration; the triune goddess of conflict, Badb, Macha, and Mórrígan; and Ogma, a warrior of great eloquence to whom is ascribed the invention of ogham. These deities, and many others, have their equivalents in British mythology and no doubt existed in continental Europe as well.

The mother of these deities and, ultimately, the ancestor of all Celts and all Druids, has remained a shadowy figure who plays little or no active part in the mythological cycle as it has come down to us. Having brought forth and nurtured an entire pantheon is surely accomplishment enough. She remains, however, firmly at the heart of Druid ritual in her role as progenitor and protector. She is revered and loved as a mother and as the spiritual hearth where Druids draw comfort, wisdom, and strength.

Other deities are accorded roles that are more specific and are worked with by Druids in specific ways, at specific times, and in specific places. Many of these deities are anonymous spirits of place, but there are others who have universal roles and with whom most Druids will work at some time or other.

With Danu in her role as hearth mother and perhaps concerned with the cerebral and spiritual aspects of life, it is the Dagda who fills much of the rest of the world with his presence. The Dagda and his equivalents (such as Bran and possibly Cernunnos) have very similar attributes. He is a formidable character who can destroy and restore to life any creature with his great club, and who can provide for all who follow him with his ever-full cauldron and his ever-laden apple trees. He also has a strong affinity with the animal kingdom and is sometimes known as the Lord of the Beasts. This is a potent force, the exemplar of Celtic society for he is an accomplished Druid, a great warrior, and a highly skilled artisan, upright and benevolent. Yet the Dagda also has a comical side. He dresses in a rough tunic that is too short to cover his buttocks, behaves in an amiably oafish way, and is extremely fond of porridge.

Guardianship of the Land requires consent of the Land for it will accept none but those who are suited to the role. Consent can only be given by the Land itself, usually by a representative goddess of sovereignty. There are many examples of specific and local goddesses of sovereignty who bear the name of the region or the country over which they hold sway.

In non-specific terms, sovereignty manifests as the *cailleach*. The modern meaning of the word, 'old woman' has also acquired the pejorative meaning of 'hag', which, whilst it has some relevance, has devalued the importance of sovereignty. Originally, the word meant 'veiled one', which is much more relevant to the original form of the goddess. A 'veiled one' might be an old woman, but it can also be a widow, or one pledged to a cause or calling. The veil sets them apart, by their own choice, and allows them the right to stay separated or to return to society as and when they please.

The veil is also a glamour. It represents the barrier that must be crossed, the understanding that must be attained by someone if they are to see the face of sovereignty and thus gain her consent. In allegorical tales concerning the *cailleach*, the glamour is a less subtle symbol. When she first appears to the hero, it is as an ugly old woman asking to be loved (emotionally and physically) or imposing an appropriate task. When love is freely given (or the task successfully undertaken), the veil dissolves to reveal a beautiful young woman.

Long-lived sovereignty will take many champions in this way, renewing each cycle of her existence and ensuring the Land is well protected. The relationship between sovereignty and her champion is sealed with a sacred or ritual marriage. Neglect of the relationship is and was a serious matter. Discord is reflected in the state of the Land. Ancestral Celts had an economy and a culture dependent on agriculture and the well-being of the Land was essential. A king who neglected his duties could be removed quite legally by the people.

Sovereignty is of great importance to Druids. To function properly as a Druid it is necessary to respect and work in service of the Land. Yet, by committing themselves to such a relationship with the goddess, they gain personal and spiritual sovereignty. This is the gift that the goddess offers in return for the work that Druids do in her name. That freedom is gained through responsibility and obligation is not unique to pagan religion or, indeed, any religion. Nevertheless, it does form an important part of the Celtic metaphysic and to achieve this through a sacred bond with the goddess of the Land is one of the ways in which Druids affirm their spiritual path and pay honour to their ancestors.

Along with the Dagda and the *cailleach*, there are two other quintessential deities important to Druids. They balance the maturity of the Good God and the Veiled One with their youth. One of these is Lug, a warrior skilled in all the crafts and arts. The other is the highly enigmatic figure of the Mabon.

Standing behind the cognate figures of Lleu Llaw Gyffes, Lug Lámfhota, and the Gaulish Lugus is the ancient and bright figure of Lug. Possibly pre-Celtic, this deity was worshipped widely. Lug means 'light' and he is often simplistically regarded as a solar deity, a representation of the sun. He is solar, in part, but he is a much more complex and subtle deity than that. As a hero of Celtic tales, he is a warrior of great renown, famed for his use of the spear (hence his name meaning 'long arm' in Irish and 'steady hand' in Welsh). Yet, as the texts make clear, he is a young man of many accomplishments – in agricultural, metalworking, woodworking, harping, magic, medicine, and as a cup bearer. He is also credited with the invention of the game *fidchell*.

Once again, we see a quintessentially Celtic character, this time in youthful form with all the confidence and vigour of early life. Yet this overlay of Celtic culture does not altogether obscure the more fundamental and perhaps much older nature of this deity. The illumination he offers as a deity of light is both physical and spiritual, and like the light, he is swift and has the power to heal. The importance of Lug to the Celts, however, is indisputable and clear. His name can be found embedded in place names from the north of Britain right through Europe to Silesia. Furthermore, in Goidelic, his name is attached to one of the great annual festivals, Lughnasad. This is a feast in celebration of harvesting the cereal crops, themselves associated with the sun. He is thought to have been especially important to Druids, a connection that is underpinned by a number of cryptic similarities between Lug and Myrddin.

Lug, however, is not the only youthful deity of importance to ancestral Celts and modern Druids. In various traditions, there are tales of a Divine Youth, one whose conception and birth or early life occur outside of time, one who is imprisoned and rescued or, alternatively, who is fostered by a sisterhood of nine and trained for his role as a great hero. We only have fragments now of what appears to have been a great cycle of stories which may have drawn parallels between the life of the hero and the cycle of the year.

In British mythology, the child is known simply as the Mabon (which means 'child') who is the son of Modron ('the mother') and he is clearly a form of the deity Maponus ('divine child') found throughout Europe. Tradition now associates his birth with the winter solstice largely because as an archetype found in many cultures, this is when the divine child enters the world. A new son is born as a new sun is born, ensuring a further year of fertility and prosperity. As the child grows, he becomes the champion of the goddess, his mother.

All these tales may have a familiar ring, even to those who are not acquainted with the rich world of Celtic mythology. This is because the tales have never stopped developing, any more than the religion to which they belong. As always, the old deities were superseded. In Britain, the tales continued to develop into the corpus now known as the Matter of Britain. The tales of Arthur and his companions bear strong resemblances to the older tales of deities and their adventures.

Celtic deities also went underground and have become increasingly confused with the inhabitants of Faerie. Reasons for this confusion are not hard to find, as faeries are Otherworldly and share many of the attributes of deity. It is not this confusion, however, that makes them worth mentioning further. Rather, it is the important place they have had in the lives and affairs of Celtic peoples as well as the role they now play in the lives of Druids.

Any mention today of faeries or of a faerie tradition will invariably conjure certain images in the popular imagination. However, faeries are not diminutive figures with gauzy wings who sit around in flowers all day, any more than they are elves (a similar, but different race). Faeries are beings who have lived alongside humans for thousands of years. They are very much like humans in appearance and stature, with many of the same concerns and habits. Their preferred colours, by which they are often identified, are green and silver. Ancestral Celts held them in great respect and avoided contact with them when they could as, for all the similarities between them and humans; they live their lives by different rules. Although they are not deliberately malevolent certain of their ways are harmful to people and if affronted they can retaliate with absolute vengeance.

The fact that the realm of faeries is said to be underground (or sometimes under water) should not be taken literally. They do not live in caves any more than they are denizens of the Christian Hell. The world of Faerie is very similar to our own; it is simply that the gateways to this world are often to be found in hillsides or where there is water. They can move between their world and ours at will.

A great deal of ancestral Celtic folklore was concerned with faerie and they were taken seriously and treated with respect. Interest in faerie has grown again in recent times, although most popular depictions are based on Victorian conceptions and most books on the subject are, frankly, drivel. Many modern Druids accept the reality of faeries. A few even try to work with them. Most, however, whilst paying due regard to a people with whom they share the planet advise caution when in their presence.

*

Although the deities of the Celtic pantheon are important to Druids, their beliefs and practices do not revolve around them alone. That is why the Druid Way is not about blind worship. Druids work with their deities, identifying what they represent and how they can empower a person to carry forward their druidic service. There is no disrespect in this. Druids look upon their deities as mentors. These deities are shown every respect, but it is clear from the myths that they have a great dislike for sycophancy.

A Druid will usually develop a personal relationship, often quite intimate, with a particular deity. This relationship will grow out of an honouring and working with that deity, rather than out of worship. Nor does this relationship exclude work with other deities. It is simply that a Druid will work most, and therefore become more closely linked, with an aspect of the divine that best suits their own work in the world. The relationship is not always the most obvious, or the one that a Druid would initially choose. Indeed, it often takes a number of years for the relationship to develop and for the purpose behind it to become apparent.

A relationship with a deity is not, for Druids, an end in itself. They work with their deities in order to come to a better understanding of the world. This understanding is also a means to an end, for the Druid uses it to do what they can in the world to bring about balance and harmony.

OGHAM

Ogham (pronounced 'o-am' [the 'o' as in 'hot'] with just the hint of a 'y' between the 'o' and the 'a') are the only known form of native Celtic letters. They probably originated in south-west Ireland and have never been found outside Ireland and Great Britain – despite claims that they have been discovered in America. The ogham 'alphabet' (more properly the 'beth-luis-nuin') consists of twenty letters, to which a further five (representing diphthongs) were added at a much later date to accommodate Latinate introductions to the language.

Many people think of the ogham as nothing more than a tree alphabet, but this is not strictly true. Part of the confusion stems from the fact that most (though not all) of the names of the letters are also the names of trees. There are other, more recent reasons, which are discussed below. Although in one system the letters do represent trees, ogham were also attached to many other systems and name lists. There are body ogham, hound ogham, cow ogham, work ogham, place ogham, and so on. However, the link with trees is early and deep as ogham were considered to be branches of the Tree of Wisdom, and were probably used as a means of teaching.

The original twenty oghams are divided into four groups or *aicme*. These consist of anything from one to five straight lines or notches cut to, or across, a stem line. This stem could be either vertical or horizontal. Where the line is horizontal, the letters are to be read from left to right. Where the line is vertical, it was the usual practice to write from top to bottom. Inscriptions that followed the outer edge of a stone slab or the inner line of an arch were generally written from bottom left, upward, across the top and then down the right-hand side.

The true or original order of the letters is now uncertain. The chart below gives what is considered to be the original order (with the diphthongs omitted), but the letters of the first group are sometimes given in the order beith-luis-fearn-saile-nuin.

The suggested pronunciations are open to question, as they do not quite accord with what is known of the development of Celtic languages. 'C', however, is always a hard letter (Celtic is pronounced 'Keltic', for example), and 's' is always soft (that is, it is not used to signify a 'z' sound – 'his' would be pronounced 'hiss' and not 'hiz').

'Q' is absent in both modern groups of languages (despite the Goidelic languages being known as Q-Celtic), and 'w' is absent from the ogham and modern Irish. This suggests that 'quert' is a later interpolation replacing some other phoneme. It has been shown here as 'cú' (pronounced 'coo').

Two other ogham are also uncertain. 'Ngetal' may be an eclipsed form of 'getal', but it is hard to understand why, as the names are ascribed phonetically and the 'g' is already taken. Some commentators assign the letter 'p', but this is also uncertain as the letter 'p' was a late introduction to the language and an extra ogham has been found on inscriptions to represent it. The double 's' given for 'straif' appears to be entirely redundant. It is highly likely that the phonetic values for these ogham follow some other form that we no longer use or for which there are other letter combinations in the Latin alphabet.

Ogham vertical	Ogham horizontal	Name	Pronunciation	Roman letter	Associated tree
		beith	BEH	b	birch
		luis	LWEESH	l	rowan
		nuin	NEE-uhn	n	ash
		fearn	FAIR-n	f	alder
		saile	SAHL-yuh	s	willow
		huathe	HOO-ah	h	hawthorn
		duir	DOO-r	d	oak
		tinne	CHIN-yuh	t	holly
		coll	CULL	c	hazel
		quert	CUAIRT	cú	apple
		muinn	MUHN	m	vine
		gort	GORT	g	ivy
		ngetal	NYEH-tl	ny/p	reed
		straif	STRAHF	ss	blackthorn
		ruis	RWEESH	r	elder
		ailm	AHL-m	a	pine
		onn	UHN	o	gorse
		ur	OO-ruh	u	heather
		edhadh	EH-yuh	e	aspen
		ido	EE-yoh	i	yew

A number of modern commentators have stated that ogham is an impractical script for anything longer than inscriptions carved on stone. This, however, seems to be a matter of the untrained eye and unpractised hand inventing difficulties where none exist. The twenty-six Latinate letters of the English alphabet are far more complex in form and they are as nothing compared to Sino-Tibetan ideographic symbols used for religious texts. And there is plenty of evidence to suggest that whole books were written using ogham script inscribed on wands of wood that were threaded together.

The Celtic peoples could and did read and write. Indeed, they were far from illiterate, being renowned for many centuries for their learning, their schools, and their civilized approach to life. As well as a native script, they also used the scripts of other peoples. Most commonly used were Greek letters although as Latin became a common language, they used Latin letters as well. The belief that Celts were illiterate stems from a misreading of Cæsar who merely stated that the Druids would not commit their teachings to writing.

Neither the Greek nor the Latin alphabets were properly suited to Celtic languages and it is possible that the native script was devised to better accommodate them. Its origins are, however, shrouded in mystery and most references to it are to be found in the Irish myths and sagas where it is intimately linked with magic and with the wisdom of the Druids.

The sagas contain many references to great libraries of bark and wooden wands carved with the ogham script. However, the bulk of extant ogham scripts, dating from the fifth and sixth centuries AD, are carved on stones. There are 369 known inscriptions, some found in Wales and Scotland. The bulk, however, are to be found in Ireland, concentrated in County Kerry where there are 121 of them. This has led to suggestions that this is where the script originated, but it could just as easily be that this is where the use of such inscriptions survived the longest.

Claims that ogham is of great antiquity are to be treated with a great deal of caution. However, it did not come into existence fully formed in the fifth and sixth centuries AD simply to be used as a form of lithic inscription. Indeed, the extant forms suggest the tail end of their use as a form of lettering. This, combined with the undoubted antiquity of some of the tales in which it features as an integral part of the action, does tend to suggest an origin at least several centuries BC.

The invention of ogham is ascribed to Ogma, god of eloquence and literature. Ogma, a son of the Dagda, was skilled in dialects (important in ancestral times, as there were many different dialects of the Celtic language) and poetry as well as being a warrior. He also had a role in conveying the souls of the dead to the Otherworld.

As well as this, he is also considered a Sun deity as he is often called Ogma Grian-aineach (Ogma of the Sunny Face) or Ogma Cermait (Ogma of the Honeyed Mouth - sweet talker, honey also a gift of the Sun). He has cognates in Britain (Ogmia) and Gaul (Ogmios) where he was also considered a Sun deity who had a role in language and conveying the dead on their long journey.

The fact that we know so little about the origins and use of ogham script has led to a great deal of wild speculation, but the most plausible explanation is that it developed from a sign language. Sign languages were thought to be common amongst students in druidic colleges as rules of silence were commonly enforced. This spilled over into Christian monastic life from an early stage. The fact that there are four groups of five letters, each composed of one to five straight lines (or fingers) lends this theory support.

For all the uncertainty that surrounds ogham, we do know that the script is very closely linked with druidic learning. Although its outward appearance is as a 'tree alphabet', each letter and each group of letters had many other associations. It certainly makes a useful basis for a mnemonic system - essential to Druids who committed their entire teachings to memory.

A text from the fourteenth century, within the *Book of Ballymote,* is devoted to ogham and gives an explanation of the characters and the various forms of ogham. Although a medieval text, and one that seems to be corrupt, examination of the content suggests that what is written down is derived from much older, orally transmitted material. That, too, suggests that it is druidic in origin.

Much of that ancient lore has been lost, although there have been a number of attempts in recent decades to try to understand more about the use and nature of ogham. Much of this is based on two sources. The first is that of the revivalists, principally Iolo

Morganwg. His work is so tainted with invention that it is difficult to be certain about any of his historical claims.

The second source is the work of Robert Graves in his book, *The White Goddess*. In this, he explores the meaning of the poem 'Cat Goddeu' (The Battle of the Trees) and many other things besides. From this, he derives a tree calendar and a number of other ideas that have often been repeated as if they were undisputed fact from ancestral times. There is no basis in history for believing there was ever a tree calendar per se. This, however, has not stopped many people jumping on the bandwagon and misleading those who have yet to develop their critical acumen.

That trees are associated with different times of the year and with different aspects of the cycle of the seasons and the hero tales of the Sun God is beyond question. That most ogham letters are named for trees is also beyond question. However, the obsession with making neat lists and associations is a modern, linear, Roman view of the world. Celts were easy going and organic in their thinking. They knew the world flowed and changed and that you could not compartmentalize things so easily. That is why Druids took nineteen years to train! That is why they never stopped learning.

There is slight evidence that Druids used four yew rods for divination in connection with ogham script but there is no known description of how this was done. It is possible the rods were used in conjunction with a pattern known as 'Fionn's Window' that is to be found in *The Book of Ballymote*. This is composed of five concentric circles that act as the stem lines. At the quarters on the outer circle are placed the first ogham of each group, each successive ogham on the next circle inward.

This pattern could be marked on the ground or on a cloth and the wands cast – a divination made from the way in which they fell. Adjacent to one diagram of Fionn's window is another circle that is quartered with elongated cuneiform shapes. These resemble metal rods found just outside Colchester in the grave of what is thought to have been a Druid.

Not knowing the meanings associated with individual characters or groups and their relative positions on the wheel, means that it is impossible to reproduce any ancestral system of divination. Any systems that are in use today are modern inventions. This does not necessarily invalidate their worth. That is a decision you will have to come to for yourself after exploring them.

Some of these modern systems have been developed after years of study; many have not. The cards, rods, or whatever other paraphernalia are used are merely aids. They act as keys to unlock what lies within the mind and experience of diviner and querent alike rather than being inherently able to divine the future. They cannot simply be picked up and used. You have to learn them and work with them over time in order to allow them to permeate your very being.

Whether or not ogham was used in ancestral times as a method of divination, and to what extent it represents a form of encoding knowledge, we will never really know. We cannot, however, ignore the fact that it is intimately connected with the tree, which stands at the heart of all that is druidic.

If nothing else, the ogham script gives us a starting point for work with trees. As you learn the script, you can learn about each tree that is associated with it. This, in turn, provides the opportunity to begin thinking about the way in which Celtic peoples viewed the world, as a flowing and universal interconnectedness, a deep forest of mystery into which we must all travel, a place where the very letters they used are living branches of the great and sacred trees that watch over us and teach us - if we can but take the time to learn.

WORKING ALONE & WORKING WITH OTHERS

There are many mysteries associated with the Druid Way, not least that which surrounds the decision to become Druid. It is not something that comes to a person in a flash of light. They have to be looking for it before they can find it; yet it is the nature of the quest that people who are searching for a spiritual path do not know precisely what they are looking for.

The mystery is compounded as the Druid Way is far from being the easiest path about which to find information. Despite the fact that the number of Druids (and pagans in general) is growing there is very little clear advice for those who are interested or who wish to explore on their own – hence this book.

Most people, on deciding to explore the Druid Way, do so alone for a while. They read books and pagan magazines, practice the workings they find, get into the countryside as much as possible, look at trees, and do generally druidic things. Eventually they come to feel that it would be nice to meet and practice with others of like mind, so expanding what they have learned so far.

Normally, the best way to meet people is at a local, open pagan meeting (often referred to as a 'moot'). You can look for adverts in pagan magazines. Alternatively, you can join one of the Druid Orders or Networks.

Druid Orders
Most Druid Orders have a hierarchy of people responsible for the running of the organization. They will often have a Chief Druid in overall charge of things, with many others in positions of responsibility within the Order. These vary, but they often use revivalist Druid titles such as Pendragon and Scribe. Any large organization has to have people working in such a way if things are to run smoothly. The membership belongs either to Groves within the Order, or they work alone.

Some Orders also offer correspondence courses to which people can subscribe. Indeed, you may not be considered a member unless you are prepared to do the course. There are people who say that you should not pay for magical or spiritual knowledge. If that is the case, should you have bought this book?

We live and work in the twenty-first century, and we are part of a money-orientated world. Paper, people's time, publishing, and postal costs all mount up, so a fee is acceptable these days.

However, do be careful and use common sense. If you think it is too expensive, try to find out what you will be getting for your money. Any Order that will not let you know what you are getting for your money is not worth dealing with. After all, you would not buy a new house or car without seeing it first.

Most courses are in three parts covering three grades – those of Bard, Ovate, and Druid. You will need to take all three to become a Druid, as they are inclined to treat each aspect of the Druid as separate and linear.

Joining an Order can be a daunting experience. Everyone knows far more than you do (so you think), everyone knows everyone else (so it seems), and the Chief Druid must be a magical master (rarely so). It is the same when we join a Grove or any other group of people in society. We want to know all that they know; be part of the whole; find a haven on the inside.

Give yourself time to consider whether you want to join an Order. It is a big step and you need to be aware of what you will gain and lose by doing so. Gather as much information as you can about the various Orders and see if you feel comfortable with what you have learned. If you are able, go away on your own for a weekend to give yourself space in which to make your decision.

Most people who join an Order also want to be part of a Grove, members of an Order who live in the same location and meet on a regular basis. These are an important part of the way in which Orders work. They can provide companionship, an opportunity for like-minded people to work and explore together, and a sense of belonging. There are many such Groves and groups affiliated with Orders. Most of these will celebrate the cycle of the year and organize other Druid activities such as camps, retreats, and initiations into the three grades.

This is, of course, the major problem. If you are the sort of person that likes to be part of a large, structured group with leaders (normally those in the Druid Grade) and regular meetings, then an Order is probably for you. If, however, you are an individual who shies away from hierarchical structures and dislikes the idea of a Chief in charge, then an Order is not going to work for you.

If that is the way you feel, but you still want the focus provided by a course, there is nothing wrong with joining an Order and confining yourself to that. You will often be assigned a tutor who should give you the support and advice you need while studying. When the course is finished, you can leave to pursue your studies and continue your work as you see fit, although you may find that you can happily exist on the fringes of the Order.

People who don't fit in with Orders are normally of two types. Firstly, there is the person who hops from group to group wanting all the answers without doing any of the work. They do not normally stay long enough to gain anything, but will often run an organization down for not giving them a 'quick fix'. These people have a long way yet to travel.

The second type (and there are many of these) are those that join to find out more about the Druid Way, but who soon realize that they already know just as much as the Order can offer, if not more. They also discover that the very presence of a large organization distracts them from being Druid. Internal politics can also be at odds with those who profess to be Druid, with backbiting and people trying to obtain power within the group.

For all that, there are many good Orders and many good things about working in an Order, especially the structured education, the company, and the sense of belonging. If, on the other hand, you really feel the need to explore your *own* vision of the Druid Way, then one of the two following options may well suit you better.

The Hedge
Let us now look at the other extreme - the Druid that works on their own. There are a number of reasons why people work alone. They may, for instance, not know any other Druids, or they may live in isolated areas where it is difficult to meet up with others. It might be that they feel other people's ideas of what one should be doing would tie them down. Of course, they may simply feel that working alone is the way they should be going at that time in their life.

Most Hedge Druids maintain contact with other Druids, usually people with whom they have become close friends. Absolute isolation would be contrary to the basic ideas of the Druid Way. Nevertheless, retreating from the World in order to become closer to the world is a time-honoured tradition.

Solo witches use the word 'hedge' more these days, but it is not originally a Craft word. Indeed, there is a long and venerable history of Hedge Druidry. When Christianity began to exert political pressure, many Druid colleges were forced to close. Druids left their groves and took to the highways and byways to practise and to teach. Hedges became their companions, their source of food, and, often, their shelter.

In fact, the majority of Druids in ancestral times would have worked alone once they had completed their training. They would have been attached to something like a ditched enclosure, a sacred site, a tribal leader, or even a village – offering their wisdom and practical skills to all who were in need of them.

The path of the Hedge Druid can be one of the most rewarding elements of the Druid Way. The person can focus on their own exploration and concentrate on their own practice without having to do what others ordain. They don't need to become involved with politics, as there is no one else with whom to fall out. They can do things how they like and when they like.

Of course, there is a down side. It is always good to be able to discuss things with others and to pass on what one has learned. Without contact, this is not possible. Moreover, it takes a particular strength of will to carry on when there is a lack of connection with an important aspect of the web of being.

This is a particular problem at the festivals. It can be very difficult to whip up the enthusiasm to do a ritual when working alone, whereas a large group can be inspiring. In addition, working with a group outside on a dark winter's night is much more likely to happen than a Hedge Druid tramping off alone into a dark wet wood. Many Hedge Druids end up doing most of their workings indoors, which is perfectly acceptable, but it does diminish the experience by removing direct contact with the natural world.

Yet another problem is that most rituals are written with groups in mind, so they need adapting. In *Arianrhod's Dance*, we provide sample rituals for solo working in order to make life a little easier for the solo practitioner.

It must be said that the Hedge Druid fulfils a very important role, and is by no means any less a Druid for not working within an Order or Grove. They often work with a particular part of the landscape, and over the years protect and heal it, which is indeed a reward in itself. They are also often much clearer and stronger in their vision, free to explore the deepest tracts of the Forest without the distraction of the concerns of Grove or Order. They practice for the Goddess and for Truth, rather than for other people.

Groves

The word Grove has several meanings in druidic practice, most of which are discussed elsewhere in this book. However, the type of Grove that will be discussed here – a collection of Druids who meet on a regular basis to work together - is probably the type of group to which most Druids would like to belong.

A Grove can be attached to an Order, or be independent. If it belongs to an Order, you will need to belong to the Order to be part of the Grove. Some Orders have Grade Groves, which means that the Druid Grove can only be attended by those in the Druid Grade, Ovate Groves welcome Ovates and Druids, while all grades can attend a Bardic Grove.

Independent Groves are not attached to any Order or group. They stand alone as a working Grove of individuals. They are often, but not always, run by a Druid who has been through the Order system.

A Grove can be as small as two people or as large as you like – although group dynamics dictate against too large a gathering being successful. When a Grove reaches a certain size it may split into sister Groves which function separately for rituals and teaching, but which come together for celebrations.

The same things are celebrated as within an Order, but any teaching that takes place is normally within the group. A Druid may take on several pupils and work with them face to face. As in other spiritual and magical traditions, some Groves advertise for new members and are known as open Groves. Others remain as closed Groves.

Closed Groves

Closed Groves have an air of mystery about them and can attract a lot of undue attention. There is nothing different about them other than the fact that entry into the Grove is by invitation only. You have to know the Druids beforehand, not easy if you are looking to make your first steps along the Way.

Most Druids who work in closed Groves will say that their involvement began with a chance meeting. This is not much help if you want to join one now and are searching! There is a degree of faith involved in this, trusting that if you are meant to be part of something it will find you.

Normally as you grow on your Druid path, you do end up meeting someone who works in a Grove. Druids are alive to the fact that others are seeking a way into the Forest. They are sensitive to those who are true seekers and will often go out of their way to point them in a direction that is appropriate for them.

If that means an involvement with a closed Grove, you might well be invited along on the clear understanding that you are a guest. The members of the Grove will have discussed this and will now want the opportunity to discover whether you and they are compatible. Only when everyone is happy that you fit in will you be invited to join.

From the outside, the process can seem patronizing although as we will see below it is nothing of the kind. If such an approach is not your scene, however, then joining an Order and working with a Grove in your locale is probably a better option. It is also less of a commitment for those who are still not completely certain of their path.

Closed Groves are usually smaller than other Groves and they work as a very tight unit. Members should bond well with each other, as this is considerably more than being friends. There is a long-term commitment to working with a small group of people on a spiritual venture – one reason why so much caution is exercised when inviting new members into the circle. Trust and loyalty are extremely important when you open yourself to others in this way.

How often they meet is up to the group. They will always celebrate the festivals, but will often meet in between as well to perform healings, meditations, and other workings as well as learning. The meetings are held at each other's houses or, more usually, outside in a grove in a wood or at a secluded spot in the countryside, well away from the general public.

Most Druids that work in a closed Grove also explore their own path in the Forest when the Grove is inactive. This gives them the best of both worlds – the opportunity for more concentrated and personal work whilst staying in close contact with their Grove brothers and sisters.

Although loyalty is a major concept of this type of Grove, a member should still be free to leave at any time they wish. People change. They may realize they need a break away from their Druid work; they may even realize they are on the wrong path. It may be that they start to lose their focus of what the Grove is, doing things that are not acceptable to other members. It is then up to someone in the Grove to speak to that person to try to sort out the problem. As a last resort, people may be asked to leave.

Given the nature of the group and the way in which it takes care over inviting new members, closed Groves rarely have such major problems. All groups have their ups and downs, but members tend to be very supportive of one another. It is this powerful dynamic that empowers members of closed Groves; it is this sense of a permanent hearth that enables members to explore deep into the Forest.

Retreats, courses, and camps
Whatever your involvement with others, you will inevitably hear of or be invited to attend a course, camp, or retreat. Spending time with others of like mind can be useful, but you need to think carefully before involving yourself with any of these. Investigate them carefully and approach them with the right frame of mind.

To begin with, consider whether you are paying a fair price. Many of these events are extremely expensive. Some consist of little more than the privilege of camping in a muddy field alongside a bunch of strangers who know little or nothing of campsite etiquette. Other events, whilst in more salubrious surroundings, seem to be part of the social calendar of a large number of those attending and it is very easy to feel left out.

You also need to consider whether any teaching that is offered is worth having. One or two teachers are worth going to listen to, but they rarely have anything to do with the usual round of events. Unfortunately, there are many more self-styled experts and 'showman shamans' at work in the world. They are charlatans with adolescent minds and have nothing of worth to offer. There is a third group that one might call 'celebrity speakers', but whatever they have to say will inevitably turn up in their next book which, if it is worth reading at all, can be borrowed from your local library and read in the comfort of your own home at pace to suit yourself.

This may be considered unduly harsh. Such events can be an opportunity for lone practitioners to meet and socialize (although there are plenty of other ways in which this can be achieved). Some of them are extremely well organized, offer value for money, and offer genuine opportunities to learn. If you are of a sociable bent, they are worth exploring. However, there are a huge number of rip-off merchants out there who want to part you from what little money you might have and we advise you to be careful.

There is another aspect of this that is rarely considered. Many of these events, especially those that are billed as retreats, can cause a great deal of harm as those who organize them have little or no understanding of the forces they can unleash. Some of them offer workings and initiations that should never be given to people who are virtual strangers.

Experiential workshops and retreats are prime examples of this. All people who take to the Druid Way undertake a retreat from the World so that they might become closer to and more integrated with the world. But this is a slow process in which we should take careful steps. An abrupt retreat from society is extremely difficult. Not only does this involve coping with new surroundings and new people, it involves a personal transition that can be emotionally taxing. Without the presence of experienced guides, this can do more harm than good.

Should you wish to make retreats, but do not feel you would fit in with organized events, you can always organize your own. A few hours at home on your own with the telephone switched off, a weekend away in the country; anywhere that you can centre on yourself without interruption is sufficient. These can be general retreats in which you eat simple foods, relax, and restore some balance in your life; or they can be focused, in which you spend the time reading and reflecting on a specific topic.

There are also ways of learning that do not involve specifically druidic courses. Working holidays in which you learn practical skills such as hedge laying or go on guided nature walks are often of much greater value than vague courses on such things as 'drumming'. After all, you take your Druid nature with you and absorb what you learn into that whilst integrating yourself with the real world.

As always, the choice is yours – we simply want you to be aware of what may be involved. It is important that you learn what you are capable of coping with and what you need at any given moment of your development.

*

If you find that you are still unsure about whether to join a Druid group - don't! Wait until the time feels right, and then choose carefully. This doesn't stop you exploring, learning, and developing. Being Druid is not, at heart, about joining a Grove or an Order for all the advantages that may bring.

The options above give an insight into working alone and working with other people. You might fancy doing both – which is always a good choice. That way you are never lonely, but you leave yourself free to grow as an individual on this path.

You might even decide to form your own Grove, either with an Order's help or as a closed Grove. If you do, be prepared for a lot of hard work of a very mundane nature. You will need to write and type up rituals, send them to members, phone around to arrange meetings, as well as sort out problems such as transport, food, ritual tools, and people's grievances whilst coping with your own life outside of the Grove.

This last point is very important. Keep everything in balance. Although being Druid will inform all that you are, you have an existence beyond the Order, the Grove, or the Hedge. Remember that your family may not be Druid and they are important as well.

BEING A DRUID IN THE WORLD

We all hope and believe that we live in a tolerant society - a place where one is free to believe and practise whatever spiritual path one chooses. Unfortunately, our hopes and the rhetoric of politicians are rarely matched by the reality. When it comes to the Druid Way and other pagan paths, tolerance levels can be extremely low.

The main problem is that the Druid Way (along with Witchcraft and the Northern Tradition) is classed as an 'occult' religion, with all that is implied by that term to those who do not know its true meaning. The media love this, and there will always be some 'showman shaman' ready to appear on television or do an interview for the newspapers to back this up.

Neither the public nor the media are interested in the truth about the Druid Way. They prefer to believe lurid stories of rituals at midnight with cowled figures, or to ridicule the whole Druid world as eccentrics in white robes who worship the Sun. When it comes to politicians, the tactic is different. They ignore paganism altogether and pretend it does not exist, effectively disenfranchising hundreds of thousands of people.

All the spirit paths that come under the umbrella word pagan are nature based. Those who follow these paths lead peace-loving lives with their families and friends. They would never dream of hurting anyone or anything – it would be against their creed. On the whole, pagans abjure material acquisitiveness and work to heal the hurts of the world. They are also tolerant of other religions.

There will always be people with severe mental problems who will perform unsavoury acts in the name of one or other of the pagan paths (just as they do in the name of the Christ or Allah or any other deity or religion you care to name). These people need professional help and are nothing to do with the Druid Way or paganism. It is a sad fact that it is this type of person the public thinks of when the occult is mentioned, and this type of person that the media chooses to write about without explaining all the facts.

There are, of course, Druids who go on television and speak very well about the Druid Way, but they are rare. Moreover, articulate as they might be, they can offer little help with one of the major problems we all face when we become Druid - how do we deal with other people in our lives when they know so little about the path we tread?

How you approach this problem depends, ultimately, on your own situation – whether you are in a long term relationship, living at home with parents, or perhaps part of an organization (like the police or armed forces) that is not known for its open-mindedness. You alone will have to consider all the factors and you alone will have to decide who needs to know of the path you have taken.

Family and friends
If you decide to tell your family or close friends that you have become a Druid or joined a Druid Order, be prepared. If you just dive in, both feet first, saying, 'I have found the Way and I stand around in a circle wearing a white nightie,' you are asking for *big* trouble. Those closest to you may already have guessed that you have taken an important step - after all, they do know you well. Others will be worried and some very interested. Whatever the case, you will need to be able answer any questions they have in a way they will understand.

One of the best ways to broach the subject is to mention briefly that you belong to an Order or Grove and that you are learning about the Druid Way. Don't lecture or proselytize - how would you like it? - and see if you can get whoever you are telling to read a small book on the Druid Way. Then let them ask their questions.

This is all very well if you live alone or at home and you are telling parents and friends, but what about a partner? Living with another person who does not follow your spiritual path can cause problems, especially if you try to keep it hidden. Consider, for example, a man who goes to work, plays with the children, watches television, and hardly ever goes out. One day, he joins a Druid Order and starts going out, wearing white robes, and tells his wife he has met all these new people, but it's all secret. Pots and pans will probably fly (and not by magic)!

If you have a partner, they need to be told. You owe them nothing less. The best time is when you first become interested. Do not leave it for five years until you have to go away for a weekend to preside over a solstice ceremony. Most couples who have different interests and beliefs live with each other's ways – it is part of being a couple. If you are close, your directions will not, in any case, be dissimilar. At the very least, your partner may be sympathetic; at best, they may wish to journey with you.

There can also be problems when children are involved. Many people would like their offspring to be carbon copies of themselves. They are not.

> You may give them your love but not your thoughts,
> For they have their own thoughts.
>
> [Kahlil Gibran – *The Prophet*]

Many religions of this world force children into a spiritual path. Druids do not, for ours is a Way of freedom. We can nurture them as any Druid should – in love and Truth – but the Druid Way is our path, not theirs. They will grow strong in the love we offer them and they will find their own Way. It is great that they join in our Grove picnics and dress up at Samhain, but they must be allowed to explore other Ways. It is frightening for the parents who want to bring up a baby Druid, but there are enough hazards in the world for young people without their parents adding to them. We can, in Truth, only guide.

Teenagers

If you are a young person reading this book and want to become Druid, who do you tell? You don't have to tell anyone, but there will doubtless be situations where being open will make life simpler. If your parents think you are being secretive about what you are doing, explain to them in a gentle way and again maybe offer them a book to read.

Just because you are young does not mean you have not spent time searching carefully and sensibly for what you want. If your parents are of a different faith, this is something you will need to sort out as a family.

Parents do worry about their children because, unfortunately, there are people in this world that take advantage of the young. With this in mind, explain that no Grove or Druid Order is likely to let you join before you are eighteen. You might find your school friends and teachers will need educating as well on what a Druid is, especially if you do not wish to join in religious meetings at your school. The law on this depends on where you live. It is well worth checking it out and being certain of your rights.

There have been cases where young pagans have been bullied by their peers, ostracized by their schools, and, in extreme cases, driven to suicide. Don't let things get out of hand. If you are being victimized, seek help.

Open Gatherings

In Druidry, there is a tradition of public gatherings (Gorseddau). These are often held in 'the eye of the Sun' in very public places, such as Primrose Hill in Central London, Avebury, or Stonehenge. If you decide to attend any of these public rituals, you will be *seen* by the public. The press is often there, including television cameras, and although it is not the done thing to take pictures of people without their permission, the public will doubtless be taking photographs. The choice is easy here. If you don't want to be seen in public, don't go to one of these public gatherings.

Druids and Christians

On the whole, Druids live in nations that are predominantly Christian. Some Christians are very tolerant and open to other faiths. Most Christians, if you tell them you are Druid, may think you a bit weird and perhaps avoid you in future. There are, however, fundamentalist Christian organizations and Evangelical Churches that see Druids in particular and pagans in general as being in league with the Devil and something to be stamped out.

The Devil belongs to Abrahamic tradition (Judaism, Christianity, and Islam). Druids do not believe in the Devil, let alone honour such a being. There *are* people who call themselves Satanists, but they are not pagans as they eschew the basic principles of pagan belief. Equally, those fundamentalists and evangelicals whose actions and words are marked by intolerance and hatred of others are not, truly speaking, Christians.

Nonetheless, these ersatz-Christians are adept at spreading their poison. People have lost their jobs, homes, and children when it has been discovered they are pagan. New-age shops and other businesses have had to close down in some areas because of repeated attacks from such people. Even sacred sites used occasionally by pagans have been vandalized, including stone circles in the UK, which are part of the nation's heritage.

Fundamentalist Christian organizations are on the increase, encouraged in their vituperation by weak political systems. These people have no interest in trying to understand Druids. They are best avoided, so saving yourself, your family, and friends from a great deal of unpleasantness. We have nothing to be ashamed of in our chosen path, but it is best to keep our own counsel unless we can be certain of those in whom we confide.

Who else should we tell?
There is really no need to tell anyone. Druidry is your *personal* spiritual way. Your Druid friends will know, of course, and you may choose to confide in you family and close friends. Beyond that, keep it to yourself.

However, there may be certain times when you are asked to state your religion – if you go into hospital, for example, or when filling in a census form. It is up to you what information you give, but it may be important to you to state the truth. This information is given in confidence, so it should not present a problem. Consider, also, if you are ever called upon to give evidence under oath. You do *not* have to swear on the Bible (and it would, in any case, be a meaningless act for a Druid). Decide what oath would have meaning for you and explain to the appropriate authorities in advance of the occasion if possible.

*

Modern Druids are not treated with the same respect accorded our ancestors so you will need to decide very carefully how you proceed through life and interact with the World. We hope that this chapter does not seem too downbeat, but we know from experience that the joy of exploring the Druid Way can be tempered by unpleasantness. It is for that reason that we suggest you proceed with discretion, sharing your inner joy with the few whilst working for the many.

PART FOUR

A CRANE BAG

GLOSSARY

BC/AD - We thought long and hard about using these terms as this is a book about the Druid Way. Many people now use BCE (Before Current/Common Era) and CE (Current/Common Era), but these are a sham. There is no common era, except in the imperialist imagination of the western scientists who invented the term. BCE and CE use the Christian year zero as their base point and mean the same as BC (Before Christ) and AD (Anno Domini). If they had meant a different date, we would have considered using them. As BC and AD are widely understood, we thought it better to be open and honest about the system we are using.

Deiseal/tuathal – Deiseal, often given in its Anglicized form of 'deosil', means 'sunwise' and is the preferred direction in druidic working. Tuathal (anticlockwise or widdershins) is the direction used for unwinding energies. This does not make tuathal a 'bad' direction, that is an invention of the Christian witch-hunters who placed a 'diabolic' interpretation on anything left-handed (*sinister* is simply the Latin word for 'left').

There are those who advocate working in the opposite direction, correctly pointing out that the Earth rotates tuathal when viewed from above the North Pole. However, if you look down on the Earth from above the South Pole, it rotates deiseal. It is all a matter of perspective.

Whilst ancestral Druids were sophisticated astronomers and knew that the Earth orbited the Sun (and consequently rotated on its own axis), the important thing for them, being inhabitants of the northern hemisphere, was the direction the sun appeared to take in the sky. If you face it as it rises, it moves to the right.

Divination - Many Druids practise some form of divination. By using the Tarot or ogham, it is possible to discover what may come to be in the future. These days there are tarot cards to suit most tastes, including Druid and Celtic decks. Ogham cards and sticks are also available commercially. You could also explore the use of runes and the *I Ching*.

Faerie - Most cultures have a faerie tradition, none more so than the Celtic peoples. Today we have demoted faeries to a childhood fantasy, but Celtic faeries are not 'Tinkerbell' creatures. They are a race of peoples who have lived alongside humans for thousands of years and who should be treated with a great deal of caution and respect. The little creatures with wings and pointy hats are largely a Victorian invention.

Druids (and most ancient peoples) would not have tried to contact the Sidhe or the denizens of Faerie. They feared them, knew them as a people who are completely other. The contacting of faeries is a very recent thing and not to be encouraged.

Faeries are a private people who live by their own rules and who tend to show themselves only when they want to be seen. Although they live in their own world, it is contiguous with ours and they can move between the two at will. They tend to appear on the borderlands of places - the edge of a wood, the seashore, the bend in the stairs, out of the corner of your eye. They are known by many names: the Gentry, the Sidhe, Fay, Fair Folk, and Shining Ones. They should not be confused with Elves who are a different race belonging to the Northern Traditions.

Forest/forest - Forest with a capital 'F' is used to denote the inner landscape of the Druid as well as being a metaphor for the world of spirit, whilst forest with a small 'f' is a collection of trees.

Goddess - The Goddess can mean many different things to people. In the Celtic pantheon, there are many types of goddess, all with tales of wonder and wisdom to impart. In Her primal aspect as the Great Goddess, we see Her as a universal triple Goddess of all nature. She is the maiden, mother, and cailleach. We know Her as Danu who gives life as the breath of spring, the fullness of the harvest. She is the death and rebirth of the year, our lives, and the universe. She is the land, the sea, and the sky. She is the mighty ocean, the silvery brook, the Moon, the stars, the dark deep forests, the poppy filled meadow. She is life. As Druids, we honour Her in our daily lives, meditations, and rituals.

Horned God - An antlered deity who is Lord of the Animals, with distinct manifestations - Herne (English), Woden (Germanic), or Cernunnos (Celtic). He is the Oak King in the summer and the Holly King in the winter. He also plays the part of the hunter and Lord of the Underworld, but later in the year at the winter solstice, He is reborn as the Mabon. As Cernunnos, He later became a god of fertility - this having more to do with sacrifice and regeneration than sex.

Magic – Druid magic is different from that used in other pagan paths. We do not cast spells or make potions. Instead, we work with the natural energies around us. This energy is found in all things - animals, trees, stones, birds, water, weather, sound, even dreams. In our rituals and meditations, we link into these energies and work with them for the good, giving out love, light, and healing.

Metaphysics - The study of the ultimate causes and underlying nature of things, especially the nature of being. A particular world view is known as a 'metaphysic'. The word derives from Aristotle's work, the *Metaphysics*, so called because it was written after (*meta*) his work on the physical world (*physics*). It is now generally taken to mean 'beyond/other than the physical'.

Mistletime/mistletide – see 'Yule'.

Northern Tradition - Religions based on Germanic, Norse, and pre-Christian Scandinavian paths. Today they tend to be put under the heading of Asatru. The Asatru movement is growing very big in Northern Europe and America, and in Iceland, it is now an official state religion. Asatru honour the principles of courage, loyalty, and fellowship, with a focus on healing and the environment.

Pagan - Paganism is a broad religious movement that encompasses shamanistic, ecstatic, polytheistic, and magical traditions along with less well-defined but generally pagan attitudes. Most of the religions termed pagan are characterized by nature-centred spirituality, a veneration of female and male deistic principles, personally developed belief systems based on a direct experience of the divine in the world, and an encouragement of tolerance and diversity. Honour, trust, and friendship are key elements.

Today approximately 300 million people are pagan and the numbers are growing. This is particularly so in the western world where many people feel that comparatively recent religions (such as Christianity) do not address their everyday concerns. They look increasingly to those religious traditions that had a particular reverence for the natural world to fill their needs. The Druid Way is just such a tradition, one that is particularly relevant to the western world as it is not only the west's heritage, but it is of direct relevance to the spiritual and material concerns of people today. Many people are pagan without actually belonging to any particular group.

Pentagram/pentacle - A pentagram is a five-pointed star. Many Druids and pagans wear such a device for protection and for an outward sign of their path. It is worn with the single point upwards, when it is considered a symbol of life.

Protection - As Druids, we do not believe in evil demons and devils. What we protect ourselves against are the negative, draining energies that are abundant in our ailing world. Healing work is especially debilitating and we need to ensure we do not deplete ourselves. That is why it is important to work within a circle and to close it properly afterwards. The same goes for making sure we are properly grounded after working.

Summerlands - A modern generic term for the Celtic lands of wonder to which we sail when we leave this world. The nineteenth century theosophist, Helena Blavatsky, saw it as the astral plane to which the dead went. Today we are more inclined to imagine it as a place of wonder and eternal youth, a paradisical Avalon.

Wicca - Wicca has been a name used since the repeal of the Witchcraft Act in 1951 when Gerald Gardner was active. He devised most of the Wiccan ritual, drawing on many different cultures, and is responsible for the movement as we know it today. Prior to this, the path was known as the Old Religion or the Craft.

Many witches today still practice the Craft, rather than follow the rites of modern Wicca, practising a form of natural magic very much akin to the work of Druids. Many other witches claim to be hereditary or traditional. Some Wiccan paths draw on Celtic religious practices and make use of Celtic deities, but Wicca itself is not inherently Celtic.

Work - Druids and most other pagans refer to the meditation, magic, ritual, and healing they perform as work. That is, they are activities in which one exerts one's physical strength and mental faculties. The path is not an easy one.

world/World – The word 'world' (with a small 'w') is generally interchangeable with the word 'universe' and means 'everything that is'. It can also be used to mean 'everything on the planet'. When 'World' (with a capital 'W') is used, it has a specialized meaning – 'the physical, ideological, and social constructs of human beings'. Druids work to mitigate the harm caused by the World.

This distinction is borrowed from the evolving Celtic metaphysic of Greywind.

Yule - The word Yule is often used by pagans to replace the word Christmas. The origin of the word is both the Old Norse *jól* and the Old English *geól*. Originally meaning 'wheel', it was used from an early date to signify the month of December and, more specifically, Christmas itself, linking it firmly with Christianity. As a personal choice, we prefer to use the terms 'Mistletime' and 'Mistletide' for the winter solstice and winter period.

RESOURCES

Druid Orders, Networks, and Groves have differing lifespans and evolutionary pathways; membership criteria can change; contact addresses alter; new groups come into existence. The same is true of magazines. Rather than put information about them here that could soon be out of date, we suggest you make an Internet search. We appreciate that not everyone has or wishes to own a computer, but most public libraries now offer access to the Internet, and have staff that will help you. A search using the word 'Druid' will result in enough information to allow you to contact a group that best suits your needs.

Organizations mentioned below are British and Irish as they are the ones we know from personal experience. Similar organizations exist worldwide. All details were correct at the time of going to press, but please double check.

Tree planting organizations
The Woodland Trust
Autumn Park, Dysart Road, Grantham, Lincolnshire, NG31 6LL
Tel: 01476 581111, Fax: 01476 590808
Website: www.woodland-trust.org.uk

The Woodland Trust Scotland
Glenruthven Mill, Abbey Road, Auchterarder, Perthshire, PH3 1DP
Tel: 01764 662554, Fax: 01764 662554

The Woodland Trust Wales (Coed Cadw)
Yr Hen Orsaf, Llanidloes, Powys, SY18 6EB
Tel: 01686 412508, Fax: 01686 413284

The Woodland Trust Northern Ireland
1 Dufferin Court, Dufferin Avenue, Bangor, County Down, BT20 3BX
Tel: 028 9127 5787, Fax: 028 9127 5942

Reforesting Scotland
62-66 Newhaven Road, Edinburgh, EH6 5QB
Tel: 0131 554 4321, Fax: 0131 554 0088
Website: http://reforestingscotland.gn.apc.org

Native Woodland Trust of Ireland
Stoneybrook, Kilteel, Co. Kildare, Republic of Ireland
Website: www.nativewoodtrust.ie

Natural Death & Green Burials
Natural Death Centre (produce the *Natural Death Handbook*)
6 Blackstock Mews, Blackstock Road, London, N4 2BT
Tel: 0871 288 2098, Fax: 020 7354 3831
Website: www.naturaldeath.org.uk

Liferites (information and advice on all rites of passage)
Gwndwn Mawr, Trelech, Carmarthenshire, SA33 6SA
Tel: 01994 484527
Website: www.liferites.org

Animal Rights/Compassionate Living
Dr Hadwen Trust
(supports research into replacing animals in medical testing)
84a Tilehouse Street, Hitchin, Herts, SG5 2DY
Tel: 01462 436819, Fax: 01462 436844
www.drhadwentrust.org.uk

League Against Cruel Sports Ltd
Sparling House, 83-87 Union Street, London, SE1 1SG
Tel: 0845 330 8486
www.league.co.uk

Viva! (Vegetarians International Voice for Animals)
8 York Court, Wilder Street, Bristol, BS2 8QH
Tel: 0117 944 1000, Fax: 0117 924 4646
www.viva.org.uk

People for the Ethical Treatment of Animals (PETA)
PO Box 36668, London, SE1 1WA
Tel: 020 7357 9229, Fax: 020 7357 0901
www.peta.org.uk

The Vegetarian Society
Parkdale, Dunham Road, Altrincham, Cheshire, WA14 4QG
Tel: 0161 925 2000, Fax: 0161 926 9182
www.vegsoc.org

Vegan Society
7 Battle Road, St Leonards on Sea, East Sussex, TN37 7AA
Tel: 01424 427393, Fax: 01424 717064
www.vegansociety.com

Tastes in music, film, and fiction are highly subjective, but we have included titles with pagan or Celtic themes that we have enjoyed and which we think are worth trying. A number of the following books are the first in or part of a series.

Music

Afro Celt Sound System (1996), *Sound Magic*, Real World Records
Altan (1993), *Island Angel*, Green Linnet
Calverly (1990), *Celtic Mysteries*, Oasis Productions
Deanta (1994), *Ready for the Storm*, Green Linnet
McKennitt, Loreena (Various), *Elemental/To Drive the Cold Winter Away/Parallel Dreams/The Visit/A Winter Garden/The Mask and the Mirror/The Book of Secrets*, Quinlan Road
Mark, J. (1993), *Celtic Story*, White Cloud
Mediaeval Babes (2000), *Undrentide*, BMG Classics
Thornton, P. (1996), *Sorcerer*, New World Music
Williamson, Robin (1994), *Songs of Love and Parting/Five Bardic Mysteries*, T.M.C.

Cinema and Television

Bedknobs and Broomsticks (1970) - Dir: Robert Stevenson
The Box of Delights (19??) - Dir: Penny Rye
Chocolat (2000) - Dir: Lasse Hallström
The Company of Wolves (1984) - Dir: Neil Jordan
Excalibur (1981) - Dir: John Boorman
The Fisher King (1991) - Dir: Terry Gilliam
Lancelot du Lac (1974) - Dir: Robert Bresson
Legend (dir. Ridley Scott)
Lord of the Rings (2001, 2002, 2003) - Dir: Peter Jackson
Mary Poppins (1964) - Dir: Robert Stevenson
Perceval le Gallois (1978) - Dir: Eric Rohmer
Princess Mononoke (1997) - Dir: Hayao Miyazaki
Silent Running (1971) - Dir: Douglas Trumbull
The Snow Spider (19??) - Dir: Pennant Roberts

Fiction

Alexander, L. (1964), *The Book of Three*, Heinemann, London
Bradley, M. (1983), *The Mists of Avalon*, Michael Joseph, London
Cooper, S. (1965), *Over Sea, Under Stone*, Puffin, Harmondsworth
Crossley-Holland, K. (2000), *Arthur: The Seeing Stone*, Orion, London
De Lint, C. (1991), *The Little Country*, William Morrow, New York

Frost, R. (1971), *The Poetry*, Jonathan Cape, London

Garner, A. (1967), *The Owl Service*, Collins, London

Hardy, T. (1981), *The Woodlanders*, Penguin, London

Holdstock, R. (1994), *Merlin's Wood*, HarperCollins, London

Jones, D. W. (1986), *Howl's Moving Castle*, Methuen, London

Le Guin, U. (1968), *A Wizard of Earthsea*, Puffin, Harmondsworth

Nimmo, J. (1986), *The Snow Spider*, Mammoth, London

O'Shea, P. (1985), *The Hounds of the Mórrígan*, Puffin, Harmondsworth

Stewart, M. (1970), *The Crystal Cave*, Hodder & Stoughton, London

Tolkien, J. R. R. (1968), *The Lord of the Rings*, George Allen & Unwin, London

Tolstoy, N. (1988), *The Coming of the King*, Bantam, London

White, T. H. (1958), *The Once and Future King*, Collins, London

Wolf, J. (1988), *The Road to Avalon*, Collins, London

Yeats, W. B. (1950), *Collected Poems*, Macmillan, London

BIBLIOGRAPHY

This list contains books we referred to whilst writing as well as those we believe to contain useful information and ideas. It is not definitive, but many of them contain useful bibliographies of their own.

Ashe, G. (1957), *King Arthur's Avalon*, Fontana, London

Ashe, G. (1977), *The Ancient Wisdom*, Macmillan, London

Ashe, G. (1982), *Avalonian Quest*, Methuen, London

Beth, R. (1990), *Hedge Witch*, Robert Hale, London

Bord J. & C. (1978), *A Guide to Ancient Sites in Britain*, Paladin, London

Bord, J. & C. (1982), *Earth Rites*, Granada, London

Bord, J. & C. (1985), *Sacred Waters*, Granada, London

Castleden, R. (1983), *The Wilmington Giant*, Turnstone Press, Wellingborough

Chadwick, N. (1971), *The Celts*, Penguin, Harmondsworth

Chetan, A. & Brueton, D. (1994), *The Sacred Yew*, Arkana, London

Coghlan, R. (1991), *The Encyclopaedia of Arthurian Legends*, Element, Shaftesbury

Cunliffe, B. (1997), *The Ancient Celts*, Oxford University Press, Oxford

Cunliffe, B. (2003), *The Celts – A Very Short Introduction*, Oxford University Press, Oxford

Dames, M. (1976), *The Silbury Treasure*, Thames & Hudson, London

Dames, M. (1977), *The Avebury Cycle*, Thames & Hudson, London

Darrah, J. (1994), *Paganism in Arthurian Romance*, D.S.Brewer, Woodbridge

Dillon, M. & Chadwick, N. (2003), *The Celtic Realms*, Castle Books, Edison, NJ

Dixon-Kennedy, M. (1996), *Celtic Myth and Legend*, Blandford, London

Ellis, P. B. (1990), *The Celtic Empire (1000BC – 51AD)*, Constable, London

Ellis, P. B. (1993), *Celt and Saxon (AD 410-937)*, Constable, London

Ellis, P. B. (1994), *The Druids*, Constable, London

Ellis, P. B. (1995), *Celtic Women*, Constable, London

Ellis, P. B. (1997), *Celt and Greek*, Constable, London

Ellis, P. B. (1998), *Celt and Roman*, Constable, London

Gifford, J. (2000), *The Celtic Wisdom of Trees*, Godsfield Press, New Alresford

Godwin, M. (1994), *The Holy Grail*, Bloomsbury, London

Green, M. (1988), *The Path through the Labyrinth*, Thoth Publications, Loughborough

Green, M. (1989), *Natural Magic*, Element, Shaftesbury

Greywind (2001), *the Voice within the Wind*, Grey House in the Woods, Ballantrae

Greywind (2005), *the Light beyond the Forest*, Grey House in the Woods, Ballantrae

Hageneder, F. (2001), *The Heritage of Trees*, Floris, Edinburgh

Heselton, P. (1991), *Earth Mysteries*, Element, Shaftesbury

Hitching, F. (1976), *Earth Magic*, Cassell & Company, London

Hopman, E. E. (1995), *A Druid's Herbal*, Destiny Books, Rochester

Hubert, H. (1992), *The History of the Celtic People*, Bracken Books, London

Humphries, C. J., et al (2004), *Trees of Britain and Europe*, Hamlyn, London

Jackson, K. H. [tr.] (1971), *A Celtic Miscellany*, Penguin, Harmondsworth

James, S. (1993), *Exploring the World of the Celts*, Thames & Hudson, London

Jones, K. (1991), *The Ancient British Goddess*, Ariadne, Glastonbury

Kendrick, T. D. (1928), *Druids and Druidism*, Dover, Mineola, NY

Koch, J. T. & Carey, J. (2003), *The Celtic Heroic Age* (4th ed), Celtic Studies Publications, Aberystwyth

Laing, L. (1979), *Celtic Britain*, Granada, St Albans

Loomis, R. S. (1926), *Celtic Myth and Arthurian Romance*, Constable, London

Loomis, R. S. (1963), *The Grail from Celtic Myth to Christian Symbol*, Constable, London

Mac Cana, P. (1983), *Celtic Mythology*, Newnes, Feltham

MacCulloch, J. A. (1911), *The Religion of the Ancient Celts*, Constable, London

MacCulloch, J. A. (1918), *Celtic Mythology*, Constable, London

MacKillop, J. (1998), *Dictionary of Celtic Mythology*, Oxford University Press, Oxford

Markale, J. [tr Mygind, A., Hauch, C. & Henry, P.] (1986), *Women of the Celts*, Inner Traditions, Rochester

Markale, J. [tr Hauch, C.] (1993), *The Celts*, Inner Traditions, Rochester

Markale, J. [tr Graham, J.] (1999), *The Druids*, Inner Traditions, Rochester

Marsh, H. (1970), *Dark Age Britain – Sources of History*, David & Charles, London

Mason, P. & Franklin, A. (1998), *The Sacred Circle Tarot*, Llewellyn, St Paul, MN

Matthews, C. (1987), *Mabon and the Mysteries of Britain*, Arkana, London

Matthews, C. (1989), *Arthur and the Sovereignty of Britain*, Arkana, London

Matthews, C. (1989), *The Celtic Tradition*, Element, Shaftesbury

Matthews, C. & J. (1989), *The Western Way*, Arkana, London

Matthews, C. & J. (1992), *Ladies of the Lake*, Thorsons, London

Matthews, C. & J. (1997), *Hallowquest*, Thorsons, London

Matthews, J. (1989), *The Arthurian Tradition*, Element, Shaftesbury

Matthews, J. (1990), *Gawain, Knight of the Goddess*, Aquarian, London

Matthews, J. (1990), *The Grail Tradition*, Element, Shaftesbury

Matthews, J. (1991), *Taliesin, Shamanism and the Bardic Mysteries in Britain and Ireland*, Aquarian, London

Matthews, J. (1996), *The Druid Source Book*, Blandford, London

Matthews, J. (1998), *The Bardic Source Book*, Blandford, London

Matthews, J. (1999), *The Celtic Seers' Source Book*, Blandford, London

Moorey, T. (2000), *Witchcraft*, Hodder & Stoughton, London

Palmer, J. D. (2001), *Animal Wisdom*, Thorsons, London

Paterson, J. M. (1996), *Tree Wisdom*, Thorsons, London

Pennick, N. (1996), *Celtic Sacred Landscapes*, Thames & Hudson, London

Piggott, S. (1975), *The Druids*, Thames & Hudson, London

Rackham, O. (2001), *Trees & Woodland in the British Landscape*, Phoenix, London

Rees, A. & B. (1961), *Celtic Heritage*, Thames & Hudson, London

Rees, B. R. (1998), *Pelagius, Life and Letters*, Boydell, Woodbridge

Rich, D. & Begg, E. (1991), *On the Trail of Merlin*, Aquarian Press, London

Richards, G. (1991), *The Philosophy of Gandhi*, Curzon Press, Richmond

Ross, A. (1967), *Pagan Celtic Britain*, Constable, London

Ross, A. (1999), *Druids*, Tempus, Stroud

Seddon, R. (1990), *The Mystery of Arthur at Tintagel*, Rudolf Steiner Press, London

Skolimowski, H. (1992), *Living Philosophy*, Arkana, London

Spence, L. (1928), *The Mysteries of Britain*, Newcastle Publishing, Van Nuys, CA

Spence, L. (1945), *The Magic Arts in Celtic Britain*, Constable, London

Spence, L. (1949), *The History and Origins of Druidism*, Newcastle Publishing, Van Nuys, CA

Stewart, R. J. (1984), *Merlin: The Prophetic Vision and the Mystic Life*, Arkana, London

Stewart, R. J. (1990), *Celtic Gods Celtic Goddesses*, Blandford, London

Sutton, D. (1990), *Trees of Britain and Europe*, Kingfisher, London

Talboys, G. K. (2005), *Way of the Druid*, O-Books, Ropley

Tolstoy, N. (1985), *The Quest for Merlin*, Hamish Hamilton, London

Versluis, A. (1986), *The Philosophy of Magic*, Arkana, London

Waite, A. E. (1933), *The Holy Grail*, Rider & Co, London

Wentz, W. Y. E. (1911), *The Fairy-Faith in Celtic Countries*, Colin Smythe, Gerrards Cross

Weston, J. (1920), *From Ritual to Romance*, Princeton University Press, Princeton

White, J. & Talboys, G. K. (2004), *Arianrhod's Dance – a Druid Ritual Handbook*, Grey House in the Woods, Ballantrae

York, M. (2003), *Pagan Theology*, New York University Press, New York

The Matter of Britain
Texts listed below are given in a very rough chronological order. Those with publishers listed are key texts, others are for the more dedicated (and some are out of print). This represents just a fraction of the material that exists.

The Matter of Britain contains works that are important to the Western Mystery Tradition in general and to Druids in particular. Not all versions and tales will appeal, but they all drew originally from Celtic sources and they all contain hidden gems of knowledge that will help us to a greater understanding of our role in the world today. The most important thing, however, is that they are first read for pleasure.

Coe, J. B. & Young, S. (1995), *The Celtic Sources for the Arthurian Legend*, Llanerch, Felinfach.
Guest, C. (1846), *The Mabinogion*, Voyager, London.
Geoffrey of Monmouth (1966), *The History of the Kings of Britain*, Penguin, Harmondsworth.
Geoffrey of Monmouth - *Vita Merlini*
Wace, R. & Layamon (1912), *Arthurian Chronicles*, Everyman, London.
Beroul - *The Romance of Tristan*
Eilhart von Oberge - *Tristan*
Brother Robert - *Tristan*
Thomas of Britain - *Tristan et Yseut*
Robert de Boron - *Joseph d'Arimathie*
Marie de France - *Lais*
Chrétien de Troyes (1987), *Arthurian Romances*, Everyman, London.
Anon - *Perlesvaus (The High Book of the Grail)*
Anon - *Lancelot do Lac*
Ulrich von Zatzikhoven - *Lanzelet*
Wolfram von Eschenbach (1980), *Parzival*, Penguin, Harmondsworth.
Anon - *Y Seint Graal*
Bromwich, R. [tr.] (1961), *Trioedd Ynys Prydein*, University of Wales Press, Cardiff.
Anon - *Gest of Sir Gawain*
Anon - *Suite de Merlin*
Anon - *Prose Merlin*
Anon - *Prophécies de Merlin*
Gottfried von Strassburg - *Tristan*
Matarasso, P. M. [tr.] (1969), *The Quest of the Holy Grail*, Penguin,

Harmondsworth.

Cable, J. [tr.] (1971), *The Death of King Arthur*, Penguin, Harmondsworth.

Anon – *Arthour & Merlin*

Anon – *Joseph of Aramathie*

Anon – *Alliterative Morte Arthur*

Tolkien, J. R. R. [tr.] (1975), *Sir Gawain and the Green Knight*, George Allen & Unwin, London.

Anon – *Sir Perceval of Gales*

Anon – *Ywain and Gawain*

Anon – *Merlin, or the Early History of King Arthur*

Malory, T. (2000), *Le Morte D'Arthur*, Cassell, London.

Related Texts

Ailred & Joceline (1989), *The Lives of Ninian and Kentigern*, Llanerch, Felinfach.

Aneirin (1994), *The Gododdin*, Llanerch, Felinfach.

Anon – *The Book of Taliesin*

Nennius (1980), *British History and The Welsh Annals*, Phillimore, Chichester.

Pennar, M. [tr.] (1988), *Taliesin Poems*, Llanerch, Felinfach.

Pennar, M. [tr.] (1989), *The Black Book of Carmarthen (Selections)*, Llanerch, Felinfach.

Williams, H. [tr.] (1899), *Two Lives of Gildas*, Llanerch, Felinfach.